Table of Contents

Foreword

This book aspires to present a coherent, readily accessible recapitulation of American constitutional law. Its approach is to combine extensive text with abstracts from seminal decisions of the United States Supreme Court. The US Constitution and other organic documents are appended.

As suggested by the title, the subject matter of constitutional law is broken into two halves: governmental power and constitutional rights. Each half is similarly bisected according to two of the most important principles that underlie the material. For government, these are the principles of separation of powers and federalism. For rights, they are liberty and equality.

This book is designed primarily for teaching, specifically for teaching relative newcomers to the common law in general, and to non-parliamentary government in particular. Consequently, the presentation attempts to capture the most essential concepts of American constitutional law, including many that Americans take for granted.

While primarily written for classroom use, the book can nonetheless be profitably read and consulted by lawyers and scholars, both of whom will welcome the systematic presentation of this vast topic. Despite its diminutive size, this book provides far more theoretical and prudential analysis than one finds in commercial student materials. However, it does not flood the reader with the minutiae found in lengthy texts and casebooks. One who wants to explore a topic more deeply should, of course, resort to these tomes. The leading academic works on American constitutional law are cited throughout the text, and are listed in the bibliography. References to periodical literature also provide the reader with recent, comprehensive treatments for further research.

Part One features a number of fundamental decisions of the Supreme Court on the structure of governmental institutions. Part Two in a like way provides edited versions of many of the leading decisions that recognize and interpret the norms we call constitutional rights. All of the case decisions reported in this book have been painstakingly edited, although a few opinions are left more or less intact. Footnotes have been omitted, with two exceptions. With few exceptions, concurring and dissenting opinions have been omitted.

There are certain tacit assumptions made in this book, and a decent respect for the opinion of the reader requires that at least a few of these be acknowledged. For one thing, these materials assume that government, and in some sense society, can be fashioned instrumentally by norms and institutions. The materials assume that more liberty is better than less. In the democratic spirit of our times, these materials do not challenge the belief that making government accountable and responsible to the "people," however defined, is generally or ultimately a good thing; or at least it is preferable to some other governmental apparatus.

More germanely perhaps, these materials might be read to assume, as does most scholarship on the subject, that societies possess a quality called "power," and that the quantity of this "power" is more or less constant, so that if it is bestowed on the government it cannot at the same time be retained by the people or held by them under the guise of "rights." In my lectures I refer to this style of thinking as "political mercantilism." It might be described more prosaically as comprehending power and rights as a "zero sum game." Either way, I do not ascribe to it. Nor do I share the view that law is best understood as a manifestation of societal power. For all we know, power may be merely a primal dynamic inbred into us by the evolutionary process, and government no more than the baroque cerebral reverberations of primitive ancestral hierarchies. Anyway I have tried to sanitize the text of my own views on this and most other subjects, so as to make the book less objectionable to lecturers who may wish to employ it in their own courses. In consolation, the footnotes contain more references to my publications than conventional modesty might otherwise allow.

This book was made possible by the combined efforts of dedicated co-workers Gina Clark-Bellak, Ilsa Klöckner, Shannon Hunt and Esther Edmondson. I would also like to thank Professors Barry Cushman, Richard A. Merrill, and Graham C. Lilly from the University of Virginia, and Richard Emory and C. Jay Robbins, IV all of whom used an earlier version of this book in their teaching in Münster, for their valuable comments.

Münster, June 2001   Thomas Lundmark

About the Author

Thomas Lundmark studied literature at San Diego State University and the University of Uppsala and holds a bachelor of arts degree in comparative literature, awarded in 1972. Mr. Lundmark studied law at the University of California, Berkeley, where he earned the juris doctor degree in 1976, and at the Albert-Ludwigs-Universität Freiburg as a Fulbright Scholar in 1976-77. Years later, in 1995, he was granted the degree Doktor der Rechte (Dr. jur.) by the Rheinische Friedrich-Wilhelms-Universität Bonn.

Returning to San Diego in 1977, Mr. Lundmark worked as a litigation and trial lawyer, first in private, then in public, practice. Coincidentally with a change in the focus of his law practice, Mr. Lundmark was appointed in 1986 an adjunct professor of law at the University of San Diego, teaching part-time until 1991, when he was appointed to a Fulbright professorship at the Rheinische Friedrich-Wilhelms-Universität Bonn. In Bonn he lectured and wrote primarily on American constitutional law. Mr. Lundmark's Fulbright status was extended for two years to enable him to teach and write on constitutional and other topics at the Universität Rostock and the Ernst Moritz Arndt Universität Greifswald. In the spring of 1995 he taught British and American constitutional law as a guest professor at the Friedrich-Schiller-Universität Jena. At the end of 1995 Mr. Lundmark returned to San Diego to practice law, teach, and write.

Mr. Lundmark was appointed a professor of law at the Westfälische Wilhelms-Universität Münster in early 1997. There he holds the chair in Common Law and Comparative Legal Theory and serves on the editorial board of the periodical *Rechtstheorie* ("Legal Theory"). He is the faculty advisor to the Foreign Law Program and regularly teaches US constitutional law. He has published widely in English and German in the areas of constitutional and environmental law, comparative law, and jurisprudence.

Introduction

This book is about democratic government and its citizens. Government possesses power. Citizens enjoy rights that protect them against untoward exercises of this power. All exercises of governmental power are traceable to, and legitimated by, the people, making them democratic.

To be meaningful and effective, democracy demands accountability. In American government, accountability is realized most immediately in the direct election of legislators. Accountability, and thereby democracy, is also fostered by the assignment of distinct governmental functions to discrete branches of government in accordance with the principle of separation of powers. Similar democratic considerations help account for the vertical division of governmental power in accordance with the principle of federalism.

But the principles of separation of powers and federalism also operate to split the monopoly of sovereign power. This splitting is believed to create a climate more hospitable to the promotion and conservation of liberty. When this device fails, judicial intervention is thought necessary to protect individual human rights from majoritarian zeal.

The materials covered in this book could be presented in any number of ways. A political scientist might stress political aspects, and focus on democracy. A historian might trace economic, political, and cultural developments. A legal theorist might begin by distinguishing law from other hierarchies, and by locating constitutional law within the resulting matrix. American constituional scholars, on the other hand, tend to emphasize ultimate questions of governmental power and constitutional rights, and to center on the role of the courts. They fashion concepts and institutions into more or less rigid frameworks. All of these approaches have their strengths and weaknesses. The constitutional lawyer's approach of plotting outer boundaries is valid and necessary because ultimate questions must often be confronted and decided in legislating, enforcing, and in interpreting law and constitutional rights. However, this approach has the unavoidable side effect of suggesting that government in fact exercises all of its power to the maximum allowable limit, and that liberty ceases at the constitutional frontier. Neither is, of course, true. In particular, by featuring constitutional rights, this approach disregards the multiplicity of far-reaching rights created by statute.

One half of this book is devoted each to governmental power and constitutional rights. The first half (Part One) sketches the structure of the federal government of the United States, focusing on the core principle of separation of powers (Subpart A). Part One also discusses so-called "checks and balances," which are deliberate departures from the principle of strict separation of powers. Federalism (Subpart B) refers to the interplay between the federal and state governments of the United States. The materials on federalism end by suggesting that democratic "localism," known in Europe as the principle of subsidiarity, be recognized as a justiciable (i.e., judicially enforceable) principle of American constitutional law.

Part One features a number of fundamental decisions of the United States Supreme Court, such as *Heart of Atlanta Motel v. United States, United States v. Lopez, McCulloch v. Maryland, Youngstown Sheet & Tube Co. v. Sawyer, Morrison v. Olson, Clinton v. Jones, Marbury v. Madison, Martin v. Hunter's Lessee,* and *Printz v. United States.* Part Two includes *Plyler v. Doe, United States v. Eichman, Brandenburg v. Ohio, Reno v. American Civil Liberties Union, R.A.V. v. City of St. Paul, Rosenberger v. Rector and Visitors of the University of Virginia, Wisconsin v. Yoder, Roe v. Wade, Korematsu v. United States, City of Richmond v. J.A. Croson Co., Washington v. Davis, Brown v. Board of Education,* and *Saenz v. Roe.*

Part Two appraises the panoply of explicit and implicit constitutional rights protected by the Constitution. In the past half century, the Supreme Court has been much more active in the subject matter of this part of the book than in that of the first. For ease of understanding and study, constitutional rights are subsumed under the concepts of liberty and equality. Liberty rights can usefully be thought of as individual rights. They include the "fundamental rights" recognized by the Constitution and by the Supreme Court, such as freedom of speech and the right of privacy. Equality rights are those enjoyed as a member of a protected group. According to reigning doctrine, the protected groups are known as "suspect" and "quasi-suspect classes." Racial classifications, for example, belong to the former group; gender classifications, to the latter.

PART ONE: GOVERNMENTAL POWER

Part One of this book addresses sovereign power and the structure of the government of the United States of America. The first of the two subparts (Subpart A) primarily treats the horizontal distribution of authority among the three limbs of the federal government. This distribution is known as separation of powers. The tactic of separating powers assigns responsibility for legislative, executive, and judicial functions to more or less independent branches, regardless of the subject matter or purpose of the governmental action. This tactic is tempered by theoretical limitations and by deliberate use of "checks and balances."

Subpart A introduces and expounds upon the theme that the federal government is one of limited, enumerated powers. This theme is taken up in Subpart B, which faces the topic of federalism, that is, the constitutional and prudential roles of the state and local governments vis-à-vis the federal government. The stratagem of federalism is to cleave federal matters from non-federal matters, to allocate the former more or less exclusively to the federal government, and to reserve the latter for more or less independent resolution by the states. Subpart B concludes by asking whether the value of democratic "localism," known in Europe as the principle of subsidiarity, ought not be recognized as a justiciable constitutional principle in the United States.

By splitting governmental authority, federalism is thought, among other things, to promote democratic accountability and to lessen the risk and gravity of undivided, extensive attacks on civil liberties. Coincidentally, these same purposes—pursuit of freedom and democracy—underpin the principle of separation of powers that is the principal focus of Subpart A.

Subpart A: The Federal Government

This book is about core principles. One such core principle is democracy. The US Constitution begins with the emphatic words "We the People." Public officials are routinely criticized for being out of touch with the will of the people, and public debate often centers on conflicting interpretations of that will. However, the US Constitution does not create a direct democracy. There is no provision for direct law-making, for example, by initiative. While federal legislators are elected, there is no provision for their recall. There is no provision for recall of the president or even for a parliamentary vote of "no confidence." Only two executive officials, the president and vice president, and none of the judges, are elected. Private individuals cannot demand enforcement of federal laws unless they have a personal stake ("standing"). While jurors hear many federal cases, they are acting in an official, representative capacity. Even then their verdict is ineffective unless reduced to judgment by a judge. All federal governmental action, whether legislative, executive, or judicial, is therefore democratically indirect.

Many fascinating questions regarding democracy, such as, Why is democracy good?, are not addressed in this book.[1] But democratic ideals are fundamental to the US Constitution and to the United States, and should not be ignored in considering the materials here presented. In particular when exploring the boundaries of constitutional rights one must ask whether the judicial safeguarding of those rights does not imply a failure of democratic institutions.

The Constitution took effect upon ratification by the ninth state on June 21, 1788, but the important states of Virginia and New York did not ratify until June 25, 1788 and July 26, 1789 respectively. The Founding Fathers of the American Constitution did not abide by the procedure called for in Article XIII of the Articles of Confederation (Attach. B). Does this mean that the Constitution is illegitimate, and that the Articles are still in effect?

The structure of the federal government of the United States is characterized by perhaps the most pronounced application of the principle of separation of powers in any country. A discussion of that principle provides a background against which the three branches of the federal government are presented. These are introduced in the order that they were created by the Constitution: the legislative, the executive, and the judiciary.

1. The Principle of Separation of Powers

The government of a state is thought to consist of three categories of powers: legislative, executive, and judicial, respectively making, enforcing, and interpreting law. Political theorist John Locke (1632-1704) favored a government of limited powers, one that was consequently less likely to violate the individual's life, health, liberty, and possessions. For the same reason, that is, the avoidance of despotic rule, Locke, in *Of Civil Government,* advocated entrusting the legislative and executive functions to distinct branches of government. The Lockian tradition of separation of powers is echoed in Justice Brandeis's dissenting opinion in *Myers v. United States*:

> The doctrine of the separation of powers was adopted by the convention of 1787 not to promote efficiency but to preclude the exercise of arbitrary power. The purpose was not to avoid friction, but, by means of the inevitable friction incident to the distribution of the governmental powers among three departments, to save the people from autocracy. . . . In America, as in England, the conviction prevailed then that the people must look to representative assemblies for the protection of their liberties. And protection of the individual . . . from the arbitrary or capricious exercise of power was then believed to be an essential of free government.[2]

---

1   See Dahl. For the author's thoughts see Lundmark, *Forms* and Lundmark, *East Germany*.
2   272 U.S. 52 (1926).

The divorcing of the judiciary from the legislature was championed most famously by Charles de Montesquieu (1689-1755) in *De l'esprit des loix*, published in 1748. When it came to the principle of separation of powers, Montesquieu's sympathies were more democratic than Locke's. According to Montesquieu, the arbitrary judicial *parlements* must be stripped of all law-making power. In turn, this power must be vested in a democratically elected and accountable legislature.[3] The theories of these two men, Locke and Montesquieu, formed the philosophical basis for the division of the federal government in the United States into three more or less distinct branches.

In the American conception of separation of powers, any governmental action requires the agreement of two branches; and any governmental action that limits an individual's constitutional rights must ordinarily navigate its way through all three organs of government, each of which must weigh the action's constitutionality. While not treated here, there is a pronounced doctrinal similarity between the federal and the state constitutional conceptions of separation of powers.[4]

The partition of powers into branches of government is not complete in the United States. This lack of complete separation is due to at least two reasons, one deliberate, and one inescapable, discussed here under the headings checks and balances and the ambiguity of the tri-partite demarcation.

a. Checks and Balances

One reason why the partition of governmental powers in the federal government is incomplete is that the US Constitution contains various "checks and balances," that is, procedures for one branch to superintend the other. While these devices may violate the letter of the principle of separation of powers, they do not violate its spirit, which is the avoidance of capricious or "despotic" rule. Indeed, the Framers of the American Constitution deliberately followed Montesquieu's exhortation when they granted the president the power to veto a bill before it becomes law,[5] an action more akin to law-making than law enforcement. Again à la Montesquieu the Framers bestowed upon the parliament (the Congress) the power to remove the president from office, although they limited the grounds for removal to conviction of "Treason, Bribery, or other high Crimes and Misdemeanors."[6] The impeachment process is hardly legislative, being a procedure more akin to criminal indictment (executive) and trial (judicial).

Other examples of deliberate checks and balances include the requirement that the president secure the approval of two-thirds of the senators to conclude a

---

3   See Merryman.
4   Gardner at p. 111.
5   Art. I, § 7.
6   Art. II, § 4.

treaty[7] and the condition that a majority of the Senate shall confirm the presidential appointment of ambassadors, federal judges, and other federal officers.[8] The popular election of the president,[9] rather than appointment by the parliament, might also be understood in this vein. So too can the institution of judicial review of legislative enactments and of executive decisions for conformity with the Constitution.

b. On the Ambiguity of the Tri-Partite Demarcation

The second reason why the separation of powers in the US is not complete is that the various powers do not lend themselves to clear theoretical and practical demarcation. In part this is true because they overlap to an uncertain, but nevertheless considerable, degree.

The theoretical division of the tripartite powers of government according to the principle of separation of powers is shaped by the proposition that the legislature, as the law giver, is the only branch that should be making law. But an internally consistent demarcation among the several powers with respect to law-making is impossible to construct. Legislation ordinarily refers to formal norms deliberately created by the legislature, which is the organ of government assembled for this purpose. The definition thus excludes custom. It also excludes the pronouncements of judicial tribunals. What then of the major areas of law that can only be found in judicial opinions? To take the crassest example: What of the many constitutional rights—privacy, for example—that are only vaguely subsumable, if at all, under textual provisions of the Constitution? Are these rights not law? Or what of "interstitial" law-making by the courts, which fills gaps sometimes left deliberately in legislation? Has the legislature somehow delegated law-making authority to the courts? And, most importantly for the United States, what of the common law, which regulated most all aspects of private law before the ascendancy of statutory law in the last century? Does anyone contend that the Framers of the American Constitution meant to demote the common law to the stature of delegated law-making or sub-law?

Legislation also differs from judicial pronouncements in that legislation looks to the future. It alters existing conditions by making a new rule for prospective application. Legislation is said to take effect *ex nunc*. *Ex post facto* laws are even specifically prohibited by the US Constitution.[10] Judicial judgments are pronounced *post factum*. One might think that the Anglo-American doctrine of *stare decisis*, which makes previous judicial decisions somehow binding on future decisions, offends this distinction and thus transgresses against the separation of powers principle. Actually, just the opposite is true. By adhering to legal rules

---

7   Art. II, § 2, cl. 2.

8   Art. II, § 2, cl. 2.

9   Art. II, § 1.

10   Art. I, §§ 9 and 10.

announced in previous decisions, judges are actually reducing the opportunity for judicial law-making and thus are promoting separation of powers. Of course judges may return to the rule and change it if it has proved to be wrong (corrective overruling). Further, they may determine that society has changed, perhaps through the passage of legislation, making a change in the rule necessary (renovative overruling). Merely changing a rule because the members of the court no longer agree with it (legislative overruling) should generally be condemned because, among other reasons, it violates notions of separation of powers.[11]

Execution of the laws means, most fundamentally, that every action of the executive must be based on law. "Law" for purposes of this truism must be read to include the Constitution, since the executive may have occasion to enforce the Constitution directly. In cases of perceived conflict between legislative and constitutional law, the executive would be required to comply with one or the other (depending upon one's conception of the state). But in making this determination, isn't the executive acting judicially? And what of instances of great public importance where the legislature has not acted? Locke would recognize executive prerogative in such cases, an innate privilege that might even supersede legislation. Here the executive would be acting legislatively. To stay with the executive for sake of example, can the executive be authorized to "legislate" interstitially, at least if based on specifically drafted authorizing legislation? Or what about informal, consistent practice of the executive in carrying out the law? Does this practice ever ripen into "law" and bind the executive? If so, can it not be said that the executive is "making law" by custom and practice? (These are issues dealt with below under the rubrics "executive privilege" and "delegation.")

Returning to the legislature, legislation ordinarily possesses general normative character. But this is not always the case. The Constitution has been interpreted to allow Congress to enact special "private" bills that benefit particular individuals, for example, by conferring the Congressional Medal of Honor, or by chartering a bank. These and other activities, though undertaken by the Congress by legislative enactment, have more of an administrative than legislative character.

Finally, the tremendous growth in the importance of administrative agencies and of federal departments in the past decades has prompted a reexamination of the accuracy of the tri-partite conception of the state, and of the efficacy of the principle of separation of powers in meeting its traditional objectives. Administrative agencies routinely exercise all three traditional governmental functions. They promulgate (legislate) regulations, they enforce (execute) these regulations and the laws on which they are based, and they adjudicate (judge) claims arising out of the application of the laws and regulations. Perhaps administrative agencies can best be understood as subordinate governmental subject-matter bodies, subordinate in the sense that municipalities are subordinate to the states. But if one

---

11   Lundmark, Juristische Technik at pp.162, 178-180.

thinks of them in this way, what has happened to democratic rule and to the constitutional guarantee of a republican form of government?[12]

2. Legislative Powers

The Congress created by the Articles of Confederation (Attach. B) was unicameral. But the present Congress has two houses, the House of Representatives and the Senate. The bifurcation, which was suggested by the bifurcation in the British Parliament into the House of Lords and House of Commons, resulted when the colonies with smaller populations refused to join a strengthened union in which their representation would be determined solely by their population. The smaller states preferred the New Jersey Plan, whereby each state would have an equal number of representatives. The New Jersey Plan was in turn rejected by the states with larger populations, like Virginia and New York. What resulted was the Great Compromise, which provided for equal representation by two representatives each in the upper house (Senate), and representation in proportion to population in the lower house (House of Representatives). In addition, the small states were guaranteed at least three votes for president and vice president in the electoral college.[13] Each state, regardless of population, is also entitled to at least one member in the House.[14]

Another (in)famous compromise concerned slavery. At the constitutional convention, the delegates from the northern states wanted the Congress to have the power to forbid trade in slaves. Most southern states opposed this. However, for purposes of representation in the House, the southern states wanted to count slaves even though slaves enjoyed neither citizenship nor the franchise (right to vote). According to the compromise, Congress was not able to forbid the foreign slave trade until 1808,[15] which it promptly did. In return, the southern states were allowed to count each slave as three-fifths of a person for purposes of representation in the House of Representatives.[16]

The Senate is composed of two senators from each state, elected for staggered, six-year terms.[17] Originally chosen by the state legislatures, senators have been popularly elected since 1913.[18] Members of the House of Representatives are elected to two-year terms,[19] the shortest of any national legislative body. In 1929 Congress fixed the total number of representatives at 435, elected in first-

---

12   See Art. IV, § 4.

13   See Art. II, § 1, cl. 2.

14   Art. I, § 2, cl. 3.

15   Art. I, § 9, cl. 1.

16   Art. I, § 2, cl. 3.

17   Art. I, § 3, cl. 1.

18   Amend. 17.

19   Art. I, § 2, cl. 1. Art. I, § 2, cl. 1

past-the-post elections in each of as many districts. The population of each district is approximately the same. Presently the average population of each congressional district is 650,000.

Each house of Congress is the judge of the qualifications of its members.[20] Each house has the power to punish its members for disorderly behavior by majority vote, and to expel a member by two-thirds' vote.[21] Both the House and the Senate have adopted procedural rules, as specifically provided in the Constitution.[22] Whereas the House rules strictly limit debate, senators, by contrast, are allowed to speak as long as they want unless 60 senators vote for closure. Abuse of this privilege to block a vote is referred to as a "filibuster."

With one exception—tax bills—a bill may originate in either house.[23] A bill becomes law only if it is passed by majority vote in both houses and is either signed by the president, ignored by the president for 10 days, or, if the bill is vetoed by the president, if the veto is overridden by a two-thirds' vote in each house of Congress.[24]

a. On the Meaning of the Term "Legislative"

In order to apply the principle of separation of powers, one must have some conception of what is meant by "legislative." One approach, employed above, is to attempt general, abstract definitions. Another, discussed in a later section, is to ask which actions of the Congress are subject to presidential veto.

The following discussion approaches the question in two additional ways. First, it explores the text of the Constitution for clues to the meaning of "legislative". Second, it examines the question of what actions are so inherently legislative that legislators enjoy absolute immunity when engaged in them.

i. The Text of the Constitution

According to the first sentence of the first article of the US Constitution, all legislative powers granted by the Constitution are vested in the Congress. The term "legislative powers" is not defined in the Constitution. Obviously, the term was chosen by the Framers of the Constitution to differentiate the legislative powers of Congress from the executive powers of the president and from the judicial powers of the supreme court.

Some inkling of what the Framers meant by "legislative powers" can be deduced from the text of the first article, which in part enumerates congressional powers.

---

20   Art. I, § 5, cl. 1.
21   Art. I, § 5, cl. 2.
22   Art. I, § 5, cl. 2.
23   Art. I, § 7, cl. 1.
24   Art. I, § 7, cl. 2.

The powers there enumerated can roughly be classified as follows (with examples in parentheses):

- Administrative powers: The power of Congress to organize its affairs (Art. I, § 2, cl. 5; Art. I, § 3, cl. 5; Art. I, § 4; Art. I, § 5; Art. I, 7, 3).

- Taxing and spending powers: The powers to raise money by imposing taxes, to borrow money, and to spend for the general welfare of the United States (Art. I, § 8, cls. 1, 2, and 6). The spending power is discussed below.

- Supervisory powers: The power to impeach, and try those officials charged with impeachable offenses (Art. I, § 2, cl. 5; Art. I, § 3, cl. 6).[25]

- Establishment powers: The powers to establish post offices, to coin money, to establish federal courts, to grant patents and copyrights (cls. 5, 7, 8, and 9), and to acquire property (Art. 4, § 3). The power to coin money includes the power to print paper money.[26]

- War power, and powers over external affairs: The powers to provide for defense, to declare war, and to punish violations of international law (cls. 10-16). This congressional authority continues after cessation of hostilities to remedy evils, such as housing shortages, attributable to the war.[27]

- Regulatory powers, including the power to investigate matters of legislative concern: The powers to regulate naturalization and bankruptcies, "To regulate Commerce with foreign Nations and among the several States, and with the Indian Tribes," and to govern the District of Columbia (Art. I, § 8, cls. 3, 4, and 17). The authority of Congress over the admission of non-citizens aliens is plenary.[28]

Of these classifications, only the last fits squarely within the definition of legislation proposed in the preceding section, that is, formal norms deliberately created by the legislature. Nevertheless, all of the specified powers, whether legislative in character or not, may, without question, constitutionally be exercised by the Congress.

Before moving on, consider the classification of the following powers that are specifically enumerated in various amendments to the Constitution:

- To enforce the amendment banning slavery (Amend. 13, § 2)

- To enforce the provisions of the 14th Amendment, which, among other things, guarantee due process and equal protection (Amend. 14, § 5)

---

25   The determination of the procedures for trying an impeached official is constitutionally entrusted to the Senate and is consequently not reviewable by the courts. Nixon v. United States, 506 U.S. 224 (1993).

26   Legal Tender Cases (Knox v. Lee), 79 U.S. 457 (1871).

27   Woods v. Cloyd W. Miller Co., 333 U.S. 138 (1948).

28   Kleindienst v. Mandel, 408 U.S. 753 (1972). The commerce clause is discussed in some detail below.

- To enforce voting rights (Amends. 15, § 2; 19, § 2; 23, § 2; 24, § 2; 26, § 2)

ii. Legislative Immunity

The distinction between legislative and non-legislative congressional activities is important for more than reasons of separation of powers. It is important in deciding what actions of the Congress are subject to presidential veto. It is also crucial to the existence and scope of congressional immunity.

The Constitution provides that, "for any Speech or Debate in either House," senators and representatives "shall not be questioned in any other Place."[29] This so-called "speech and debate clause" has been construed to forbid criminal or civil proceedings against members of Congress for "legislative acts."[30] The clause has also been extended to protect congressional aides who engage in acts that would be immune if performed by the legislator.[31]

To enjoy the protection of congressional immunity under the speech and debate clause, the conduct must be "legislative." Legislative conduct includes, in addition to statements on the floor of the Congress, matters such as conducting committee hearings, introducing material into the record at such hearings, and preparing committee reports; but it does not extend to the public distribution of committee reports, even when authorized by statute.[32] Nor does it extend to republication of defamatory statements originally made on the floor of the Congress.[33] And, while the speech and debate clause ordinarily protects a legislator's motivation for her legislative acts from judicial sanction, the clause does not prevent prosecution for bribery to influence legislation.[34]

b. Enumeration of Powers

The federal government is one of limited jurisdiction (power). This characteristic is felt most keenly in Article I, section 8, in which specified ("enumerated") powers are delegated by the individual states to the newly formed federal state. Copyrights, patents, bankruptcies, national defense, and "piracies and felonies committed on the high seas" possessed sufficient national import to merit inclusion among the enumerated powers. Criminal law and private law, which fell under the jurisdiction of the common law (state) courts, did not.

There is one broad exception to the doctrine that the federal government's powers are limited to those specifically enumerated in the Constitution. This exception encompasses external and foreign affairs, where the federal government's

---

29   Art. I, § 6, cl. 1.
30   United States v. Johnson, 383 U.S. 169 (1966).
31   Gravel v. United States, 408 U.S. 606 (1972).
32   Doe v. McMillan, 412 U.S. 306 (1973).
33   Hutchinson v. Proxmire, 443 U.S. 111 (1979).
34   United States v. Brewster, 408 U.S. 501 (1972).

powers are considered inherent and plenary despite not being expressly recited in the Constitution.[35] This exception is discussed below.

As mentioned above, the Constitution was drafted against the backdrop of the Articles of Confederation (Attach. B). The federal government formed by the Articles was seen as too weak because, among other things, it lacked the powers to tax and to regulate interstate commerce. As a result, that first federal government was dependent on voluntary contributions of money from the states. These in turn had taken to imposing import taxes on goods from other states, in effect competing against each other. As shown in the following subsections, both of these shortcomings were addressed in the new constitution in, respectively, the taxing and spending clauses and the commerce clause. The discussion below also addresses the necessary and proper clause of Article I, section 8, clause 18.

i. Taxing Power

In the words of the Constitution, "The Congress shall have Power To lay and collect Taxes, Duties, Imposts and Excises, to pay the Debts and provide for the common Defence and general Welfare of the United States."[36] "Duties" are import taxes. "Excises" or "excise taxes" are taxes on the sale, use, and production of goods, and sometimes on the privilege of doing business. "Imposts" is a term that generally includes both duties and excise taxes.

The Supreme Court was confronted for the first time in 1869 with the question whether the taxing power could be used to regulate. At issue was a federal law that imposed a tax on banknotes issued by state banks. The tax had the effect, and most certainly the intent, of taxing state-issued banknotes out of existence. The Court upheld the tax under Congress's power to "regulate the Value" of money.[37] The Congress may do indirectly by taxation that which it might have done directly by regulation.[38]

What then of a tax that cannot be justified by resort to an enumerated power? Here one must look to the dominant intent of the tax to determine whether its objective is to raise revenue or to regulate or prohibit specific activities. However, the Supreme Court has not been consistent in applying this test. For example, it upheld a tax on yellow margarine that was 40 times higher than the tax on white margarine despite the obvious purpose of supporting the dairy industry.[39]

In 1894 Congress enacted the federal government's first income tax law, one which taxed income derived from property. The Supreme Court ruled the tax unconstitutional because, as a "direct tax," it must be apportioned according to

---

35   United States v. Curtiss-Wright Export Corp., 299 U.S. 304 (1936).

36   Art. I, § 8, cl. 1.

37   Art. I, § 5.

38   Veazie Bank v. Fenno, 75 U.S. 533 (1869).

39   McCray v. United States, 195 U.S. 27 (1904).

Railway Co.[62] Professors Nowak and Rotunda described the state of affairs in their textbook *Constitutional Law* in 1991: "The Supreme Court today interprets the commerce clause as a complete grant of power."[63]

CASE: United States v. Lopez
514 U.S. 549 (1995)

CHIEF JUSTICE REHNQUIST delivered the opinion of the Court.

In the Gun-Free School Zones Act of 1990, Congress made it a federal offense "for any individual knowingly to possess a firearm at a place that the individual knows, or has reasonable cause to believe, is a school zone." The Act neither regulates a commercial activity nor contains a requirement that the possession be connected in any way to interstate commerce. We hold that the Act exceeds the authority of Congress "to regulate Commerce . . . among the several States. . . ."

We start with first principles. The Constitution creates a Federal Government of enumerated powers. See U.S. Const., Art. I, 8. As James Madison wrote, "[t]he powers delegated by the proposed Constitution to the federal government are few and defined. Those which are to remain in the State governments are numerous and indefinite." The Federalist No. 45, pp. 292-293 (C. Rossiter ed. 1961). This constitutionally mandated division of authority "was adopted by the Framers to ensure protection of our fundamental liberties." *Gregory v. Ashcroft*. . . . "Just as the separation and independence of the coordinate branches of the Federal Government serves to prevent the accumulation of excessive power in any one branch, a healthy balance of power between the States and the Federal Government will reduce the risk of tyranny and abuse from either front." Ibid.

The Constitution delegates to Congress the power "[t]o regulate Commerce with foreign Nations, and among the several States, and with the Indian Tribes." The Court, through Chief Justice Marshall, first defined the nature of Congress' commerce power in *Gibbons v. Ogden*. . . .

> Commerce, undoubtedly, is traffic, but it is something more: it is intercourse. It describes the commercial intercourse between nations, and parts of nations, in all its branches, and is regulated by prescribing rules for carrying on that intercourse.

---

62   295 U.S. 330 (1935).

63   At p. 154.

The commerce power "is the power to regulate; that is, to prescribe the rule by which commerce is to be governed. This power, like all others vested in Congress, is complete in itself, may be exercised to its utmost extent, and acknowledges no limitations, other than are prescribed in the constitution." . . . The Gibbons Court, however, acknowledged that limitations on the commerce power are inherent in the very language of the Commerce Clause.

> It is not intended to say that these words comprehend that commerce, which is completely internal, which is carried on between man and man in a State, or between different parts of the same State, and which does not extend to or affect other States. Such a power would be inconvenient, and is certainly unnecessary.

> Comprehensive as the word 'among' is, it may very properly be restricted to that commerce which concerns more States than one. . . . The enumeration presupposes something not enumerated; and that something, if we regard the language or the subject of the sentence, must be the exclusively internal commerce of a State. . . .

In 1887, Congress enacted the Interstate Commerce Act, and in 1890, Congress enacted the Sherman Antitrust Act. These laws ushered in a new era of federal regulation under the commerce power. . . .

Jones & Laughlin Steel, Darby, and *Wickard* ushered in an era of Commerce Clause jurisprudence that greatly expanded the previously defined authority of Congress under that Clause. In part, this was a recognition of the great changes that had occurred in the way business was carried on in this country. Enterprises that had once been local or at most regional in nature had become national in scope. But the doctrinal change also reflected a view that earlier Commerce Clause cases artificially had constrained the authority of Congress to regulate interstate commerce.

But even these modern-era precedents which have expanded congressional power under the Commerce Clause confirm that this power is subject to outer limits. In *Jones & Laughlin Steel,* the Court warned that the scope of the interstate commerce power "must be considered in the light of our dual system of government and may not be extended so as to embrace effects upon interstate commerce so indirect and remote that to embrace them, in view of our complex society, would effectually obliterate the distinction between what is national and what is local and create a completely centralized government." . . .

Consistent with this structure, we have identified three broad categories of activity that Congress may regulate under its commerce power. First, Congress may regulate the use of the channels of interstate commerce. . . . Second, Congress is empowered to regulate and protect the instrumentalities of interstate commerce, or persons or things in interstate commerce, even though the threat may come only from intrastate activities. . . . Finally, Congress' commerce authority includes the power to regulate those activities having a substantial relation to interstate commerce, *Jones & Laughlin Steel*, i.e., those activities that substantially affect interstate commerce. [*Wirtz*]

Within this final category, admittedly, our case law has not been clear whether an activity must "affect" or "substantially affect" interstate commerce in order to be within Congress' power to regulate it under the Commerce Clause. . . . We conclude, consistent with the great weight of our case law, that the proper test requires an analysis of whether the regulated activity "substantially affects" interstate commerce.

We now turn to consider the power of Congress, in the light of this framework, to enact § 922(q). The first two categories of authority may be quickly disposed of: § 922(q) is not a regulation of the use of the channels of interstate commerce, nor is it an attempt to prohibit the interstate transportation of a commodity through the channels of commerce; nor can § 922(q) be justified as a regulation by which Congress has sought to protect an instrumentality of interstate commerce or a thing in interstate commerce. Thus, if § 922(q) is to be sustained, it must be under the third category as a regulation of an activity that substantially affects interstate commerce.

First, we have upheld a wide variety of congressional Acts regulating intrastate economic activity where we have concluded that the activity substantially affected interstate commerce. Examples include the regulation of intrastate coal mining [*Hodel*], intrastate extortionate credit transactions [*Perez*], restaurants utilizing substantial interstate supplies [*McClung*], inns and hotels catering to interstate guests [*Heart of Atlanta Motel*], and production and consumption of home-grown wheat [*Wickard*]. These examples are by no means exhaustive, but the pattern is clear. Where economic activity substantially affects interstate commerce, legislation regulating that activity will be sustained.

Even *Wickard*, which is perhaps the most far reaching example of Commerce Clause authority over intrastate activity, involved economic activity in a way that the possession of a gun in a school zone does not. Roscoe Filburn operated a small farm in Ohio, on which, in the year involved, he raised 23 acres of wheat. It was his practice to sow winter wheat in the fall, and after harvesting it in July to sell a portion of the crop, to feed part of it to poultry and livestock on the farm, to use some in making flour for home consumption, and to keep the remainder for seeding future crops. The Secretary of Agriculture assessed a penalty against him under the

Agricultural Adjustment Act of 1938 because he harvested about 12 acres more wheat than his allotment under the Act permitted. The Act was designed to regulate the volume of wheat moving in interstate and foreign commerce in order to avoid surpluses and shortages, and concomitant fluctuation in wheat prices, which had previously obtained. The Court said, in an opinion sustaining the application of the Act to Filburn's activity:

> One of the primary purposes of the Act in question was to increase the market price of wheat and to that end to limit the volume thereof that could affect the market. It can hardly be denied that a factor of such volume and variability as home-consumed wheat would have a substantial influence on price and market conditions. This may arise because being in marketable condition such wheat overhangs the market and, if induced by rising prices, tends to flow into the market and check price increases. But if we assume that it is never marketed, it supplies a need of the man who grew it which would otherwise be reflected by purchases in the open market. Home-grown wheat in this sense competes with wheat in commerce.

Section 922(q) is a criminal statute that by its terms has nothing to do with "commerce" or any sort of economic enterprise, however broadly one might define those terms. Section 922(q) is not an essential part of a larger regulation of economic activity, in which the regulatory scheme could be undercut unless the intrastate activity were regulated. It cannot, therefore, be sustained under our cases upholding regulations of activities that arise out of or are connected with a commercial transaction, which viewed in the aggregate, substantially affects interstate commerce.

Second, § 922(q) contains no jurisdictional element which would ensure, through case-by-case inquiry, that the firearm possession in question affects interstate commerce. For example, in *United States v. Bass*, . . . the Court interpreted former 18 U.S.C. § 1202(a), which made it a crime for a felon to "receiv[e], posses[s], or transpor[t] in commerce or affecting commerce . . . any firearm." . . . The Court interpreted the possession component of § 1202(a) to require an additional nexus to interstate commerce both because the statute was ambiguous and because "unless Congress conveys its purpose clearly, it will not be deemed to have significantly changed the federal-state balance." . . . Unlike the statute in Bass, § 922(q) has no express jurisdictional element which might limit its reach to a discrete set of firearm possessions that additionally have an explicit connection with or effect on interstate commerce. . . .

The Government's essential contention, *in fine*, is that we may determine here that § 922(q) is valid because possession of a firearm in a local school zone does indeed substantially affect interstate commerce. The Government argues that possession of a firearm in a school zone may result in violent crime and that violent crime can be expected to affect the functioning of the national economy in two ways. First, the costs of violent crime are substantial, and, through the mechanism of insurance, those costs are spread throughout the population. Second, violent crime reduces the willingness of individuals to travel to areas within the country that are perceived to be unsafe. Cf. Heart of Atlanta Motel. . . . The Government also argues that the presence of guns in schools poses a substantial threat to the educational process by threatening the learning environment. A handicapped educational process, in turn, will result in a less productive citizenry. That, in turn, would have an adverse effect on the Nation's economic well-being. As a result, the Government argues that Congress could rationally have concluded that § 922(q) substantially affects interstate commerce.

We pause to consider the implications of the Government's arguments. The Government admits, under its "costs of crime" reasoning, that Congress could regulate not only all violent crime, but all activities that might lead to violent crime, regardless of how tenuously they relate to interstate commerce. Similarly, under the Government's "national productivity" reasoning, Congress could regulate any activity that it found was related to the economic productivity of individual citizens: family law (including marriage, divorce, and child custody), for example. Under the theories that the Government presents in support of § 922(q), it is difficult to perceive any limitation on federal power, even in areas such as criminal law enforcement or education where States historically have been sovereign. Thus, if we were to accept the Government's arguments, we are hard-pressed to posit any activity by an individual that Congress is without power to regulate.

. . .

These are not precise formulations, and in the nature of things they cannot be. But we think they point the way to a correct decision of this case. The possession of a gun in a local school zone is in no sense an economic activity that might, through repetition elsewhere, substantially affect any sort of interstate commerce. Respondent was a local student at a local school; there is no indication that he had recently moved in interstate commerce, and there is no requirement that his possession of the firearm have any concrete tie to interstate commerce.

To uphold the Government's contentions here, we would have to pile inference upon inference in a manner that would bid fair to convert congressional authority under the Commerce Clause to a general police power of the sort retained by the States. Admittedly, some of our prior cases have taken long steps down that road, giving great deference to congressional action. . . . The broad language in these opinions has suggested the possibility of additional expansion, but we decline here to proceed any further. To do so would require us to conclude that the Constitution's enumeration of powers does not presuppose something not enumerated, . . . and that there never will be a distinction between what is truly national and what is truly local. . . . This we are unwilling to do.

For the foregoing reasons the judgment of the Court of Appeals is affirmed.

JUSTICE KENNEDY, with whom JUSTICE O'CONNOR joins, concurring.

. . .

Of the various structural elements in the Constitution, separation of powers, checks and balances, judicial review, and federalism, only concerning the last does there seem to be much uncertainty respecting the existence, and the content, of standards that allow the judiciary to play a significant role in maintaining the design contemplated by the Framers. Although the resolution of specific cases has proved difficult, we have derived from the Constitution workable standards to assist in preserving separation of powers and checks and balances. . . . These standards are by now well accepted. Judicial review is also established beyond question, *Marbury v. Madison* . . . , and though we may differ when applying its principles, its legitimacy is undoubted. Our role in preserving the federal balance seems more tenuous.

There is irony in this, because of the four structural elements in the Constitution just mentioned, federalism was the unique contribution of the Framers to political science and political theory. Though on the surface the idea may seem counterintuitive, it was the insight of the Framers that freedom was enhanced by the creation of two governments, not one. "In the compound republic of America, the power surrendered by the people is first divided between two distinct governments, and then the portion allotted to each subdivided among distinct and separate departments. Hence a double security arises to the rights of the people. The different governments will control each other, at the same time that each will be controlled by itself." The Federalist No. 51.

The theory that two governments accord more liberty than one requires for its realization two distinct and discernable lines of political accountability: one between the citizens and the Federal Government; the second between the citizens and the States. If, as Madison expected, the federal and state governments are to control each other, see The Federalist No. 51, and hold each other in check by competing for the affections of the people, see The Federalist No. 46, those citizens must have some means of knowing which of the two governments to hold accountable for the failure to perform a given function. [Were] the Federal Government to take over the regulation of entire areas of traditional state concern, areas having nothing to do with the regulation of commercial activities, the boundaries between the spheres of federal and state authority would blur and political responsibility would become illusory. The resultant inability to hold either branch of the government answerable to the citizens is more dangerous even than devolving too much authority to the remote central power.

. . .

An interference of these dimensions occurs here, for it is well established that education is a traditional concern of the States. The proximity to schools, including of course schools owned and operated by the States or their subdivisions, is the very premise for making the conduct criminal. In these circumstances, we have a particular duty to insure that the federal-state balance is not destroyed.

While it is doubtful that any State, or indeed any reasonable person, would argue that it is wise policy to allow students to carry guns on school premises, considerable disagreement exists about how best to accomplish that goal. In this circumstance, the theory and utility of our federalism are revealed, for the States may perform their role as laboratories for experimentation to devise various solutions where the best solution is far from clear. See [New State Ice Co.] (Brandeis, J., dissenting).

If a State or municipality determines that harsh criminal sanctions are necessary and wise to deter students from carrying guns on school premises, the reserved powers of the States are sufficient to enact those measures. Indeed, over 40 States already have criminal laws outlawing the possession of firearms on or near school grounds.

Other, more practicable means to rid the schools of guns may be thought by the citizens of some States to be preferable for the safety and welfare of the schools those States are charged with maintaining. These might include inducements to inform on violators where the information leads to arrests or confiscation of the guns, programs to encourage the voluntary surrender of guns with some provision for amnesty, penalties imposed on parents or guardians for failure to supervise the child, laws providing for suspension or expulsion of gun-toting students, or programs for expulsion with assignment to special facilities.

The statute now before us forecloses the States from experimenting and exercising their own judgment in an area to which States lay claim by right of history and expertise, and it does so by regulating an activity beyond the realm of commerce in the ordinary and usual sense of that term. The tendency of this statute to displace state regulation in areas of traditional state concern is evident from its territorial operation. There are over 100,000 elementary and secondary schools in the United States. Each of these now has an invisible federal zone extending 1,000 feet beyond the (often irregular) boundaries of the school property. In some communities no doubt it would be difficult to navigate without infringing on those zones. Yet throughout these areas, school officials would find their own programs for the prohibition of guns in danger of displacement by the federal authority unless the State chooses to enact a parallel rule. . . .

[Other concurring and dissenting opinions omitted.]

dd. The Fallout from *Lopez*

The magnitude of the fallout from the *Lopez* decision is not mathematically quantifiable. More than 100 federal laws in the United States Code, including more that 25 criminal provisions, employ the words "affecting commerce" in defining the reach of the law. In addition, many laws which are based on the commerce clause, like the Gun-Free School Zone Act, do not mention the commerce clause at all. Because of these facts, and because of the breadth of the topic, the following discussion can make only observations of a general nature.

Federal social programs—such as old-age benefits (Social Security), medical care for the poor (Medicaid), and medical care for the aged and handicapped (Medicare)—are based on the federal spending power and as such are not directly affected by the *Lopez* decision. Federal anti-discrimination laws, even if based on the commerce clause, are not threatened by *Lopez* because they regulate the channels of commerce, such as hotels, restaurants, and the workplace. Tax laws enjoy their own base of federal legislative jurisdiction, even when employed as instruments of indirect regulation.[64]

Federal criminal law is concerned to a great extent with interstate and international crimes, such as drug smuggling, and crimes which employ the channels of commerce, including telephones and the post office. Consequently, post-*Lopez* courts have upheld federal convictions for carjacking,[65] possession of a machine gun,[66] and blocking access to an abortion clinic.[67] However, a few challenges based on *Lopez* have been successful. In *United States v. Denalli*,[68] the court refused to allow federal prosecution for arson on a private residence, and in *United*

---

64   Sonzinsky v. United States, 300 U.S. 506 (1937), rev'd on other grounds.

65   United States v. Bishop, 66 F.3d 569 (3d Cir. 1995).

66   United States v. Wilks, 58 F.3d 1518 (10th Cir. 1995).

67   Cheffer v. Reno, 55 F.3d 1517 (11th Cir. 1995).

68   73 F.3d 328 (11th Cir. 1996).

States v. Pappadopoulos,[69] the court declared the application of a federal law prohibiting arson on a building used in interstate commerce, and providing for greater penalties for the use of fire in committing other felonies, unconstitutional. And in the *United States v. Morrison*[70] the Supreme Court held that neither the commerce clause nor the enforcement clause of the 14th Amendment empowered Congress to create a cause of action for gender-motivated torts.

Federal family law is a field in which the impact of *Lopez* has already been felt: federal district courts in the Third, Fourth, and Ninth Circuits have ruled that Congress exceeded its regulatory powers under the commerce clause in enacting the Child Support Recovery Act of 1992, which establishes a national program to aid states in developing and implementing child support enforcement policies and procedures.[71] But the California Court of Appeal and federal district courts in the First, Second, Third, Fourth, Seventh, Tenth, and Eleventh Circuits have upheld the act.[72]

Other family law legislation appears constitutional under *Lopez* either because (1) it regulates the "channels of commerce,"[73] (2) it employs the grant of Congressional power under the 14th Amendment enforce that Amendment's prohibition of state discrimination,[74] or (3) it employs the spending power of Congress.[75]

The *Lopez* case will have little effect on the constitutionality of federal environmental legislation because most of the laws are not based exclusively on the "affecting commerce" aspect of the commerce clause. If they are, then jurisdictional problems may arise in the application of an otherwise constitutional statute. The Clean Water Act seeks to control the discharge of pollutants into the "waters of the United States." Overzealous administrative extension of this territorial juris-

---

69   64 F.3d 522 (9th Cir. 1995).

70   United States v. Morrison, 529 U.S. 598 (2000), striking down the Violence Against Women Act.

71   United States v. Mussari, 894 F. Supp. 1360 (D. Ariz. 1995); United States v. Schroeder, 894 F. Supp. 360, 364 (D. Ariz. 1995).

72   United States v. Lewis, 936 F. Supp. 1093 (D.R.I. 1996); United States v. Nichols, 928 F. Supp. 302 (S.D.N.Y. 1996); United States v. Hampshire, 892 F. Supp. 1327 (D. Kan 1995), aff'd 95 F.3d 999 (10th Cir. 1996); United States v. Sims, 936 F. Supp. 817 (N.D. Okla. 1996); Kilroy v. Winter, 54 Cal. App. 4th 793 (1997); United States v. Hopper, 899 F. Supp. 389, 393 (S.D. Ind. 1995); United States v. Murphy, 893 F. Supp. 614, 616-17 (W.D. Va. 1995); United States v. Parker, 911 F. Supp. 830 (E.D. Pa. 1995); and United States v. Bailey, 902 F. Supp. 727 (W.D. Tex. 1995); see generally Gottovi.

73   E.g., Safe Homes for Women Act of 1994, which makes domestic abuse a federal crime when the perpetrator crosses state lines.

74   E.g., Howard M. Metzenbaum Multi-Ethnic Placement Act of 1994, which prohibits state agencies from denying foster or adoptive placements solely on the basis of race.

75   Child Abuse Prevention and Treatment Act, which establishes a comprehensive federal program directed toward the prevention and treatment of child abuse and neglect. See generally Hasday, *et al.*

diction can bring invalidity of an action.[76] Another very important piece of environmental legislation, the Clean Air Act, is not affected by the reasoning of the *Lopez* decision because it employs a system of incentives to the states to entice them to prepare and enforce State Implementation Plans. The Endangered Species Act can in part be considered an exercise of the power of the federal government to enter into treaties with foreign countries.[77] Federal laws implementing treaties are binding on the states without a separate ground of federal legislative jurisdiction.[78] The National Environmental Policy Act, like many federal environmental laws, affects federal agencies and projects that are supported by federal funds, in other words, projects which would fall under Congress's spending power. As such they are not affected by the *Lopez* decision.

Other federal environmental laws, on the other hand, are exclusively based on the interstate commerce clause. Exemplary is the Surface Mining Control and Reclamation Act of 1977, which dictates mining practices for open-space mining and requires restoration after mining. In 1981 the Supreme Court upheld the constitutionality of the law despite the fact that it only indirectly (if at all) regulated interstate commerce.[79] The Supreme Court would likely reach the same result today, because mining is a commercial activity with a substantial impact on interstate and foreign commerce.

iv. Necessary and Proper Clause

The final power enumerated in Article I, section 8, is clause 18:

> [The Congress shall have Power] To make all Laws which shall be necessary and proper for carrying into Execution the foregoing Powers, and all other Powers vested by this Constitution in the Government of the United States, or in any Department thereof.

This clause was construed by the United States Supreme Court in the famous and historically fascinating case of *McCulloch v. Maryland*,[80] which has been consistently followed ever since. The Congress had chartered (created) a bank called the Bank of the United States in 1790, to lend money to the new government and to assist with collection of taxes. Jefferson was among those who opposed creation. He argued, "[T]he constitution allows only the means which are necessary, not merely 'convenient,' for effectuating the enumerated powers. If such a latitude of construction be allowed to this phrase as to give any non-enumerated power [to Congress,] it would swallow up all the delegated powers, and reduce the whole to one power."[81] That bank's charter expired in 1811. The bank was

---

76   E.g., Hoffman Homes, Inc. v. EPA, 999 F.2d 256, 261 (7th Cir. 1993).

77   Missouri v. Holland, 252 U.S. 416 (1920).

78   Ware v. Hylton, 3 U.S. 199 (1796).

79   Hodel v. Virginia Surface Mining & Reclamation Assn., Inc., 452 U.S. 264 (1981).

80   17 U.S. 316 (1819).

81   Stone at p.67

recreated in 1816, with the federal government owning 20 percent. The bank was unpopular with the states and with state-chartered banks. Some states enacted laws prohibiting the Bank of the United States from transacting business on state soil. Other states, such as Maryland, taxed it. When the Bank of the United States refused to pay the tax, claiming to be a federal institution and therefore immune from taxation, Maryland sued McCulloch, who was the bank's cashier in Baltimore, Maryland. McCulloch and his federal employer, who lost in the Maryland courts, appealed to the United States Supreme Court, which had ruled three years earlier, in *Martin v Hunter's Lessee*, repeated below, that it had jurisdiction to review the constitutionality of judgments from the state courts. Before ruling that the state could not constitutionally tax a federal facility, the Supreme Court had to rule on the constitutionality of the bank's creation.

The Supreme Court marshalled three arguments to sustain the creation of the bank. First, the Supreme Court indicated that the unchallenged existence of the bank had in effect conferred a presumption of constitutionality upon it. Second, the Court broadly construed the powers of Congress under Article I. Even though the Constitution does not enumerate a power to create a bank, Chief Justice Marshall wrote:

> A constitution, to contain an accurate detail of all the subdivisions of which its great powers will admit, and of all the means by which thy may be carried into execution, would partake of the prolixity of a legal code, and could scarcely be embraced by the human mind. . . . In considering this question, then, we must never forget that this is a constitution we are expounding.

In short, Marshall was pleading for a liberal interpretation of the Constitution in favor of grants of power to the federal government.

The third argument, and the one that concerns us here, is that Congress may incorporate a national bank as a "necessary and proper" means of carrying out its delegated powers to lay and collect taxes (Art. I, §8, cl. 1), borrow money (cl. 2), regulate commerce among the several states (cl. 3), declare and conduct war (cl. 11), and raise and support armies and a navy (cls. 12 and 13).

CASE: McCulloch v. Maryland
17 U.S. 316 (1819)

MARSHALL, Ch. J., delivered the opinion of the court.

In the case now to be determined, the defendant, a sovereign state, denies the obligation of a law enacted by the legislature of the Union, and the plaintiff, on his part, contests the validity of an act which has been passed by the legislature of that state. The constitution of our country, in its most interesting and vital parts, is to be considered; the conflicting powers of the government of the Union and of its members, as marked in that constitution, are to be discussed; and an opinion given, which may essentially influence the great operations of the government. No tribunal can approach such a question without a deep sense of its importance, and of the awful responsibility involved in its decision. But it must be decided peacefully, or remain a source of hostile legislation, perhaps, of hostility of a still more serious nature; and if it is to be so decided, by this tribunal alone can the decision be made. On the supreme court of the United States has the constitution of our country devolved this important duty.

The first question made in the cause is, has congress power to incorporate a bank?

It has been truly said, that this can scarcely be considered as an open question, entirely unprejudiced by the former proceedings of the nation respecting it. The principle now contested was introduced at a very early period of our history, has been recognized by many successive legislatures, and has been acted upon by the judicial department, in cases of peculiar delicacy, as a law of undoubted obligation.

It will not be denied, that a bold and daring usurpation might be resisted, after an acquiescence still longer and more complete than this. But it is conceived, that a doubtful question, one on which human reason may pause, and the human judgment be suspended, in the decision of which the great principles of liberty are not concerned, but the respective powers of those who are equally the representatives of the people, are to be adjusted; if not put at rest by the practice of the government, ought to receive a considerable impression from that practice. An exposition of the constitution, deliberately established by legislative acts, on the faith of which an immense property has been advanced, ought not to be lightly disregarded.

The power now contested was exercised by the first congress elected under the present constitution. The bill for incorporating the Bank of the United States did not steal upon an unsuspecting legislature, and pass unobserved. Its principle was completely understood, and was opposed with equal zeal and ability. After being resisted, first, in the fair and open field of debate, and afterwards, in the executive cabinet, with as much persevering talent as any measure has ever experienced, and being supported by arguments which convinced minds as pure and as intelligent as this country can boast, it became a law. The original act was permitted to expire; but a short experience of the embarrassments to which the refusal to revive it exposed the government, convinced those who were most prejudiced against the measure of its necessity, and induced the passage of the present law. It would require no ordinary share of intrepidity, to assert that a measure adopted under these circumstances, was a bold and plain usurpation, to which the constitution gave no countenance.

These observations belong to the cause; but they are not made under the impression, that, were the question entirely new, the law would be found irreconcilable with the constitution.

In discussing this question, the counsel for the state of Maryland have deemed it of some importance, in the construction of the constitution, to consider that instrument, not as emanating from the people, but as the act of sovereign and independent states. The powers of the general government, it has been said, are delegated by the states, who alone are truly sovereign; and must be exercised in subordination to the states, who alone possess supreme dominion.

It would be difficult to sustain this proposition. The convention which framed the constitution was indeed elected by the state legislatures. But the instrument, when it came from their hands, was a mere proposal, without obligation, or pretensions to it. It was reported to the then existing congress of the United States, with a request that it might 'be submitted to a convention of delegates, chosen in each state by the people thereof, under the recommendation of its legislature, for their assent and ratification.' This mode of proceeding was adopted; and by the convention, by congress, and by the state legislatures, the instrument was submitted to the people. They acted upon it in the only manner in which they can act safely, effectively and wisely, on such a subject, by assembling in convention. It is true, they assembled in their several states—and where else should they have assembled? No political dreamer was ever wild enough to think of breaking down the lines which separate the states, and of compounding the American people into one common mass. Of consequence, when they act, they act in their states. But the measures they adopt do not, on that account, cease to be the measures of the people themselves, or become the measures of the state governments.

From these conventions, the constitution derives its whole authority. The government proceeds directly from the people; is 'ordained and established,' in the name of the people; and is declared to be ordained, 'in order to form a more perfect union, establish justice, insure domestic tranquillity, and secure the blessings of liberty to themselves and to their posterity.' The assent of the states, in their sovereign capacity, is implied, in calling a convention, and thus submitting that instrument to the people. But the people were at perfect liberty to accept or reject it; and their act was final. It required not the affirmance, and could not be negatived, by the state governments. The constitution, when thus adopted, was of complete obligation, and bound the state sovereignties. . . .

The government of the Union, then (whatever may be the influence of this fact on the case), is, emphatically and truly, a government of the people. In form, and in substance, it emanates from them. Its powers are granted by them, and are to be exercised directly on them, and for their benefit.

This government is acknowledged by all, to be one of enumerated powers. The principle, that it can exercise only the powers granted to it, [is] now universally admitted. But the question respecting the extent of the powers actually granted, is perpetually arising, and will probably continue to arise, so long as our system shall exist.

In discussing these questions, the conflicting powers of the general and state governments must be brought into view, and the supremacy of their respective laws, when they are in opposition, must be settled.

If any one proposition could command the universal assent of mankind, we might expect it would be this—that the government of the Union, though limited in its powers, is supreme within its sphere of action. This would seem to result, necessarily, from its nature. It is the government of all; its powers are delegated by all; it represents all, and acts for all. Though any one state may be willing to control its operations, no state is willing to allow others to control them. The nation, on those subjects on which it can act, must necessarily bind its component parts. But this question is not left to mere reason: the people have, in express terms, decided it, by saying, 'this constitution, and the laws of the United States, which shall be made in pursuance thereof,' 'shall be the supreme law of the land,' and by requiring that the members of the state legislatures, and the officers of the executive and judicial departments of the states, shall take the oath of fidelity to it. . . .

Among the enumerated powers, we do not find that of establishing a bank or creating a corporation. But there is no phrase in the instrument which, like the articles of confederation [Art. II], excludes incidental or implied powers; and which requires that everything granted shall be expressly and minutely described. Even the 10th amendment, which was framed for the purpose of quieting the excessive jealousies which had been excited, omits the word 'expressly,' and declares only, that the powers 'not delegated to the United States, nor prohibited to the states, are reserved to the states or to the people;' thus leaving the question, whether the particular power which may become the subject of contest, has been delegated to the one government, or prohibited to the other, to depend on a fair construction of the whole instrument. The men who drew and adopted this amendment had experienced the embarrassments resulting from the insertion of this word in the articles of confederation, and probably omitted it, to avoid those embarrassments. A constitution, to contain an accurate detail of all the subdivisions of which its great powers will admit, and of all the means by which they may be carried into execution, would partake of the prolixity of a legal code, and could scarcely be embraced by the human mind. It would, probably, never be understood by the public. Its nature, therefore, requires, that only its great outlines should be marked, its important objects designated, and the minor ingredients which compose those objects, be deduced from the nature of the objects themselves. That this idea was entertained by the framers of the American constitution, is not only to be inferred from the nature of the instrument, but from the language. Why else were some of the limitations, found in the 9th section of the 1st article, introduced? It is also, in some degree, warranted, by their having omitted to use any restrictive term which might prevent its receiving a fair and just interpretation. In considering this question, then, we must never forget that it is a constitution we are expounding.

Although, among the enumerated powers of government, we do not find the word 'bank' or 'incorporation,' we find the great powers, to lay and collect taxes; to borrow money; to regulate commerce; to declare and conduct a war; and to raise and support armies and navies. The sword and the purse, all the external relations, and no inconsiderable portion of the industry of the nation, are intrusted to its government. It can never be pretended, that these vast powers draw after them others of inferior importance, merely because they are inferior. Such an idea can never be advanced. But it may with great reason be contended, that a government, intrusted with such ample powers, on the due execution of which the happiness and prosperity of the nation so vitally depends, must also be intrusted with ample means for their execution. The power being given, it is the interest of the nation to facilitate its execution. It can never be their interest, and cannot be presumed to have been their intention, to clog and embarrass its execution, by withholding the most appropriate means. Throughout this vast republic, from the St. Croix to the Gulf of Mexico, from the Atlantic to the Pacific, revenue is to be collected and expended, armies are to be marched and supported. The exigencies of the nation may require, that the treasure raised in the north should be transported to the south, that raised in the east, conveyed to the west, or that this order should be reversed. Is that construction of the constitution to be preferred, which would render these operations difficult, hazardous and expensive? Can we adopt that construction (unless the words imperiously require it), which would impute to the framers of that instrument, when granting these powers for the public good, the intention of impeding their exercise, by withholding a choice of means? . . .

It is not denied, that the powers given to the government imply the ordinary means of execution. That, for example, of raising revenue, and applying it to national purposes, is admitted to imply the power of conveying money from place to place, as the exigencies of the nation may require, and of employing the usual means of conveyance. . . .

But the constitution of the United States has not left the right of congress to employ the necessary means, for the execution of the powers conferred on the government, to general reasoning. To its enumeration of powers is added, that of making 'all laws which shall be necessary and proper, for carrying into execution the foregoing powers, and all other powers vested by this constitution, in the government of the United States, or in any department thereof.'

The counsel for the state of Maryland have urged various arguments, to prove that this clause, though, in terms, a grant of power, is not so, in effect; but is really restrictive of the general right, which might otherwise be implied, of selecting means for executing the enumerated powers. . . .

[The] argument on which most reliance is placed, is drawn from that peculiar language of this clause. Congress is not empowered by it to make all laws, which may have relation to the powers confered on the government, but such only as may be 'necessary and proper' for carrying them into execution. The word 'necessary' is considered as controlling the whole sentence, and as limiting the right to pass laws for the execution of the granted powers, to such as are indispensable, and without which the power would be nugatory. That it excludes the choice of means, and leaves to congress, in each case, that only which is most direct and simple.

Is it true, that this is the sense in which the word 'necessary' is always used? Does it always import an absolute physical necessity, so strong, that one thing to which another may be termed necessary, cannot exist without that other? We think it does not. If reference be had to its use, in the common affairs of the world, or in approved authors, we find that it frequently imports no more than that one thing is convenient, or useful, or essential to another. To employ the means necessary to an end, is generally understood as employing any means calculated to produce the end, and not as being confined to those single means, without which the end would be entirely unattainable. Such is the character of human language, that no word conveys to the mind, in all situations, one single definite idea; and nothing is more common than to use words in a figurative sense. Almost all compositions contain words, which, taken in a their rigorous sense, would convey a meaning different from that which is obviously intended. It is essential to just construction, that many words which import something excessive, should be understood in a more mitigated sense—in that sense which common usage justifies. The word 'necessary' is of this description. It has not a fixed character, peculiar to itself. It admits of all degrees of comparison; and is often connected with other words, which increase or diminish the impression the mind receives of the urgency it imports. A thing may be necessary, very necessary, absolutely or indispensably necessary. To no mind would the same idea be conveyed by these several phrases. The comment on the word is well illustrated by the passage cited at the bar, from the 10th section of the 1st article of the constitution. It is, we think, impossible to compare the sentence which prohibits a state from laying 'imposts, or duties on imports or exports, except what may be *absolutely* necessary for executing its inspection laws,' with that which authorizes congress 'to make all laws which shall be necessary and proper for carrying into execution' the powers of the general government, without feeling a conviction, that the convention understood itself to change materially the meaning of the word 'necessary,' by prefixing the word 'absolutely.' This word, then, like others, is used in various senses; and, in its construction, the subject, the context, the intention of the person using them, are all to be taken into view.

Let this be done in the case under consideration. The subject is the execution of those great powers on which the welfare of a nation essentially depends. It must have been the intention of those who gave these powers, to insure, so far as human prudence could insure, their beneficial execution. This could not be done, by confiding the choice of means to such narrow limits as not to leave it in the power of congress to adopt any which might be appropriate, and which were conducive to the end. This provision is made in a constitution, intended to endure for ages to come, and consequently, to be adapted to the various crises of human affairs. To have prescribed the means by which government should, in all future time, execute its powers, would have been to change, entirely, the character of the instrument, and give it the properties of a legal code. It would have been an unwise attempt to provide, by immutable rules, for exigencies which, if foreseen at all, must have been seen dimly, and which can be best provided for as they occur. To have declared, that the best means shall not be used, but those alone, without which the power given would be nugatory, would have been to deprive the legislature of the capacity to avail itself of experience, to exercise its reason, and to accommodate its legislation to circumstances. If we apply this principle of construction to any of the powers of the government, we shall find it so pernicious in its operation that we shall be compelled to discard it. . . .

So, with respect to the whole penal code of the United States: whence arises the power to punish, in cases not prescribed by the constitution? All admit, that the government may, legitimately, punish any violation of its laws; and yet, this is not among the enumerated powers of Congress. The right to enforce the observance of law, by punishing its infraction, might be denied, with the more plausibility, because it is expressly given in some cases. Congress is empowered 'to provide for the punishment of counterfeiting the securities and current coin of the United States,' and 'to define and punish piracies and felonies committed on the high seas, and offences against the law of nations.' The several powers of congress may exist, in a very imperfect state, to be sure, but they may exist and be carried into execution, although no punishment should be inflicted, in cases where the right to punish is not expressly given.

Take, for example, the power 'to establish post-offices and post-roads.' This power is executed, by the single act of making the establishment. But, from this has been inferred the power and duty of carrying the mail along the post-road, from one post-office to another. And from this implied power, has again been inferred the right to punish those who steal letters from the post-office, or rob the mail. It may be said, with some plausibility, that the right to carry the mail, and to punish those who rob it, is not indispensably necessary to the establishment of a post-office and post-road. This right is indeed essential to the beneficial exercise of the power, but not indispensably necessary to its existence. So, of the punishment of the crimes of stealing or falsifying a record or process of a court of the United States, or of perjury in such court. To punish these offences, is certainly conducive to the due administration of justice. But courts may exist, and may decide the causes brought before them, though such crimes escape punishment.

The baneful influence of this narrow construction on all the operations of the government, and the absolute impracticability of maintaining it, without rendering the government incompetent to its great objects, might be illustrated by numerous examples drawn from the constitution, and from our laws. . . .

In ascertaining the sense in which the word 'necessary' is used in this clause of the constitution, we may derive some aid from that with which it is associated. Congress shall have power 'to make all laws which shall be necessary and proper to carry into execution' the powers of the government. If the word 'necessary' was used in that strict and rigorous sense for which the counsel for the state of Maryland contend, it would be an extraordinary departure from the usual course of the human mind, as exhibited in composition, to add a word, the only possible effect of which is, to qualify that strict and rigorous meaning; to present to the mind the idea of some choice of means of legislation, not strained and compressed within the narrow limits for which gentlemen contend.

But the argument which most conclusively demonstrates the error of the construction contended for by the counsel for the state of Maryland, is founded on the intention of the convention, as manifested in the whole clause. To waste time and argument in proving that, without it, congress might carry its powers into execution, would be not much less idle, than to hold a lighted taper to the sun. As little can it be required to prove, that in the absence of this clause, congress would have some choice of means. That it might employ those which, in its judgment, would most advantageously effect the object to be accomplished. That any means adapted to the end, any means which tended directly to the execution of the constitutional powers of the government, were in themselves constitutional. This clause, as construed by the state of Maryland, would abridge, and almost annihilate, this useful and necessary right of the legislature to select its means. That this could not be intended, is, we should think, had it not been already controverted, too apparent for controversy.

We think so for the following reasons:

1st. The clause is placed among the powers of Congress, not among the limitations on those powers.

2d. Its terms purport to enlarge, not to diminish the powers vested in the government. It purports to be an additional power, not a restriction on those already granted. No reason has been, or can be assigned, for thus concealing an intention to narrow the discretion of the national legislature, under words which purport to enlarge it. . . .

The result of the most careful and attentive consideration bestowed upon this clause is, that if it does not enlarge, it cannot be construed to restrain the powers of Congress, or to impair the right of the legislature to exercise its best judgment in the selection of measures to carry into execution the constitutional powers of the government. If no other motive for its insertion can be suggested, a sufficient one is found in the desire to remove all doubts respecting the right to legislate on that vast mass of incidental powers which must be involved in the constitution, if that instrument be not a splendid bauble.

We admit, as all must admit, that the powers of the government are limited, and that its limits are not to be transcended. But we think the sound construction of the constitution must allow to the national legislature that discretion, with respect to the means by which the powers it confers are to be carried into execution, which will enable that body to perform the high duties assigned to it, in the manner most beneficial to the people. Let the end be legitimate, let it be within the scope of the constitution, and all means which are appropriate, which are plainly adapted to that end, which are not prohibited, but consist with the letter and spirit of the constitution, are constitutional. . . .

If a corporation may be employed, indiscriminately with other means, to carry into execution the powers of the government, no particular reason can be assigned for excluding the use of a bank, if required for its fiscal operations. To use one, must be within the discretion of Congress, if it be an appropriate mode of executing the powers of government. That it is a convenient, a useful, and essential instrument in the prosecution of its fiscal operations, is not now a subject of controversy. All those who have been concerned in the administration of our finances, have concurred in representing its importance and necessity; and so strongly have they been felt, that statesmen of the first class, whose previous opinions against it had been confirmed by every circumstance which can fix the human judgment, have yielded those opinions to the exigencies of the nation. Under the confederation, Congress, justifying the measure by its necessity, transcended, perhaps, its powers, to obtain the advantage of a bank; and our own legislation attests the universal conviction of the utility of this measure. The time has passed away, when it can be necessary to enter into any discussion, in order to prove the importance of this instrument, as a means to effect the legitimate objects of the government.

But were its necessity less apparent, none can deny its being an appropriate measure; and if it is, the decree of its necessity, as has been very justly observed, is to be discussed in another place. Should congress, in the execution of its powers, adopt measures which are prohibited by the constitution; or should congress, under the pretext of executing its powers, pass laws for the accomplishment of objects not intrusted to the government; it would become the painful duty of this tribunal, should a case requiring such a decision come before it, to say, that such an act was not the law of the land. But where the law is not prohibited, and is really calculated to effect any of the objects intrusted to the government, to undertake here to inquire into the decree of its necessity, would be to pass the line which circumscribes the judicial department, and to tread on legislative ground. This court disclaims all pretensions to such a power. . . .

It being the opinion of the court, that the act incorporating the bank is constitutional; and that the power of establishing a branch in the state of Maryland might be properly exercised by the bank itself, we proceed to inquire—

2. Whether the State of Maryland may, without violating the constitution, tax that branch?

That the power of taxation is one of vital importance; that it is retained by the States; that it is not abridged by the grant of a similar power to the government of the Union; that it is to be concurrently exercised by the two governments: are truths which have never been denied. . . .

. . .

That the power of taxing it by the States may be exercised so as to destroy it, is too obvious to be denied. . . .

. . .

That the power to tax involves the power to destroy; that the power to destroy may defeat and render useless the power to create ; that there is a plain repugnance in conferring on one government a power to control the constitutional measures of another, which other, with respect to those measures, is declared to be supreme over that which exerts the control, are propositions not to be denied. But all inconsistencies are to be reconciled by the magic of the word CONFIDENCE. Taxation, it is said, does not necessarily and unavoidably destroy. To carry it to the excess of destruction, would be an abuse, to presume which, would banish that confidence which is essential to all government.

But is this a case of confidence? Would the people of any one State trust those of another with a power to control the most insignificant operations of their State government? We know they would not. Why, then, should we suppose, that the people of any one State should be willing to trust those of another with a power to control the operations of a government to which they have confided their most important and most valuable interests? In the legislature of the Union alone, are all represented. The legislature of the Union alone, therefore, can be trusted by the people with the power of controlling measures which concern all, in the confidence that it will not be abused. This, then, is not a case of confidence, and we must consider it is as it really is. . . .

If we apply the principle for which the State of Maryland contends, to the constitution, generally, we shall find it capable of changing totally the character of that instrument. We shall find it capable of arresting all the measures of the government, and of prostrating it at the foot of the States. . . . If the states may tax one instrument, . . . they may tax any and every other instrument. [The] American people [did] not design to make their government dependent on the states. . . .

It has also been insisted, that, as the power of taxation in the general and State governments is acknowledged to be concurrent, every argument which would sustain the right of the general government to tax banks chartered by the States, will equally sustain the right of the States to tax banks chartered by the general government.

But the two cases are not on the same reason. The people of all the States have created the general government, and have conferred upon it the general power of taxation. The people of all the States, and the States themselves, are represented in Congress, and, by their representatives, exercise this power. When they tax the chartered institutions of the States, they tax their constituents; and these taxes must be uniform. But when a State taxes the operations of the government of the United States, it acts upon institutions created, not by their own constituents, but by people over whom they claim no control. It acts upon the measures of a government created by others as well as themselves, for the benefit of others in common with themselves. The difference is that which always exists, and always must exist, between the action of the whole on a part, and the action of a part on the whole—between the laws of a government declared to be supreme, and those of a government which, when in opposition to those laws, is not supreme.

. . .

[We] conclude that the states have no power, by taxation or otherwise, to retard, impede, burden, or in any manner control, the operations of the constitutional laws enacted by Congress. . . .

This opinion does not deprive the States of any resources which they originally possessed. It does not extend to a tax paid by the real property of the bank, in common with the other real property within the State, nor to a tax imposed on the interest which the citizens of Maryland may hold in this institution, in common with other property of the same description throughout the State. But this is a tax on the operations of the bank, and is, consequently, a tax on the operation of an instrument employed by the government of the Union to carry its powers into execution. Such a tax must be unconstitutional.

[Reversed.]

To summarize *McCulloch v. Maryland* on the major point that concerns us here, the Court held that "necessary and proper" means "any appropriate or proper means" to achieve the ends specified in an enumerated power. Restated somewhat differently: Resort to the necessary and proper clause does not obviate the need for a constitutionally enumerated ends; but the "necessity" of the means in this context is for Congress to judge.

When we get to constitutional rights we will see that, when a law infringes a constitutionally protected right, the necessity of the means does become subject to judicial review.

3. Executive Power

The second article of the Constitution provides for and governs the executive power of the United States government. Clause 1 reads:

The executive Power shall be vested in a President of the United States of America.

There is a textual discrepancy between the constitutional creation of the presidency, on the one hand, and the Congress and the Supreme Court on the other. In creating the Congress, the Constitution reads, "All legislative Powers herein granted," and for the Supreme Court, "The judicial Power of the United States." Does this subtle difference in wording betray an intent on behalf of the Framers to create, or at least to recognize the existence of, inherent presidential powers? This position was taken by no less a constitutional expert than Alexander Hamilton, chief author of the essays *The Federalist*. The contrary, and historically more likely, view was espoused by James Madison, who has been dubbed the "Father of the Constitution" for his pivotal role at the Constitutional Convention. According to Madison, the addition of the words "of the United States" in the first clause of the second article would have been superfluous, since it is obvious that the federal government is one of limited powers.[82] Further, the president is specifically commanded to "take Care that the Laws be faithfully executed."[83]

The debate between Hamilton and Madison concerned the power of President George Washington, the first president elected under the Constitution, to issue a Neutrality Proclamation declaring that the United States would remain neutral in a European war. In the centuries since that debate, commentators and courts have come to accept that the federal government—and not just the president alone—enjoys inherent power over foreign affairs. The Constitution grants Congress the power to regulate foreign commerce, to punish offenses against international law, to raise and support military forces, and to declare war; and the Constitution names the president commander in chief of the army and navy,[84] grants him (with the advice and consent of the Senate) certain treaty-making powers,[85] and provides that he appoint (with advice and consent of the Senate) ambassadors and receive foreign ambassadors.[86] Conceptually, these and other powers over foreign affairs were never possessed by the colonies turned states; rather, they passed directly to the federal government as a sovereign nation from the sovereign nation of Great Britain.

---

82   Chemerinsky, Constitutional Law, at pp. 243-244
83   Art. II, § 3.
84   Art. II, § 2, cl. 1.
85   Art. II, § 2, cl. 2.
86   Art. II, § 2, cl. 2.

a. Foreign Affairs

Having determined that the federal power over foreign affairs is plenary and exclusive, it is another matter to demarcate the scope of the respective powers of the Congress and the president over foreign affairs. The following discussion confines itself to the making of treaties and to military interventions.

i. Treaties and Executive Agreements

The Constitution empowers the president, "by and with the Advice and Consent of the Senate, to make Treaties, provided two thirds of the Senators present concur."[87] Treaties that do not expressly or impliedly require Congress to enact effectuating legislation are self-executing, that is, they create judicially enforceable rights and liabilities without the necessity of further action by Congress. Where there is a conflict between a treaty and an act of Congress, they are of equal weight. Thus, the last expression will control.[88] The United States government might, however, remain accountable under a superseded treaty according to international law; but the dispute will not be justiciable in American courts.[89]

Formal treaties are much less common than so-called "executive agreements" that the president enters into with foreign countries. Because these agreements are not considered to be treaties, they do not require the consent of the Senate. In *United States v. Belmont*[90] and *United States v. Pink*[91] the Supreme Court upheld the Litvinov Agreement, by which the United States recognized the Soviet Union as a nation in exchange for the Soviet Union's assignment of its interests in the assents of a nationalized Russian insurance company in New York, whose assets were used to pay claims of the US and others against the Soviet Union. A more recent example is the agreement that President Carter negotiated with Iran by which Iran would release American hostages in return for the lifting of a (presidentially ordered) freeze on Iranian assets in the United States.[92]

Executive agreements have a dignity "similar" to that of treaties in that they can be self-executing, and they prevail over inconsistent state law.[93] However, unlike treaties, an executive agreement will not prevail over inconsistent federal legislation.[94]

---

87   Art. II, § 2, cl. 2. The Senate has approved 1,523 treaties and rejected 20. Int'l Herald Trib., Oct. 15, 1999, p.8, col.1.

88   Head Money Cases, 112 U.S. 580 (1884).

89   Clark v. Allen, 331 U.S. 503 (1947).

90   301 U.S. 324 (1937).

91   315 U.S. 203 (1942).

92   Dames & Moore v. Regan, 453 U.S. 654 (1981).

93   United States v. Pink, 315 U.S. 203 (1942).

94   United States v. Guy W. Capps, Inc., 204 F.2d 655 (4th Cir. 1953), aff'd on other grounds, 438 U.S. 296 (1955); see Lundmark & McNeece.

ii. Foreign Military Interventions

As detailed above, the Constitution splits power to commit foreign troops abroad between the Congress and the president. By committing the powers to appropriate money, to raise armies, and to declare war (Is this power legislative or executive?) to the Congress, the Constitution is giving the Congress the upper hand. But what of insurrection or invasion? May the president deploy military forces without waiting for a congressional declaration of war? This question was answered in the affirmative in the *Prize Cases*,[95] which upheld the presidential blockade of southern ports during the Civil War in the absence of a congressional declaration of war. The court wrote:

> If a war be made by invasion of a foreign nation, the president is not only authorized but bound to resist force by force. He does not initiate the war, but is bound to accept the challenge without waiting for any special legislative authority. And whether the hostile party be a foreign invader, or States organized in rebellion, it is nonetheless a war, although the declaration of it be unilateral.[96]

In 1973 Congress enacted a statute entitled "The War Powers Resolution," abstracted below, over President Nixon's veto. Critics claim that this law unconstitutionally limits the president's prerogatives as commander in chief, and enacts an impermissible legislative veto. Since its passage it has often been ignored.[97] All presidents since its passage have asserted that the War Powers Resolution is unconstitutional.[98]

STATUTE: The War Powers Resolution
P.L. 93-148

SECTION 2. PURPOSE AND POLICY

(a) It is the purpose of this joint resolution to fulfill the intent of the framers of the Constitution of the United States and insure that the collective judgment of both the Congress and the President will apply to the introduction of United States Armed Forces into hostilities, or into situations where imminent involvement in hostilities is clearly indicated by the circumstances, and to the continued use of such forces in hostilities or in such situations.

(b) Under article I, section 8, of the Constitution, it is specifically provided that the Congress shall have the power to make all laws necessary and proper for carrying into execution, not only its own powers but also all other powers vested by the Constitution in the Government of the United States, or in any department or officer thereof.

---

95   67 U.S. 635 (1863).

96   At p. 668.

97   Koh at pp. 39-40.

98   Treanor at p. 704.

(c) The constitutional powers of the President as Commander-in-Chief to introduce United States Armed Forces into hostilities, or into situations where imminent involvement in hostilities is clearly indicated by the circumstances, are exercised only pursuant to (1) a declaration of war, (2) specific statutory authorization, or (3) a national emergency created by attack upon the United States, its territories or possessions, or its armed forces.

SECTION 3. CONSULTATION

The President in every possible instance shall consult with Congress before introducing United States Armed Forces into hostilities or into situations where imminent involvement in hostilities is clearly indicated by the circumstances, and after every such introduction shall consult regularly with the Congress until United States Armed Forces are no longer engaged in hostilities or have been removed from such situations.

SECTION 4. REPORTING

(a) In the absence of a declaration of war, in any case in which United States Armed Forces are introduced—

(1) into hostilities or into situations where imminent involvement in hostilities is clearly indicated by the circumstances;

(2) into the territory, airspace or waters of a foreign nation, while equipped for combat, except for deployments which relate solely to supply, replacement, repair, or training of such forces; or

(3) in numbers which substantially enlarge United States Armed Forces equipped for combat already located in a foreign nation; the president shall submit within 48 hours to the Speaker of the House of Representatives and to the President pro tempore of the Senate a report, in writing, setting forth [the circumstances necessitating the introduction of armed forces other information requested by the Congress].

SECTION 5. CONGRESSIONAL ACTION

. . .

(b) Within sixty calendar days after a report is submitted or is required to be submitted pursuant to section 4(a)(1), whichever is earlier, the President shall terminate any use of Untied States Armed Forces with respect to which such report was submitted (or required to be submitted), unless the Congress (1) has declared war or has enacted a specific authorization for such use of United States Armed Forces, (2) has extended by law such sixty-day period, or (3) is physically unable to meet as a result of an armed attack upon the United States. Such sixty-day period shall be extended for not more than an additional thirty days if the President determines and certifies to the Congress in writing that unavoidable military necessity respecting the safety of United States Armed Forces requires the continued use of such armed forces in the course of bringing about a prompt removal of such forces.

(c) Notwithstanding subsection (b), at any time that United States Armed Forces are engaged in hostilities outside the territory of the United States, [without] a declaration of war or specific statutory authorization, such forces shall be removed by the President if the Congress so directs by concurrent [resolution].

SECTION 8. INTERPRETATION OF JOINT RESOLUTION

(a) Authority to introduce United States Armed Forces into hostilities or into situations wherein involvement in hostilities is clearly indicated by the circumstances shall not be inferred—

(1) from any provision of law (whether or not in effect before the date of the enactment of this joint resolution), including any provision contained in any appropriation Act, unless such provision specifically authorizes the introduction of United States Armed Forces into hostilities or into such situations and stating that it is intended to constitute specific statutory authorization within the meaning of this joint resolution; or

(2) from any treaty heretofore or hereafter ratified unless such treaty is implemented by legislation specifically authorizing the introduction of United States Armed Forces into hostilities or into such situations and stating that it is intended to constitute specific statutory authorization within the meaning of this joint [resolution].

. . .

(d) Nothing in this joint resolution—

(1) is intended to alter the constitutional authority of the Congress or of the President, or the provision of existing treaties; or

(2) shall be construed as granting any authority to the President with respect to the introduction of United States Armed Forces into hostilities or into situations wherein involvement in hostilities is clearly indicated by the circumstances which authority he would not have had in the absence of this joint [resolution.]

b. Domestic Affairs ("Emergency" Power)

At this juncture we consider whether the president might not enjoy some inherent power to act domestically even in the absence of express constitutional or statutory authority. The leading case addressing the existence and scope of any such power is *Youngstown Sheet & Tube Co. v. Sawyer.*[99] That case arose in 1952 when the United Steelworkers Union announced a nationwide strike during the hostilities in Korea. Congress took no action. Fearing that the strike would endanger national defense and jeopardize the war effort, President Truman ordered his Secretary of Commerce to take possession of the steel mills and to keep them running. The Supreme Court, by a 6-3 vote, in seven different opinions, declared the seizure unconstitutional.

In the majority opinion, authored by Justice Black, the Court denies the existence of any inherent presidential power: "The President's power, if any, to issue the order must stem either from an act of Congress or from the Constitution itself."[100] Considering the case before him, Justice Black found neither, and therefore declared the action unconstitutional. Justice Jackson voted with the majority that the seizure was unconstitutional. His opinion, abstracted below, delineates three categories of presidential power.

CASE: Youngstown Sheet & Tube Co. v. Sawyer
[Steel Seizure Case]
343 U.S. 579 (1952)

MR. JUSTICE BLACK delivered the opinion of the Court.

[We] are asked to decide whether [President Truman] was acting within his constitutional power when he issued an order directing the Secretary of Commerce [Sawyer] to take possession of and operate most of the Nation's steel mills. The mill owners argue that the President's order amounts to lawmaking, a legislative function which the Constitution has expressly confided to the Congress and not to the President. The Government's position is that the order was made on findings of the President that his action was necessary to avert a national catastrophe which would inevitably result from a stoppage of steel production, and that in meeting this grave emergency the President was acting within the aggregate of his constitutional powers as the Nation's Chief Executive and the Commander in Chief of the [Armed Forces]. The issue emerges here from the following series of events:

In the latter part of 1951 [during the Korean War], a dispute arose between the steel companies and their employees [for] new collective bargaining agreements. [Efforts to settle the

---

99   343 U.S. 579 (1952).
100   At p. 585.

dispute—including reference to the Federal Wage Stabilization Board—failed.] On April 4, 1952, the [Steelworkers'] Union gave notice of a nation-wide strike called to begin [on] April 9. The indispensability of steel as a component of substantially all weapons and other war materials led the President to believe that the proposed work stoppage would immediately jeopardize our national defense and that governmental seizure of the steel mills was necessary in order to assure the continued availability of steel. [Accordingly,] the President, a few hours before the strike was to begin, issued Executive Order 10340, [directing] the Secretary of Commerce to take possession of most of the steel mills and keep them running. The Secretary immediately issued his own possessory orders, calling upon the presidents of the various seized companies to serve as operating managers for the United States. [The] next morning the President sent a message to Congress reporting his [action]. Congress has taken no action. Obeying the Secretary's orders under protest, the companies brought proceedings against him in the District Court, [which] on April 30 issued a preliminary injunction restraining the Secretary from "continuing the seizure and possession of the plants [and] from acting under the purported authority of Executive Order No. 10340." On the same day the Court of Appeals stayed the District Court's injunction. Deeming it best that the issues raised (? promptly decided by this Court, we granted certiorari on May 3 and set the cause for argument on May 12. [This decision was announced soon after, on June 2, 1952.]

The President's power, if any, to issue the order must stem either from an act of Congress or from the Constitution itself. There is no statute that expressly authorizes the President to take possession of property as he did here. Nor is there any act of Congress to which our attention has been directed from which such a power can fairly be implied. . . .

It is clear that if the President had authority to issue the order he did, it must be found in some provision of the Constitution. And it is not claimed that express constitutional language grants this power to the President. The contention is that presidential power should be implied from the aggregate of his powers under the Constitution. Particular reliance is placed on provisions in Article II which say that "The executive Power shall be vested in a President . . ."; that "he shall take Care that the Laws be faithfully executed"; and that he "shall be Commander in Chief of the [Army and Navy]." The order cannot properly be sustained as an exercise of the President's military power as Commander in Chief of the Armed Forces. The Government attempts to do so by citing [cases] upholding broad powers in military commanders engaged in day-to-day fighting in a theater of war. Such cases need not concern us here. Even though "theater of war" be an expanding concept, we cannot with faithfulness to our constitutional system hold that the Commander in Chief of the Armed Forces has the ultimate power as such to take possession of private property in order to keep labor disputes from stopping production. This is a job for the Nation's lawmakers, not for its military authorities. Nor can the seizure order be sustained because of the several constitutional provisions that grant executive power to the President. In the framework of our Constitution, the President's power to see that the laws are faithfully executed refutes the idea that he is to be a lawmaker. The Constitution limits his functions in the lawmaking process to the recommending of laws he thinks wise and the vetoing of laws he thinks bad. And the Constitution is neither silent nor equivocal about who shall make laws which the President is to execute. . . .

. . .

It is said that other Presidents without congressional authority have taken possession of private business enterprises in order to settle labor disputes. But even if this be true, Congress has not thereby lost its exclusive constitutional authority to make laws necessary and proper to carry out the powers vested by the Constitution "in the Government of the United States, or any Department or Officer thereof." The Founders of this Nation entrusted the lawmaking power to the Congress alone in both good and bad times. It would do no good to recall the historical events, the fears of power and the hopes for freedom that lay behind their choice. Such a review would but confirm our holding that this seizure order cannot stand.

[Affirmed.]

MR. JUSTICE JACKSON, concurring in the judgment and opinion of the Court.

[A] judge, like an executive adviser, may be surprised at the poverty of really useful and unambiguous authority applicable to concrete problems of executive power as they actually present themselves. Just what our forefathers did envision, or would have envisioned had they foreseen modern conditions, must be divined from materials almost as enigmatic as the dreams Joseph was called upon to interpret for Pharaoh. A century and a half of partisan debate and scholarly speculation yields no net result but only supplies more or less apt quotations from respected sources on each side of any question. They largely cancel each other. And court decisions are indecisive because of the judicial practice of dealing with the largest questions in the most narrow way. The actual art of governing under our Constitution does not and cannot conform to judicial definitions of the power of any of its branches based on isolated clauses or even single Articles torn from context. While the Constitution diffuses power the better to secure liberty, it also contemplates that practice will integrate the dispersed powers into a workable government. It enjoins upon its branches separateness but interdependence, autonomy but reciprocity. Presidential powers are not fixed but fluctuate, depending upon their disjunction or conjunction with those of Congress. We may well begin by a somewhat over-simplified grouping of practical situations in which a President may doubt, or others may challenge, his powers, and by distinguishing roughly the legal consequences of this factor of relativity.

1. When the President acts pursuant to an express or implied authorization of Congress, his authority is at its maximum, for it includes all that he possesses in his own right plus all that Congress can delegate. In these circumstances, and in these only, may he be said (for what it may be worth) to personify the federal sovereignty. If his act is held unconstitutional under these circumstances, it usually means that the Federal Government as an undivided whole lacks power. A seizure executed by the President pursuant to an Act of Congress would be supported by the strongest of presumptions and the widest latitude of judicial interpretation, and the burden of persuasion would rest heavily upon any who might attack it.

2. When the President acts in absence of either a congressional grant or denial of authority, he can only rely upon his own independent powers, but there is a zone of twilight in which he and Congress may have concurrent authority, or in which its distribution is uncertain. Therefore, congressional inertia, indifference or quiescence may sometimes, at least as a practical matter, enable, if not invite, measures on independent presidential responsibility. In this area, any actual test of power is likely to depend on the imperatives of events and contemporary imponderables rather than on abstract theories of law.

3. When the President takes measures incompatible with the expressed or implied will of Congress, his power is at its lowest ebb, for then he can rely only upon his own constitutional powers minus any constitutional powers of Congress over the matter. Courts can sustain exclusive presidential control in such a case only by disabling the Congress from acting upon the subject. Presidential claim to a power at once so conclusive and preclusive must be scrutinized with caution, for what is at stake is the equilibrium established by our constitutional system.

Into which of these classifications does this executive seizure of the steel industry fit? It is eliminated from the first by admission, for it is conceded that no congressional authorization exists for this seizure. [Can] it then be defended under flexible tests available to the second category? It seems clearly eliminated from that class because Congress has not left seizure of private property an open field but has covered it by three statutory policies inconsistent with this seizure. [This] leaves the current seizure to be justified only by the severe tests under the third grouping, where it can be supported only by any remainder of executive power after subtraction of such powers as Congress may have over the subject. In short, we can sustain the President only by holding that seizure of such strike-bound industries is within his domain and beyond control by Congress.

The Solicitor General seeks the power of seizure in three clauses of the Executive Article, the first reading, "The executive Power shall be vested in a [President]." [The Government argues:] "In our view, this clause constitutes a grant of all the executive powers of which the Government is capable." If that be true, it is difficult to see why the forefathers bothered to add several specific items, including some trifling ones. . . . I cannot accept the view that this clause is a grant in bulk of all conceivable executive power but regard it as an allocation to the presidential office of the generic powers thereafter stated. The clause on which the Government next relies is that "The President shall be Commander in Chief of the Army and Navy of the United States. . . ." [T]his loose appellation is sometimes advanced as support for any presidential action, internal or external, involving use of force, the idea being that it vests power to do anything, anywhere, that can be done with an army or navy. That seems to be the logic of an argument tendered at our bar—that the President having, on his own responsibility, sent American troops abroad derives from that act "affirmative power" to seize the means of producing a supply of steel for them. [No] doctrine that the Court could promulgate would seem to me more sinister and alarming than that a President whose conduct of foreign affairs is so largely uncontrolled, and often even is unknown, can vastly enlarge his mastery over the internal affairs of the country by his own commitment of the Nation's armed forces to some foreign venture. I do not, however, find it necessary or appropriate to consider the legal status of the Korean enterprise to discountenance argument based on it.

[The] Constitution expressly places in Congress power "to raise and *support* Armies" and "to *provide* and *maintain* a Navy." (Emphasis supplied.) This certainly lays upon Congress primary responsibility for supplying the armed forces. Congress alone controls the raising of revenues and their appropriation and may determine in what manner and by what means they shall be spent for military and naval procurement. [There] are indications that the Constitution did not contemplate that the title Commander in Chief of the Army and Navy will constitute him also Commander in Chief of the country, its industries and its inhabitants. He has no monopoly of "war powers," whatever they are. [That] military powers of the Commander in Chief were not to supersede representative government of internal affairs seems obvious from the Constitution and from elementary American history. The third clause in which the Solicitor General finds seizure powers is that "he shall take Care that the Laws be faithfully executed. . . ." That authority must be matched against [the due process clause of the Fifth Amendment]. One gives a governmental authority that reaches so far as there is law, the other gives a private right that authority shall go no farther. These signify about all there is of the principle that ours is a government of laws, not of men, and that we submit ourselves to rulers only if under rules.

The Solicitor General lastly grounds support of the seizure upon nebulous, inherent powers never expressly granted but said to have accrued to the office from the customs and claims of preceding administrations. The plea is for a resulting power to deal with a crisis or an emergency according to the necessities of the case, the unarticulated assumption being that necessity knows no law. Loose and irresponsible use of adjectives colors all nonlegal and much legal discussion of presidential powers. "Inherent" powers, "implied" powers, "incidental" powers, "plenary" powers, "war" powers and "emergency" powers are used, often interchangeably and without fixed or ascertainable meanings. The vagueness and generality of the clauses that set forth presidential powers afford a plausible basis for pressures within and without an administration for presidential action beyond that supported by those whose responsibility it is to defend his actions in court. The claim of inherent and unrestricted presidential powers has long been a persuasive dialectical weapon in political controversy. While it is not surprising that counsel should grasp support from such unadjudicated claims of power, a judge cannot accept self-serving press statements of the attorney for one of the interested parties as authority in answering a constitutional question, even if the advocate was himself. But prudence has counseled that actual reliance on such nebulous claims stop short of provoking a judicial [test].

In view of the ease, expedition and safety with which Congress can grant and has granted large emergency powers, certainly ample to embrace this crisis, I am quite unimpressed with the argument that we should affirm possession of them without statute. Such power either has no beginning or it has no end. If it exists, it need submit to no legal restraint. I am not alarmed that it would plunge us straightway into dictatorship, but it is at least a step in that wrong direction. As to whether there is imperative necessity for such powers, it is relevant to note the gap that exists between the

President's paper powers and his real powers. The Constitution does not disclose the measure of the actual controls wielded by the modern presidential [office]. Vast accretions of federal power, eroded from that reserved by the States, have magnified the scope of presidential [activity].

Executive power has the advantage of concentration in a single head in whose choice the whole Nation has a part, making him the focus of public hopes and expectations. In drama, magnitude and finality his decisions so far overshadow any others that almost alone he fills the public eye and ear. No other personality in public life can begin to compete with him in access to the public mind through modern methods of communications. By his prestige as head of state and his influence upon public opinion he exerts a leverage upon those who are supposed to check and balance his power which often cancels their effectiveness. Moreover, rise of the party system has made a significant extra constitutional supplement to real executive power. [I] have no illusion that any decision by this Court can keep power in the hands of Congress if it is not wise and timely in meeting its problems. A crisis that challenges the President equally, or perhaps primarily, challenges Congress. If not good law, there was worldly wisdom in the maxim attributed to Napoleon that "The tools belong to the man who can use them." We may say that power to legislate for emergencies belongs in the hands of Congress, but only Congress itself can prevent power from slipping through its [fingers]. With all its defects, delays and inconveniences, men have discovered no technique for long preserving free government except that the Executive be under the law, and that the law be made by parliamentary deliberations. Such institutions may be destined to pass away. But it is the duty of the Court to be last, not first, to give them up.

[Other concurring and dissenting opinions omitted.]

Can the president impound (i.e., refuse to spend) money that Congress has mandated be spent? Would doing so violate the principle of separation of powers? The Impoundment Control Act of 1974[101] effectively forbids the practice.[102]

c. Presidential Legislative Prerogatives

This section addresses two abashedly legislative functions discharged by the executive branch of the federal government. One, the veto power, is expressly

---

101   31 U.S.C. § 1301.
102   See Train v. New York, 420 U.S. 35 (1975).

provided for in the Constitution. The other, the delegation of legislative power to the executive, finds no textual support in the Constitution.

i. Presidential Veto

The presidential veto power is expressly provided for in Article I, section 7, clause 2:

> Every Bill which shall have passed the House of Representatives and the Senate, shall, before it becomes a Law, be presented to the President of the United States; If he approve he shall sign it, but if not he shall return it, with his Objections to that House in which it shall have originated. . . . If any Bill shall not be returned by the President within ten Days (Sundays excepted) after it shall have been presented to him, the Same shall be a Law, in like Manner as if he had signed it, unless the Congress by their Adjournment prevent its Return, in which Case it shall not be a Law.

The veto power extends to legislative measures ("Bills") that are presented to the president before they become law. The veto power also extends to "Every Order, Resolution, or Vote to which the Concurrence of the Senate and House of Representatives may be necessary (except on a question of Adjournment)."[103] The veto power therefore does not extend to actions by the Congress that are not legislative, at least if they are not in the form of a bill. Exceptions from the president's veto power therefore include (non-binding) resolutions, adoption of procedures to organize Congress's affairs, and acts that are committed to the discretion of the Congress. This last group (comprising congressional acts excluded from the reach of the president's veto power) includes declarations of war, consent to treaties and appointments, and impeachment proceedings.

Governmental officials are subject to official and unofficial oversight by Congress. This oversight ranges from informal telephonic inquiries to the submission of reports and testimony before congressional committees. One provision of the Immigration and Nationality Act allowed either house of Congress to overturn a decision of the Immigration and Naturalization Service to suspend deportation. The provision was declared unconstitutional on separation of powers grounds.[104]

ii. Delegation of Legislative Power

While extremely difficult to justify on separation of powers grounds, and while arguably unconstitutional for violation of the opening sentence of Article I of the Constitution, delegations of regulatory power to administrative agencies is a 20th and 21st century necessity. In light of the complexity of the law and the need for specialized knowledge, the only alternative would be to increase the staff of the Congress manyfold and to force members of Congress to vote on volumes of measures that they could never hope to comprehend.

---

103   Art. I, § 7, cl. 3.
104   Immigration and Naturalization Service v. Chadha, 462 U.S. 919 (1983).

During the 1930s, Congress would sometimes, at the president's request, make wholesale delegations to the executive. The National Industrial Recovery Act, for example, authorized the president to adopt "codes of fair competition" for various industries. When these delegations reached the courts, they were condemned as unconstitutional abdications of legislative authority.[105]

It is popular among constitutional scholars to say that the delegation doctrine is dead. While it is true that no decision since 1935 has invalidated a congressional delegation of power, and that the Supreme Court has been liberal with what it considers "intelligible standards," a resurrection of the doctrine cannot be ruled out. Should it be ruled out? Is there no chance that even broad-based agencies might act capriciously or despotically? Are the courts a sufficient final refuge if they do?

d. Election, Appointment, Removal, and Immunity

The qualifications of the president are prescribed in Article II, section 1, clause 5:

> No Person except a natural born Citizen, or a Citizen of the United States, at the time of the Adoption of this Constitution, shall be eligible to the Office of President; neither shall any person be eligible to that Office who shall not have attained to the Age of thirty five Years, and been fourteen Years a Resident within the United States

The youngest person to become president was forty-year-old Theodore Roosevelt.

i. Election and Appointment

The president is not appointed by the Congress. Rather, he is popularly, but indirectly, elected. At the time the Constitution was drafted, representatives chosen by the states would travel great distances on horseback or by carriage to the electoral college to cast their votes. The voters of the states, then as now, voted by proxy via the electoral college. As part of a political compromise to gain the consent of the small states, representation in the electoral college for each state is equivalent to the sum of its senators and representatives.[106] The electoral college still basically operates on a "winner takes all" rule. This is an extra-constitutional practice, codified in the laws of all of the states except two, by which the candidate who receives the largest number of votes in a state receives all of that state's electoral votes.[107] It has come to pass four times that candidates with more

---

105 E.g., Panama Refining Co. v. Ryan, 293 U.S. 388 (1935) and Schechter Poultry Corp. v. United States, 295 U.S. 495 (1935). To survive judicial review, the legislative delegation must contain "intelligible standards" that confine the discretion of the agency. Yankus v. United States, 321 U.S. 414 (1944). For an example of the use by a state court of the non-delegation doctrine, see Bayside Timber Co. v. Board of Supervisors, 20 Cal. App. 3d 1 (1971), discussed in Lundmark, *Regulation*.

106 U.S. Const., Art.II §1, cl.2; Williams v. Rhodes 393 U.S. 23 (1968) at page 43, note 2.

107 Mikva at p. 800.

popular votes have lost to candidates with more electoral college votes. Three instances were in the 19th century. The most recent occurrence was in November 2000, in which George W. Bush defeated Albert Gore, Jr.

The procedure for the election of the president has been changed once by amendment to the Constitution. Since the ratification of the 12th Amendment in 1804, electors must vote for one person as president and for another as vice president. The amendment resulted from the presidential election of 1800, which saw two men, Aaron Burr and Thomas Jefferson, tie. Previously, the candidate with the most votes became president; the runner-up became vice president. Incidentally, the tie vote between Burr and Jefferson was broken by a vote in the House of Representatives.

Elections and voting rights have been the chief topic addressed in the 17 amendments ratified since the Bill of Rights (the first 10 amendments). In addition to the amendments granting the suffrage to former slaves,[108] to women,[109] to citizens of the District of Columbia to vote for president and vice president, but not for members of Congress,[110] and to 18-year-olds,[111] other amendments have been ratified to abolish poll (head) taxes as a qualification for voting[112] and to govern the election of senators[113] and of the president.

The date on which the newly elected president and vice president would begin serving was moved up to the 20th day of January by the 20th Amendment, ratified in 1933. Until Franklin D. Roosevelt, no other president had run for election to more than two consecutive terms. The 22nd Amendment wrote this custom into the Constitution. The 25th Amendment, ratified in 1967, provides a procedure for presidential appointment, and congressional confirmation, of a replacement vice president. (Previously vacancies had remained unfilled until the next election.) In 1973 Gerald Ford became the first person chosen to be vice president under the 25th Amendment. The following year, Ford became president upon President Nixon's resignation. Nelson Rockefeller was chosen vice president under the same procedure.

ii. Removal (Impeachment)

The government of the United States is not parliamentary. There is no procedure for a vote of no confidence. There is no procedure for popular referendum to re-

---

108   Amend. 15.
109   Amend. 19.
110   Amend. 23.
111   Amend. 26.
112   Amend. 24.
113   Amend. 17.

move a wayward president. The exclusive means of removal is set forth in Article II, section 4, of the Constitution:

> The President, Vice President and all civil Officers of the United States, shall be removed from Office on Impeachment for, and Conviction of, Treason, Bribery, or other high Crimes and Misdemeanors.

Impeachment consists of an act of the House of Representatives charging the official with "Treason, Bribery, or other high Crimes and Misdemeanors." History is vague on what this originally meant, and commentators have varied widely in their interpretations. Many people share the conviction of (then Congressman) Gerald Ford when he said, "An impeachable offense is whatever a majority of the House of Representatives considers it to be."

The Senate must try the president on the charges in the impeachment resolution. The original proposal was to have the Supreme Court try the president, but this was changed to make the impeachment procedure more democratic. A two-thirds' vote of the members present is required to convict and remove the president from office.[114] Conviction does not bring a prison term or monetary fine:

> Judgment in Cases of Impeachment shall not extend further than to removal from Office, and disqualification to hold and enjoy any Office of honor, Trust or Profit under the United States: but the Party convicted shall nevertheless be liable and subject to Indictment, Trial, Judgment and Punishment, according to Law.[115]

Five federal judges have been removed by impeachment and conviction. The last was district court judge Walter Nixon, who was convicted of making false statements to a grand jury, and was sentenced to prison. The House impeached Nixon. Rather than hold a trial with all of its members present, the Senate created a committee which held hearings and made recommendations to the full Senate. By two-thirds' vote of the members present,[116] the Senate removed Judge Nixon from office. The Supreme Court refused to set aside the conviction, ruling the procedure valid, or at least nonjusticiable.[117]

President Andrew Johnson, who became president on the death of Abraham Lincoln, was impeached in 1867 for firing Secretary of War Edwin Stanton who had openly challenged the president's authority. The House charged that, in doing so, Johnson had violated the Tenure in Office Act, which specifically provided that the firing of a department head would be deemed a "high misdemeanor."[118] The Senate failed by one vote to convict Johnson on the charge. President Nixon resigned after the House Judiciary Committee voted three articles of impeachment

---

114   Art. I, § 3, cl. 6.

115   Art. I, § 3, cl. 7.

116   Art. I, § 3.

117   Nixon v. United States, 506 U.S. 224 (1993).

118   Years later the Supreme Court invalidated the Tenure in Office Act on separation of powers grounds. Myers v. United States, 272 U.S. 52 (1926).

against him, but before he was impeached by the House. (The articles charged the president with obstruction of justice in connection with the Watergate cover-up, using government agencies, such as the FBI and the IRS, for political purposes, and failing to comply with subpoenas.) The only elected president ever to have been impeached was President Clinton, who was charged in 1998 by the House of Representatives with committing perjury and obstruction of justice. The Senate failed to convict him on the charges.

In the wake of the Watergate Scandal under President Nixon, Congress enacted the Ethics in Government Act of 1978[119] which allows for the appointment of an "independent counsel" to investigate and prosecute wrongdoing by high executive officials on the assumption that the executive itself could not be counted on to do so. Nevertheless, the first step in the process must be taken by the Attorney General, a presidential appointee. If, following a preliminary investigation, she determines that there are "reasonable grounds to believe that further investigation is warranted," she refers the matter to a panel of federal judges, chosen from different courts, one of which must be the Court of Appeals for the District of Columbia Circuit. These three judges in turn appoint the independent counsel and define her prosecutorial jurisdiction.

The constitutionality of the appointment procedures of the Ethics in Government Act was attacked on the grounds that they (1) violated the appointments clause,[120] (2) breached the limitations placed on federal judges by Article III, and (3) unconstitutionally interfered with executive functions and therefore contravened the principle of separation of powers. The Supreme Court upheld the law, with only one dissenting vote, in the following case.

CASE: Morrison v. Olson
487 U. S. 654 (1988)

CHIEF JUSTICE REHNQUIST delivered the opinion of the Court.

This case presents us with a challenge to the independent counsel provisions of the Ethics in Government Act of 1978. [We] hold today that these provisions of the Act do not violate the Appointments Clause [or] the limitations of Article III, nor do they impermissibly interfere with the President's authority under Article II in violation of the constitutional principle of separation of powers. . . .

[After a lengthy recitation of the factual and procedural background, Chief Justice Rehnquist's opinion addresses the claim that the statutory procedure for naming the

---

119   28 U.S.C. §§ 591-599.
120   Art. II, § 2, cl. 2.

independent counsel violates the letter of the Appointments Clause, which states:

> [B]y and with the Advice and Consent of the Senate, [the President] shall appoint Ambassadors, other public Ministers and Consuls, Judges of the supreme Court, and all other Officers of the United States, whose Appointments are not herein otherwise provided for, and which shall be established by Law: but the Congress may by Law vest the Appointment of such inferior Officers, as they think proper, in the President alone, in the Courts of Law, or in the Heads of Departments.[121]

The court rejected this claim, holding that the tenure, duration, and duties of the office established that the independent counsel, Alexia Morrison, was an "inferior" officer and as such need not be named by the president.

[Next the court rejected a claim that the judges' power to define the jurisdiction of the independent counsel conflicted with Article III. Rehnquist stressed that the appointing judges had no power whatsoever to supervise the independent counsel in the exercise of her investigative and prosecutorial authority.]

. . .

B. The final question to be addressed is whether the Act, taken as a whole, violates the principle of separation of powers by unduly interfering with the role of the Executive Branch. [We] observe first that this case does not involve an attempt by Congress to increase its own powers at the expense of the Executive Branch. Unlike some of our previous cases, most recently [Bowsher], this case simply does not pose a "dange[r] of congressional usurpation of Executive Branch functions." . . . [Congress's] role under the Act is [largely] limited to receiving reports or other information and oversight of the independent counsel's activities, functions that we have recognized generally as being incidental to the legislative function of Congress. Similarly, we do not think that the Act works any *judicial* usurpation of properly executive functions. [Once] the court has appointed a counsel and defined his or her jurisdiction, it has no power to supervise or control the activities of the counsel. [T]he various powers delegated to the [Special] Division are not supervisory or administrative, nor are they functions that the Constitution requires be performed by officials within the Executive Branch. [Finally,] we do not think that the Act "impermissibly undermine[s]" the powers of the Executive Branch, or "disrupts the proper balance between the

---

121   Art. II, § 2, cl. 2.

coordinate branches [by] prevent[ing] the Executive Branch from accomplishing its constitutionally assigned functions." It is undeniable that the Act reduces the amount of control or supervision that the Attorney General and, through him, the President exercises over the investigation and prosecution of a certain class of alleged criminal activity. [Nonetheless], the Act does give the Attorney General several means of supervising or controlling the prosecutorial powers that may be wielded by an independent counsel. Most importantly, the Attorney General retains the power to remove the counsel for "good cause." [Notwithstanding] the fact that the counsel is to some degree "independent" and free from executive supervision to a greater extent than other federal prosecutors, in our view [the] Act give the Executive Branch sufficient control over the independent counsel to ensure that the President is able to perform his constitutionally assigned [duties].

[Reversed.]

JUSTICE SCALIA, dissenting. [Justice Scalia was the sole dissenter. Justice Kennedy did not participate in the case.]

. . .

If to describe this case is not to decide it, the concept of a government of separate and coordinate powers no longer has meaning. [Article II, § 1, cl. 1] of the Constitution provides: "The executive Power shall be vested in a President of the United States." [This] does not mean *some* of the executive power, but *all of* the executive power. It seems to me, therefore, that the decision [in the court below] invalidating the present statute must be upheld on fundamental separation-of-powers principles if the following two questions are answered affirmatively: (1) Is the conduct of a criminal prosecution (and of an investigation to decide whether to prosecute) the exercise of purely executive power? (2) Does the statute deprive the President of the United States of exclusive control over the exercise of that power? Surprising to say, the Court appears to concede an affirmative answer to both questions, but seeks to avoid the inevitable conclusion that since the statute vests some purely executive power in a person who is not the President of the United States it is void. The Court concedes that "[t]here is no real dispute that the functions performed by the independent counsel are 'executive'." Governmental investigation and prosecution of crimes is a quintessentially executive function. As for the second question, whether the statute before us deprives the President of exclusive control over that quintessentially executive activity: The Court does not, and could not possibly, assert that it does not. That is indeed the whole object of the statute. Instead, the Court points out that the President, through his Attorney General, has at least *some* control. That concession is alone enough to invalidate the statute, but I cannot refrain from pointing out that the Court greatly exaggerates the extent of that "some" Presidential [control]. [It] is ultimately irrelevant how much the statute reduces Presidential control. [It] is not for us to determine, and we have never presumed to determine, *how much* of the purely executive powers of government must be within the full control of the President. The Constitution prescribes that they *all* are.

. . .

The purpose of the separation and equilibration of powers in general, and of the unitary Executive in particular, was not merely to assure effective government but to preserve individual freedom. Those who hold or have held offices covered by the Ethics in Government Act are entitled to that protection as much as the rest of us, and I conclude my discussion by considering the effect of the Act upon the fairness of the process they receive. [Under] our system of government, the primary check against prosecutorial abuse is a political one. The prosecutors who exercise this awesome discretion are selected and can be removed by a President, whom the people have trusted enough to elect. Moreover, when crimes are not investigated and prosecuted fairly, nonselectively, with a reasonable sense of proportion, the President pays the cost in political damage to his administration. [That] is the system of justice the rest of us are entitled to, but what of that select class consisting of present or former high-level Executive Branch officials? If an allegation is made against them of any violation of any federal criminal law [the] Attorney General must give it his attention. That in itself is not objectionable. But if, after a 90-day investigation without the benefit of normal investigatory tools, the Attorney General is unable to say that there are "no reasonable grounds to believe" that further investigation is warranted, a process is set in motion that is *not* in the full control of persons "dependent on the people," and whose flaws cannot be blamed on the President. An independent counsel is selected, and the scope of his or her authority prescribed, by a panel of judges. What if they are politically partisan, as judges have been known to be, and select a prosecutor antagonistic to the [administration]? There is no remedy for that, not even a political one.

[The] ad hoc approach to constitutional adjudication has real attraction, even apart from its work-saving potential. It is guaranteed to produce a result, in every case, that will make a majority of the Court happy with the law. The law is, by definition, precisely what the majority thinks, taking all things into account, it *ought* to be. I prefer to rely upon the judgment of the wise men who constructed our system, and of the people who approved it, and of two centuries of history that have shown it to be sound. Like it or not, that judgment says, quite plainly, that "[t]he executive Power shall be vested in a President of the United States."

iii. Privilege and Immunity

Although not expressly mentioned in the Constitution, the Supreme Court has recognized a privilege to prevent disclosure of confidential communications made between the president and his advisors. The claim of executive privilege is given utmost deference by the courts when the communications relate to military, diplomatic, or sensitive national security secrets.[122] Executive privilege does not extend to evidence of meetings, or to conversations overheard by third persons, such as bodyguards.[123]

In the civil context, the president, whether sitting or former, enjoys absolute immunity from claims predicated on his official acts.[124] Can a sitting president can be criminally prosecuted? Does a sitting president enjoy immunity from civil law suits arising before taking office, or based on unofficial acts? Consider the following case.

CASE: Clinton v. Jones
520 U.S. 681 (1997)

Justice Stevens delivered the opinion of the Court.

This case raises a constitutional and a prudential question concerning the Office of the President of the United States. Respondent, a private citizen, seeks to recover damages from the current occupant of that office based on actions allegedly taken before his term began. The President submits that in all but the most exceptional cases the Constitution requires federal courts to defer such litigation until his term ends and that, in any event, respect for the office warrants such a stay. Despite the force of the arguments supporting the President's submissions, we conclude that they must be rejected.

Petitioner, William Jefferson Clinton, was elected to the Presidency in 1992, and re-elected in 1996. His term of office expires on January 20, 2001. In 1991 he was the Governor of the State of Arkansas. Respondent, Paula Corbin Jones, is a resident of California. In 1991 she lived in Arkansas, and was an employee of the Arkansas Industrial

---

122   United States v. Nixon, 418 U.S. 683 (1974).

123   In re Sealed Case, 148 F.3d 1073 (D.C. Cir. 1998), cert. denied in Rubin v. United States, 531 U.S. 1301 (1998).

124   Nixon v. Fitzgerald, 457 U.S. 731 (1982).

Development Commission. On May 6, 1994, she commenced this action in the United States District Court for the Eastern District of Arkansas by filing a complaint naming petitioner and Danny Ferguson, a former Arkansas State Police officer, as defendants. The complaint alleges two federal claims, and two state law claims over which the federal court has jurisdiction because of the diverse citizenship of the parties. As the case comes to us, we are required to assume the truth of the detailed—but as yet untested—factual allegations in the complaint.

Those allegations principally describe events that are said to have occurred on the afternoon of May 8, 1991, during an official conference held at the Excelsior Hotel in Little Rock, Arkansas. The Governor delivered a speech at the conference; respondent—working as a state employee—staffed the registration desk. She alleges that Ferguson persuaded her to leave her desk and to visit the Governor in a business suite at the hotel, where he made "abhorrent" sexual advances that she vehemently rejected. She further claims that her superiors at work subsequently dealt with her in a hostile and rude manner, and changed her duties to punish her for rejecting those advances. Finally, she alleges that after petitioner was elected President, Ferguson defamed her by making a statement to a reporter that implied she had accepted petitioner's alleged overtures, and that various persons authorized to speak for the President publicly branded her a liar by denying that the incident had occurred.

Respondent seeks actual damages of $75,000, and punitive damages of $100,000. Her complaint contains four counts. The first charges that petitioner, acting under color of state law, deprived her of rights protected by the Constitution, in violation of . . . 42 U.S.C. § 1983. The second charges that petitioner and Ferguson engaged in a conspiracy to violate her federal rights, also actionable under federal law. See . . . 42 U.S.C. § 1985. The third is a state common law claim for intentional infliction of emotional distress, grounded primarily on the incident at the hotel. The fourth count, also based on state law, is for defamation, embracing both the comments allegedly made to the press by Ferguson and the statements of petitioner's agents. Inasmuch as the legal sufficiency of the claims has not yet been challenged, we assume, without deciding, that each of the four counts states a cause of action as a matter of law. With the exception of the last charge, which arguably may involve conduct within the outer perimeter of the President's official responsibilities, it is perfectly clear that the alleged misconduct of petitioner was unrelated to any of his official duties as President of the United States and, indeed, occurred before he was elected to that office.

In response to the complaint, petitioner promptly advised the District Court that he intended to file a motion to dismiss on grounds of Presidential immunity, and requested the court to defer all other pleadings and motions until after the immunity issue was resolved. . . .

Petitioner's principal submission—that "in all but the most exceptional cases" . . ., the Constitution affords the President temporary immunity from civil damages litigation arising out of events that occurred before he took office—cannot be sustained on the basis of precedent.

Only three sitting Presidents have been defendants in civil litigation involving their actions prior to taking office. Complaints against Theodore Roosevelt and Harry Truman had been dismissed before they took office; the dismissals were affirmed after their respective inaugurations. Two companion cases arising out of an automobile accident were filed against John F. Kennedy in 1960 during the Presidential campaign. After taking office, he unsuccessfully argued that his status as Commander in Chief gave him a right to a stay under the Soldiers' and Sailors' Civil Relief Act of 1940. . . . The motion for a stay was denied by the District Court, and the matter was settled out of court. Thus, none of those cases sheds any light on the constitutional issue before us.

. . .

As a starting premise, petitioner contends that he occupies a unique office with powers and responsibilities so vast and important that the public interest demands that he devote his undivided time and attention to his public duties. He submits that—given the nature of the office—the doctrine of separation of powers places limits on the authority of the Federal Judiciary to interfere with the Executive Branch that would be transgressed by allowing this action to proceed.

. . .

It does not follow, however, that separation of powers principles would be violated by allowing this action to proceed. The doctrine of separation of powers is concerned with the allocation of official power among the three co-equal branches of our Government. The Framers "built into the tripartite Federal Government . . . a self executing safeguard against the encroachment or aggrandizement of one branch at the expense of the other. . . . Thus, for example, the Congress may not exercise the judicial power to revise final judgments . . ., or the executive power to manage an airport. . . . Similarly, the President may not exercise the legislative power to authorize the seizure of private property for public use. Youngstown. . . . And, the judicial power to decide cases and controversies does not include the provision of purely advisory opinions to the Executive, or permit the federal courts to resolve nonjusticiable questions.

Of course the lines between the powers of the three branches are not always neatly defined. . . . But in this case there is no suggestion that the Federal Judiciary is being asked to perform any function that might in some way be described as "executive." Respondent is merely asking the courts to exercise their core Article III jurisdiction to decide cases and controversies. Whatever the outcome of this case, there is no possibility that the decision will curtail the scope of the official powers of the Executive Branch. The litigation of questions that relate entirely to the unofficial conduct of the individual who happens to be the President poses no perceptible risk of misallocation of either judicial power or executive power.

. . .

Of greater significance, petitioner errs by presuming that interactions between the Judicial Branch and the Executive, even quite burdensome interactions, necessarily rise to the level of constitutionally forbidden impairment of the Executive's ability to perform its constitutionally mandated functions. "[O]ur . . . system imposes upon the Branches a degree of overlapping responsibility, a duty of interdependence as well as independence the absence of which 'would preclude the establishment of a Nation capable of governing itself effectively.'" . . . As Madison explained, separation of powers does not mean that the branches "ought to have no partial agency in, or no controul over the acts of each other." The fact that a federal court's exercise of its traditional Article III jurisdiction may significantly burden the time and attention of the Chief Executive is not sufficient to establish a violation of the Constitution. Two long settled propositions, first announced by Chief Justice Marshall, support that conclusion.

First, we have long held that when the President takes official action, the Court has the authority to determine whether he has acted within the law. Perhaps the most dramatic example of such a case is our holding [in Youngstown Sheet] that President Truman exceeded his constitutional authority when he issued an order directing the Secretary of Commerce to take possession of and operate most of the Nation's steel mills in order to avert a national catastrophe. . . . Our holding was an application of the principle established in *Marbury v. Madison* . . . , that "[i]t is emphatically the province and duty of the judicial department to say what the law is."

Second, it is also settled that the President is subject to judicial process in appropriate circumstances. Although Thomas Jefferson apparently thought otherwise, Chief Justice Marshall, when presiding in the treason trial of Aaron Burr, ruled that a subpoena duces tecum could be directed to the

President. . . . We unequivocally and emphatically endorsed Marshall's position when we held that President Nixon was obligated to comply with a subpoena commanding him to produce certain tape recordings of his conversations with his aides. . . . As we explained, "neither the doctrine of separation of powers, nor the need for confidentiality of high level communications, without more, can sustain an absolute, unqualified Presidential privilege of immunity from judicial process under all circumstances."

Sitting Presidents have responded to court orders to provide testimony and other information with sufficient frequency that such interactions between the Judicial and Executive Branches can scarcely be thought a novelty. President Monroe responded to written interrogatories . . ., President Nixon—as noted above—produced tapes in response to a subpoena duces tecum . . ., President Ford complied with an order to give a deposition in a criminal trial . . ., and President Clinton has twice given videotaped testimony in criminal proceedings. . . . Moreover, sitting Presidents have also voluntarily complied with judicial requests for testimony. President Grant gave a lengthy deposition in a criminal case under such circumstances . . . and President Carter similarly gave videotaped testimony for use at a criminal trial. . . .

In sum, "[i]t is settled law that the separation of powers doctrine does not bar every exercise of jurisdiction over the President of the United States." . . . If the Judiciary may severely burden the Executive Branch by reviewing the legality of the President's official conduct, and if it may direct appropriate process to the President himself, it must follow that the federal courts have power to determine the legality of his unofficial conduct. The burden on the President's time and energy that is a mere by-product of such review surely cannot be considered as onerous as the direct burden imposed by judicial review and the occasional invalidation of his official actions. We therefore hold that the doctrine of separation of powers does not require federal courts to stay all private actions against the President until he leaves office.

. . .

The decision to postpone the trial was, furthermore, premature. The proponent of a stay bears the burden of establishing its need. . . . In this case, at the stage at which the District Court made its ruling, there was no way to assess whether a stay of trial after the completion of discovery would be warranted. Other than the fact that a trial may consume some of the President's time and attention, there is nothing in the record to enable a judge to assess the potential harm that may ensue from scheduling the trial promptly after discovery is concluded. We think the District Court may have given undue weight to the concern that a trial might generate unrelated civil actions that could conceivably hamper the President in conducting the duties of his office. If and when that should occur, the court's discretion would permit it to manage those actions in such fashion (including deferral of trial) that interference with the President's duties would not occur. But no such impingement upon the President's conduct of his office was shown here.

. . .

The Federal District Court has jurisdiction to decide this case. Like every other citizen who properly invokes that jurisdiction, respondent has a right to an orderly disposition of her claims. Accordingly, the judgment of the Court of Appeals is affirmed.

It is so ordered.

[Concurring opinion omitted.]

In accordance with the Supreme Court's decision, Paula Jones was allowed to prosecute her civil action against the president. At a deposition, the president was asked about an alleged affair with Monica Lewinsky. The federal judge presiding over the deposition, Susan Webber Wright, who had been appointed by President Clinton, ruled the question relevant. Rather than refuse to answer, and risk losing the case brought by Paula Jones, the president denied the affiar under oath. DNA analysis of semen stains on Monica Lewinsky's dress proved that the president had been telling less than the whole truth at his deposition. His involvement of governmental officials, including the Secretary of State, in covering up the affair formed the basis of the charge in the articles of impeachment that he had obstructed justice.

Judge Wright held Mr. Clinton in contempt of court for lying, fining him $90,000, and making him pay her expenses for traveling to Washington to preside over his "tainted deposition."[125] Clinton settled the case by paying Paula Jones $850,000, most of which came from insurance.[126]

4. Judicial Power

The federal courts are provided for in Article III of the Constitution. It would be more accurate to say that the Supreme Court is provided for, as becomes clear from the first sentence of clause 1:

The judicial Power of the United States, shall be vested in one supreme Court, and in such inferior Courts as the Congress may from time to time ordain and establish.

---

125   Jones v. Clinton, 36 F.Supp. 2d 1118 (E.D. Ark. 1999); Rotunda at note 14.
126   Pittsburgh Post-Gazette, National section, May 23, 2000.

Thus, the Constitution does not require the Congress to establish inferior federal courts; but, of course, it has done so, as it is specifically empowered to do.[127] Nor, for that matter, must Congress confer on the inferior courts jurisdiction to decide all matters within the federal judicial power.[128]

Federal judges are appointed by the president, and confirmed by the Senate (called the "advice and consent" procedure).[129] The Constitution specifies no particular qualifications for appointment, nor standards for confirmation, and the Senate occasionally refuses to confirm presidential appointments.[130] The last nomination to be rejected was Republican President Reagan's nomination of Robert Bork, whom the Democratic Senate considered too conservative.[131]

As provided in the Constitution, all federal "Article III" judges "hold their Offices during good Behaviour, and shall, at stated Times, receive for their Services, a Compensation, which shall not be diminished during their Continuance in Office."[132] This means that federal judges' salaries cannot be reduced, and federal judges cannot be forced to retire or leave office. The only avenue available to remove them is by impeachment, as with the president.

The Constitution does not prescribe the size of the Supreme Court, and in the early years, the size fluctuated. The number of judges (called "Justices") was set by law at nine in 1869.[133]

a. Express Grants of (and Limitations on) Judicial Power

Article III of the Constitution provides not only for the establishment of the Supreme Court and inferior courts, it also specifies what matters these courts may decide. A three-step procedure is warranted in judging whether federal courts have jurisdiction to decide any particular dispute. The first issue to address is the nature of the dispute, that is, whether it falls with the subject matter jurisdiction of the federal court. Thereafter one must consider whether the dispute meets the "case or controversy" requirement of Article III. Third, it must be asked whether the dispute, though federal and otherwise justiciable under the "case or controversy" clause, is nonetheless beyond the purview of the courts because its resolution is constitutionally committed to the "political" branches of government (the "political question" doctrine).

---

127   See also Art. I, § 8, cl. 9.

128   Sheldon v. Sill, 49 U.S. 441 (1850).

129   Art. II, § 2, cl. 2.

130   Massey.

131   Ross at p. 993.

132   Art. III. § 1.

133   Act of March 3, 1863, chap. C, § 1, 12 Stat. 794.

i. Heads of Federal Judicial Power (Subject Matter Jurisdiction)

The federal judiciary, like the federal government as a whole, enjoys jurisdiction only in cases enumerated in the Constitution. By definition these are cases in which the federal government has some particular interest. For ease of discussion, these instances of federal judicial jurisdiction are gathered under two heads: diversity jurisdiction and federal question jurisdiction.

The federal courts possess federal question jurisdiction over cases or controversies:[134]

- "arising under this Constitution, the Laws of the United States, and Treaties made, or which shall be made, under their authority [28 U.S.C. § 1331]; . . .

- affecting Ambassadors, other public Ministers and Counsels [original, "trial" jurisdiction in the Supreme Court pursuant to Art. III, § 2, cl. 2]; . . .

- [involving] admiralty and maritime Jurisdiction [exclusive federal jurisdiction, 28 U.S.C. § 1333]; . . .

- to which the United States shall be a Party [28 U.S.C. § 1345]; . . .

- between two or more States [original jurisdiction with the Supreme Court, 28 U.S.C. § 1251]."

The federal courts exercise diversity of citizenship jurisdiction (where the amount in controversy must generally exceed $50,000) over cases or controversies:[135]

- "between Citizens of different States [28 U.S.C. § 1332(a)(1), which includes permanent foreign residents];

- between Citizens of the same State claiming Lands under Grants of different States, and between a State, or the Citizens thereof, and foreign States [28 U.S.C. §§ 1330 and 1332(a)(4)]."

Cases that do not fall under one of these heads of jurisdiction are not justiciable in the federal courts, but they may well be in the state courts. The courts of the states are not limited by the constraints of Article III.

There are very few cases that can be brought only in the federal, and not in the state, courts. These include admiralty, bankruptcy, patent and copyright, and claims arising under the securities exchange and federal antitrust laws.[136] In all other cases the federal and state courts have concurrent jurisdiction.

---

134   Art. III, § 2, cl. 1.

135   Art. III, § 2, cl. 1.

136   28 U.S.C. §§ 1333, 1334 1338, 78aa, 1337, and 18 U.S.C. § 3231.

The common law tradition of judicial law-making is considered to be "policy-making" and therefore in part legislative.[137] Since, according to the Constitution, *all* legislative power is vested in Congress, does that mean that there can be no federal common law?[138]

ii. Limitation of Jurisdiction to "Cases or Controversies"

Article III, section 2 limits the jurisdiction of the federal court to "cases" or "controversies." The terms, which mean the same thing, have been construed to require that the matter in controversy be "definite and concrete, touching the legal relations of parties having adverse legal interests. It must be a real and substantial controversy admitting of specific relief through a decree of a conclusive character."[139]

The "case or controversy" requirement has spawned a host of sometimes sophisticated doctrines and distinctions, the most important of which—advisory opinions, ripeness, mootness, and standing—are sketched here.

The requirement that there be a "real and substantial controversy" has come to mean, most fundamentally, that neither the Supreme Court nor the lower federal courts will render advisory opinions on statutory interpretation, constitutionality of proposed legislation, or any other matter. This restraint in effect tells the Congress and president that they should not enact legislation if they harbor doubts about its constitutionality. Whether this makes for better government or not is open to debate. For the same reason the federal courts will not hear collusive or "friendly" suits, that is, where one side finances and controls the whole litigation.[140]

Ripeness, as its name suggests, refers to the temporal readiness of the matter for judicial determination. In large part, the reticence of the federal courts to decide matters that are not yet ripe is due to "prudential principles of judicial self-restraint."[141] A brewing controversy is not enough to invoke federal judicial relief. The threatened harm must be real and immediate, not hypothetical. For example, in one case the Supreme Court refused to rule on the constitutionality of a statute that outlawed contraceptives where the law had been on the books for 80 years but had not been enforced despite "ubiquitous, open, public sales" of contraceptives.[142]

If ripeness is the locomotive on the train of time, then mootness is the temporal caboose. The federal courts will not review cases that have been resolved, for

---

137   See Gregory v. Ashcroft, 501 U.S. 452 (1991).

138   See Kramer.

139   Aetna Life Insurance Co. v. Haworth, 300 U.S. 227 (1937).

140   Chicago & Grand Trunk Railway v. Wellman, 143 U.S. 339 (1892).

141   Rescue Army v. Municipal Court, 331 U.S. 549 (1949).

142   Poe v. Ullman, 367 U.S. 497 (1961).

there is no longer a case or controversy.[143] However, having served one's criminal sentence does not end collateral legal consequences, such as loss of voting rights.[144] By the same token, if a claim, although ostensibly moot, is "capable of repetition, yet evading review," the case or controversy requirement will not be a bar to review. Examples of the latter exception include pregnancy and voting.[145]

The requirement of "standing" has produced a large number of decisions, and a tremendous literature. In standing cases, there is seldom a problem with ripeness or mootness or even of advisory opinions; rather, the particular plaintiff is perceived not to possess "such a personal stake in the outcome of the controversy as to assure that concrete adverseness which sharpens the presentation of issues."[146] The personal stake need not be particularly high to satisfy the Supreme Court. In *United States v. SCRAP*[147] a group of law students was held to have standing to challenge a policy of the Interstate Commerce Commission which discouraged recycling and therefore, it was alleged, diminished the quality of the students' physical environment. One major exception to the standing requirement has been created for taxpayer challenges to federal spending programs that are alleged to exceed specific constitutional limitations, such as the Establishment Clause of the First Amendment.[148]

The case or controversy requirement is imposed by the Constitution, not by statutory law. Therefore it cannot be ameliorated by a statute which purports to allow any person, regardless of interest or injury, to challenge alleged statutory violations.[149]

b. Implied Grants of (and Limitations on) Judicial Power

The Constitution does not specifically provide for the judicial review of the constitutionality of governmental acts, whether they be legislative, executive, or administrative. In this way the American Constitution differs textually from those of, for example, Austria, Germany, and Spain, that specifically provide for constitutional courts. Efforts to create a Council of Revision to review with the authority to judge the constitutionality of legislative and executive acts of Congress before they went into effect were unsuccessful at the Constitutional Convention.[150]

---

143   Liner v. Jafco, Inc., 375 U.S. 301 (1964).
144   Sibron v. New York, 392 U.S. 40 (1968).
145   Moore v. Ogilvie, 394 U.S. 814 (1969).
146   Baker v. Carr, 369 U.S. 186 (1962).
147   412 U.S. 669 (1973).
148   Flast v. Cohen, 392 U.S. 83 (1968).
149   Lujan v. Defenders of Wildlife, 504 U.S. 555 (1992).
150   Farrand at p. 21.

With the authority to judge the constitutionality of legislative and executive acts comes the corresponding responsibility not to usurp legislative and constitutional authority. This responsibility, founded upon the principle of separation of powers, is termed the "political question" doctrine. Discussion of this doctrine follows an exposition of the institution of judicial review.

i. Judicial Review of Constitutionality

The catalogue of the Supreme Court's judicial province, discussed above, speaks only of cases "arising under this Constitution."[151] The closest textual suggestion of a judicial power to rule on the constitutionality of legislation is the Supremacy Clause, Article IV, section 2, which reads:

> This Constitution, and the Laws of the United States which shall be made in Pursuance thereof; and all Treaties made, or which shall be made, under the Authority of the United States, shall be the supreme Law of the Land; and the Judges in every State shall be bound thereby, any Thing in the Constitution or Laws of any State to the Contrary notwithstanding.

Admittedly, this clause does not stipulate what body should determine whether the laws are made "in Pursuance" of the Constitution. The final clause might also be read to indicate that the courts were only supposed to consider the conformity of state law to federal law.

In England courts had occasionally refused to enforce acts of Parliament. Lord Coke, in *Dr. Bonham's Case*,[152] stated that "the common law will controul acts of Parliament, adjudge them to be utterly void [when they are] against common right and reason."[153] But this was not descriptive of British practice in the 18th century. The Privy Council had employed the principle of *ultra vires* to invalidate colonial acts, and state courts had set aside acts of state legislatures for incompatibility with their constitutions. Legal historians have searched in vain for evidence that the Framers of the Constitution did not expect the courts to rule on constitutionality. Professor Bickel writes[154] that the Framers "tacitly" intended such a power. Still, it is curious from a historical standpoint that the power was first confirmed in a case where the Supreme Court concluded that it had no jurisdiction. That case, perhaps the most famous case in American constitutional jurisprudence, follows.

Marbury filed suit directly in the United States Supreme Court seeking a writ of mandamus, a species of court order, to compel Madison to deliver his commission and thus allow him to begin serving as a judge. Marbury premised his petition on section 13 of the Judiciary Act of 1789. This legislation bestowed upon the Supreme Court jurisdiction to issue writs of mandamus "to persons holding

---

151   Art. III, § 2, cl. 1.

152   8 Rep. 118a (C.P. 1610).

153   Gunther & Sullivan at p. 14.

154   At p. 15.

office under the authority of the United States." In doing so, the Judiciary Act purported to enlarge the original jurisdiction of the Supreme Court beyond that provided in Article III of the Constitution, which mentions only cases or controversies "affecting Ambassadors, other public Ministers and Counsels, and those in which a State shall be a Party."

By way of background, after suffering a defeat in the elections of 1800, the outgoing Congress created 42 new positions as justices of the peace in the District of Columbia. President John Adams, who had been defeated in the election by Thomas Jefferson, wanted to fill all vacant judicial positions with federally minded judges. He appointed his Secretary of State, John Marshall, to the vacant seat as Chief Justice at the United States Supreme Court. William Marbury and others were confirmed by the Senate on the day before Jefferson took office. Jefferson's Secretary of State, respondent Madison, refused to deliver the commissions, the formal documents evidencing the appointments.

CASE: Marbury v. Madison
5 U.S. 137 (1803)

Opinion of the court [by Chief Justice Marshall]

At the last term, on the affidavits then read and filed with the clerk, a rule was granted in this case, requiring the secretary of state to show cause why a mandamus should not issue, directing him to deliver to William Marbury his commission as a justice of the peace for the county of Washington, in the district of Columbia.

No cause has been shown, and the present motion is for a mandamus. The peculiar delicacy of this case, the novelty of some of its circumstances, and the real difficulty attending the points which occur in it, require a complete exposition of the principles on which the opinion to be given by the court is founded.

In the order in which the court has viewed this subject, the following questions have been considered and decided.

    1st. Has the applicant a right to the commission he demands?

    2dly. If he has a right, and that right has been violated, do the laws of his country afford him a remedy?

    3dly. If they do afford him a remedy, is it a mandamus issuing from this court?

The first object of inquiry is,

1st. Has the applicant a right to the commission he demands?

His right originates in an act of congress passed in February 1801, concerning the district of Columbia. . . .

The last act to be done by the president, is the signature of the commission. He has then acted on the advice and consent of the senate to his own nomination. The time for deliberation has then passed. . . .

It is therefore decidedly the opinion of the court, that when a commission has been signed by the president, the appointment is made; and that the commission is complete when the seal of the United States has been affixed to it by the secretary of state.

Where an officer is removable at the will of the executive, the circumstance which completes his appointment is of no concern; because the act is at any time revocable; and the commission may be arrested, if still in the office. But when the officer is not removable at the will of the executive, the appointment is not revocable and cannot be annulled. It has conferred legal rights which cannot be resumed. [To] withhold the commission, therefore, is an act deemed by the court not warranted by law, but violative of a vested legal right.

2. This brings us to the second inquiry; which is: If he has a right, and that right has been violated, do the laws of his country afford him a remedy? The very essence of civil liberty certainly consists in the right of every individual to claim the protection of the laws, whenever he receives an injury. One of the first duties of government is to afford that protection. In Great Britain the king himself is sued in the respectful form of a petition, and he never fails to comply with the judgment of his court.

The government of the United States has been emphatically termed a government of laws, and not of men. It will certainly cease to deserve this high appellation, if the laws furnish no remedy for the violation of a vested legal right. If this obloquy is to be cast on the jurisprudence of our country, it must arise from the peculiar character of the case.

It behooves us then to inquire whether there be in its composition any ingredient which shall exempt from legal investigation, or exclude the injured party from legal redress. . . .

The conclusion from this reasoning is, that where the heads of departments are the political or confidential agents of the executive, merely to execute the will of the president, or rather to act in cases in which the executive possesses a constitutional or legal discretion, nothing can be more perfectly clear than that their acts are only politically examinable. But where a specific duty is assigned by law, and individual rights depend upon the performance of that duty, it seems equally clear that the individual who considers himself injured has a right to resort to the laws of his country for a remedy.

The question whether a right has vested or not, is, in its nature, judicial, and must be tried by the judicial authority, If, for example, Mr. Marbury had taken the oaths of a magistrate, and proceeded to act as one; in consequence of which a suit had been instituted against him, in which his defence had depended on his being a magistrate; the validity of his appointment must have been determined by judicial authority. So, if he conceives that by virtue of his appointment he has a legal right either to the commission which has been made out for him or to a copy of that commission, it is equally a question examinable in a court, and the decision of the court upon it must depend on the opinion entertained of his appointment. That question has been discussed, and the opinion is, that the latest point of time which can be taken as that at which the appointment was complete, and evidenced, was when, after the signature of the president, the seal of the United States was affixed to the commission.

It is then the opinion of the court: 1st. That by signing the commission of Mr. Marbury, the president of the United States appointed him a justice of peace for the county of Washington in the district of Columbia; and that the seal of the United States, affixed thereto by the secretary of state, is conclusive testimony of the verity of the signature, and of the completion of the appointment; and that the appointment conferred on him a legal right to the office for the space of five years. 2d. That, having this legal title to the office, he has a consequent right to the commission; a refusal to deliver which is a plain violation of that right, for which the laws of his country afford him a remedy.

3. It remains to be inquired whether he is entitled to the remedy for which he applies?

. . .

The act to establish the judicial courts of the United States [the Judiciary Act of 1789] authorizes the supreme court 'to issue writs of mandamus, in cases warranted by the principles and usages of law, to any courts appointed, or persons holding office, under the authority of the United States.'

The secretary of state, being a person, holding an office under the authority of the United States, is precisely within the letter of the description; and if this court is not authorized to issue a writ of mandamus to such an officer, it must be because the law is unconstitutional, and therefore absolutely incapable of conferring the authority, and assigning the duties which its words purport to confer and assign.

The constitution vests the whole judicial power of the United States in one supreme court, and such inferior courts as congress shall, from time to time, ordain and establish. This power is expressly extended to all cases arising under the laws of the United States; and consequently, in some form, may be exercised over the present case; because the right claimed is given by a law of the United States.

In the distribution of this power it is declared that 'the supreme court shall have original jurisdiction in all cases affecting ambassadors, other public ministers and consuls, and those in which a state shall be a party. In all other cases, the supreme court shall have appellate jurisdiction.'

It has been insisted at the bar, that as the original grant of jurisdiction to the supreme and inferior courts is general, and the clause, assigning original jurisdiction to the supreme court, contains no negative or restrictive words; the power remains to the legislature to assign original jurisdiction to that court in other cases than those specified in the article which has been recited; provided those cases belong to the judicial power of the United States.

If it had been intended to leave it in the discretion of the legislature to apportion the judicial power between the supreme and inferior courts according to the will of that body, it would certainly have been useless to have proceeded further than to have defined the judicial power, and the tribunals in which it should be vested. The subsequent part of the section is mere surplusage, is entirely without meaning, if such is to be the construction. If congress remains at liberty to give this court appellate jurisdiction, where the constitution has declared their jurisdiction shall be original; and original jurisdiction where the constitution has declared it shall be appellate; the distribution of jurisdiction made in the constitution, is form without substance.

Affirmative words are often, in their operation, negative of other objects than those affirmed; and in this case, a negative or exclusive sense must be given to them or they have no operation at all.

It cannot be presumed that any clause in the constitution is intended to be without effect; and therefore such construction is inadmissible, unless the words require it. . . .

When an instrument organizing fundamentally a judicial system, divides it into one supreme, and so many inferior courts as the legislature may ordain and establish; then enumerates its powers, and proceeds so far to distribute them, as to define the jurisdiction of the supreme court by declaring the cases in which it shall take original jurisdiction, and that in others it shall take appellate jurisdiction, the plain import of the words seems to be, that in one class of cases its jurisdiction is original, and not appellate; in the other it is appellate, and not original. If any other construction would render the clause inoperative, that is an additional reason for rejecting such other construction, and for adhering to the obvious meaning.

To enable this court then to issue a mandamus, it must be shown to be an exercise of appellate jurisdiction, or to be necessary to enable them to exercise appellate jurisdiction.

It has been stated at the bar that the appellate jurisdiction may be exercised in a variety of forms, and that if it be the will of the legislature that a mandamus should be used for that purpose, that will must be obeyed. This is true; yet the jurisdiction must be appellate, not original.

It is the essential criterion of appellate jurisdiction, that it revises and corrects the proceedings in a cause already instituted, and does not create that case. Although, therefore, a mandamus may be directed to courts, yet to issue such a writ to an officer for the delivery of a paper, is in effect the same as to sustain an original action for that paper, and therefore seems not to belong to appellate, but to original jurisdiction. Neither is it necessary in such a case as this, to enable the court to exercise its appellate jurisdiction.

The authority, therefore, given to the supreme court, by the act establishing the judicial courts of the United States, to issue writs of mandamus to public officers, appears not to be warranted by the constitution; and it becomes necessary to inquire whether a jurisdiction, so conferred, can be exercised.

The question, whether an act, repugnant to the constitution, can become the law of the land, is a question deeply interesting to the United States; but, happily, not of an intricacy proportioned to its interest. It seems only necessary to recognize certain principles, supposed to have been long and well established, to decide it.

That the people have an original right to establish, for their future government, such principles as, in their opinion, shall most conduce to their own happiness, is the basis on which the whole American fabric has been erected. The exercise of this original right is a very great exertion; nor can it nor ought it to be frequently repeated. The principles, therefore, so established are deemed fundamental. And as the authority, from which they proceed, is supreme, and can seldom act, they are designed to be permanent.

This original and supreme will organizes the government, and assigns to different departments their respective powers. It may either stop here; or establish certain limits not to be transcended by those departments.

The government of the United States is of the latter description. The powers of the legislature are defined and limited; and that those limits may not be mistaken or forgotten, the constitution is written. To what purpose are powers limited, and to what purpose is that limitation committed to writing; if these limits may, at any time, be passed by those intended to be restrained? The distinction between a government with limited and unlimited powers is abolished, if those limits do not confine the persons on whom they are imposed, and if acts prohibited and acts allowed are of equal obligation. It is a proposition too plain to be contested, that the constitution controls any legislative act repugnant to it; or, that the legislature may alter the constitution by an ordinary act.

Between these alternatives there is no middle ground. The constitution is either a superior, paramount law, unchangeable by ordinary means, or it is on a level with ordinary legislative acts, and like other acts, is alterable when the legislature shall please to alter it.

If the former part of the alternative be true, then a legislative act contrary to the constitution is not law: if the latter part be true, then written constitutions are absurd attempts, on the part of the people, to limit a power in its own nature illimitable.

Certainly all those who have framed written constitutions contemplate them as forming the fundamental and paramount law of the nation, and consequently the theory of every such government must be, that an act of the legislature repugnant to the constitution is void.

This theory is essentially attached to a written constitution, and is consequently to be considered by this court as one of the fundamental principles of our society. It is not therefore to be lost sight of in the further consideration of this subject.

If an act of the legislature, repugnant to the constitution, is void, does it, notwithstanding its invalidity, bind the courts and oblige them to give it effect? Or, in other words, though it be not law, does it constitute a rule as operative as if it was a law? This would be to overthrow in fact what was established in theory; and would seem, at first view, an absurdity too gross to be insisted on. It shall, however, receive a more attentive consideration.

It is emphatically the province and duty of the judicial department to say what the law is. Those who apply the rule to particular cases, must of necessity expound and interpret that rule. If two laws conflict with each other, the courts must decide on the operation of each.

So if a law be in opposition to the constitution: if both the law and the constitution apply to a particular case, so that the court must either decide that case conformably to the law, disregarding the constitution; or conformably to the constitution, disregarding the law: the court must determine which of these conflicting rules governs the case. This is of the very essence of judicial duty. If then the courts are to regard the constitution; and he constitution is superior to any ordinary act of the legislature; the constitution, and not such ordinary act, must govern the case to which they both apply.

Those then who controvert the principle that the constitution is to be considered, in court, as a paramount law, are reduced to the necessity of maintaining that courts must close their eyes on the constitution, and see only the law.

This doctrine would subvert the very foundation of all written constitutions. It would declare that an act, which, according to the principles and theory of our government, is entirely void, is yet, in practice, completely obligatory. It would declare, that if the legislature shall do what is expressly forbidden, such act, notwithstanding the express prohibition, is in reality effectual. It would be giving to the legislature a practical and real omnipotence with the same breath which professes to restrict their powers within narrow limits. It is prescribing limits, and declaring that those limits may be passed at pleasure.

That it thus reduces to nothing what we have deemed the greatest improvement on political institutions—a written constitution, would of itself be sufficient, in America where written constitutions have been viewed with so much reverence, for rejecting the construction. But the peculiar expressions of the constitution of the United States furnish additional arguments in favor of its rejection.

The judicial power of the United States is extended to all cases arising under the constitution.

Could it be the intention of those who gave this power, to say that, in using it, the constitution should not be looked into? That a case arising under the constitution should be decided without examining the instrument under which it arises?

This is too extravagant to be maintained.

In some cases then, the constitution must be looked into by the judges. And if they can open it at all, what part of it are they forbidden to read, or to obey?

There are many other parts of the constitution which serve to illustrate this subject.

It is declared that 'no tax or duty shall be laid on articles exported from any state.' Suppose a duty on the export of cotton, of tobacco, or of flour; and a suit instituted to recover it. Ought judgment to be rendered in such a case? *Ought* the judges to close their eyes on the constitution, and only see the law.

The constitution declares that 'no bill of attainder or ex post facto law shall be passed.'

If, however, such a bill should be passed and a person should be prosecuted under it, must the court condemn to death those victims whom the constitution endeavours to preserve?

'No person,' says the constitution, 'shall be convicted of treason unless on the testimony of two witnesses to the same overt act, or on confession in open court.'

Here the language of the constitution is addressed especially to the courts. It prescribes, directly for them, a rule of evidence not to be departed from. If the legislature should change that rule, and declare *one* witness, or a confession *out* of court, sufficient for conviction, must the constitutional principle yield to the legislative act?

From these and many other selections which might be made, it is apparent, that the framers of the constitution contemplated that instrument as a rule for the government of *courts*, as well as of the legislature.

Why otherwise does it direct the judges to take an oath to support it? This oath certainly applies, in an especial manner, to their conduct in their official character. How immoral to impose it on them, if they were to be used as the instruments, and the knowing instruments, for violating what they swear to support!

The oath of office, too, imposed by the legislature, is completely demonstrative of the legislative opinion on this subject. It is in these words: 'I do solemnly swear that I will administer justice without respect to persons, and do equal right to the poor and to the rich; and that I will faithfully and impartially discharge all the duties incumbent on me as according to the best of my abilities and understanding, agreeably to the *constitution* and laws of the United States.'

Why does a judge swear to discharge his duties agreeably to the constitution of the United States, if that constitution forms no rule for his government, if it is closed upon him and cannot be inspected by him. If such be the real state of things, this is worse than solemn mockery. To prescribe, or to take this oath, becomes equally a crime.

It is also not entirely unworthy of observation, that in declaring what shall be the *supreme* law of the land, the *constitution* itself is first mentioned; and not the laws of the United States generally, but those only which shall be made in *pursuance* of the constitution, have that rank.

Thus, the particular phraseology of the constitution of the United States confirms and strengthens the principle, supposed to be essential to all written constitutions, that a law repugnant to the constitution is void, and that courts, as well as other departments, are bound by that instrument.

The rule must be discharged.

To recapitulate, all the judges of the US Supreme Court (there were five at the time) ruled that Madison was acting unlawfully in withholding Marbury's commission, but they refused to order Madison to comply with the law because, they held in the narrow sense, that the Constitution did not give them the jurisdiction to decide the case, at least in the first instance (original jurisdiction). Congress's attempt to enlarge that jurisdiction was "repugnant to the constitution [and] void." Accordingly, the "courts, as well as other departments, are bound by" the Constitution first, and statutes second. In result, then, the Supreme Court held section 13 of the Judiciary Act of 1789 unconstitutional.

Politically, Chief Justice Marshall's opinion was brilliant. Although Marbury was left without a judicial remedy, had Marshall ruled in his favor, the Jefferson administration would surely have ignored the order.[155] In addition, there was a real risk that Jefferson might seek the impeachment of more Federalist judges. One, an insane drunkard, had been impeached in early 1802, and was removed from office by conviction in the Senate in March 1804.[156] One day later the House impeached Supreme Court Justice Samuel Chase for political activity incompatible with his office. The Senate failed to convict Chase on "Treason, Bribery, or other high Crimes and Misdemeanors" as required by Article II, section 4, of the Constitution.

A few years after *Marbury v. Madison* the Supreme Court confirmed its constitutional power to judge the constitutionality of state legislation.[157] Shortly thereafter it was confronted with the question of whether the Constitution conferred upon it the power to review the judgments of state courts in cases that fall within the jurisdiction of the federal courts. At issue was the forerunner of section 1257(a) of title 28 of the United States Code:

> Final judgments or decrees rendered by the highest court of a State in which a decision could be had, may be reviewed by the Supreme Court by writ of certiorari where the validity of a treaty or statute of the United States is drawn in question or where the validity of a statute of any State is drawn in question on the ground of its being repugnant to the Constitution, treaties, or laws of the United States. . . .

By way of background, in 1789 the Commonwealth of Virginia had confiscated land owned by the plaintiff Martin's uncle, a British subject, and granted it to Hunter. Martin filed suit in the Virginia court against Hunter and his lessee, contending that the confiscation violated a treaty between the United States and Great Britain. The Virginia Court of Appeals ruled for the defendant on the ground that the confiscation had preceded the treaties. The plaintiff sought review by the United States Supreme Court under section 25 of the Judiciary Act, and that court reversed, holding that the Commonwealth of Virginia had not

---

155   From Chemerinsky, Constitutional Law at p. 43.
156   From Gunther & Sullivan at p. 12.
157   Fletcher v. Peck, 10 U.S. 87 (1810).

perfected its title in time. The Virginia court refused to acknowledge the reversal, claiming that Congress had no power to extend the jurisdiction of the Supreme Court to review judgments of state courts.

CASE: Martin v. Hunter's Lessee
14 U.S. 304 (1816)

STORY, J., delivered the opinion of the court. . . .

[The] appellate power is not limited by the terms of the third article to any particular courts. The words are, 'the judicial power (which includes appellate power) shall extend to *all cases*,' &c., and 'in all other cases before mentioned the supreme court shall have appellate jurisdiction.' It is the *case*, then, and not the *court*, that gives the jurisdiction. If the judicial power extends to the case, it will be in vain to search in the letter of the constitution for any qualification as to the tribunal where it depends. [If] the text be clear and distinct, no restriction upon its plain and obvious import ought to be admitted, unless the inference be irresistible.

If the constitution meant to limit the appellate jurisdiction to cases pending in the courts of the United States, it would necessarily follow that the jurisdiction of these courts would, in all the cases enumerated in the constitution, be exclusive of state tribunals. How otherwise could the jurisdiction extend to *all* cases arising under the constitution, laws, and treaties of the United States, or to all cases of admiralty and maritime jurisdiction? If some of these cases might be entertained by state tribunals, and no appellate jurisdiction as to them should exist, then the appellate power would not extend to *all*, but to *some*, cases. If state tribunals might exercise concurrent jurisdiction over all or some of the other classes of cases in the constitution without control, then the appellate jurisdiction of the United States might, as to such cases, have no real existence, contrary to the manifest intent of the constitution. [This] construction would abridge the jurisdiction of such court far more than has been ever contemplated in any act of congress. . . .

[It] is plain that the framers of the constitution did contemplate that cases within the judicial cognizance of the United States not only might but would arise in the state courts, in the exercise of their ordinary jurisdiction. With this view the sixth article declares, that 'this constitution, and the laws of the United States which shall be made in pursuance thereof, and all treaties made, or which shall be made, under the authority of the United States, shall be the supreme law of the land, and the judges in every state shall be bound thereby, any thing in the constitution or laws of any state to the contrary notwithstanding.' It is obvious that this obligation is imperative upon the state judges in their official, and not merely in their private, capacities. From the very nature of their judicial duties they would be called upon to pronounce the law applicable to the case in judgment. They were not to decide merely according to the laws or constitution of the state, but according to the constitution, laws and treaties of the United States—'the supreme law of the land.'

A moment's consideration will show us the necessity and propriety of this provision in cases where the jurisdiction of the state courts is unquestionable. Suppose a contract for the payment of money is made between citizens of the same state, and performance thereof is sought in the courts of that state; no person can doubt that the jurisdiction completely and exclusively attaches, in the first instance, to such courts. Suppose at the trial the defendant sets up in his defence a tender under a state law, making paper money a good tender, or a state law, impairing the obligation of such contract, which law, if binding, would defeat the suit. The constitution of the United States has declared that no state shall make any thing but gold or silver coin a tender in payment of debts, or pass a law impairing the obligation of contracts. If congress shall not have passed a law providing for the removal of such a suit to the courts of the United States, must not the state court proceed to hear and determine it? [Suppose] an indictment for a crime in a state court, and the defendant should allege in his defence that the crime was created by an ex post facto act of the state, must not the state court, in the exercise of a jurisdiction which has already rightfully attached, have a right to pronounce on the validity and sufficiency of the defence? It would be extremely difficult, upon any legal principles, to give a negative answer to these inquiries. Innumerable instances of the same sort might be stated, in illustration of the position; and unless the state courts could sustain jurisdiction in such cases, this clause of the sixth article would be without meaning or effect, and public mischiefs, of a most enormous magnitude, would inevitably ensue.

It must, therefore, be conceded that the constitution not only contemplated, but meant to provide for cases within the scope of the judicial power of the United States, which might yet depend before state tribunals. It was foreseen that in the exercise of their ordinary jurisdiction, state courts would incidentally take cognizance of cases arising under the constitution, the laws, and treaties of the United States. Yet to all these cases the judicial power, by the very terms of the constitution, is to extend. It cannot extend by original jurisdiction if that was already rightfully and exclusively attached in the state courts, which (as has been already shown) may occur; it must, therefore, extend by appellate jurisdiction, or not at all. It would seem to follow that the appellate power of the United States must, in such cases, extend to state tribunals; and if in such cases, there is no reason why it should not equally attach upon all others within the purview of the constitution.

It has been argued that such an appellate jurisdiction over state courts is inconsistent with the genius of our governments, and the spirit of the constitution. That the latter was never designed to act upon state sovereignties, but only upon the people, and that if the power exists, it will materially impair the sovereignty of the states, and the independence of their courts. . . .

It is a mistake that the constitution was not designed to operate upon states, in their corporate capacities. It is crowded with provisions which restrain or annul the sovereignty of the states in some of the highest branches of their prerogatives. The tenth section of the first article contains a long list of disabilities and prohibitions imposed upon the states. Surely, when such essential portions of state sovereignty are taken away, or prohibited to be exercised, it cannot be correctly asserted that the constitution does not act upon the states. The language of the constitution is also imperative upon the states as to the performance of many duties. It is imperative upon the state legislatures to make laws prescribing the time, places, and manner of holding elections for senators and representatives, and for electors of president and vice-president. And in these, as well as some other cases, congress have a right to revise, amend, or supercede the laws which may be passed by state legislatures. When, therefore, the states are stripped of some of the highest attributes of sovereignty, and the same are given to the United States; when the legislatures of the states are, in some respects, under the control of congress, and in every case are, under the constitution, bound by the paramount authority of the United States; it is certainly difficult to support the argument that the appellate power over the decisions of state courts is contrary to the genius of our institutions. The courts of the United States can, without question, revise the proceedings of the executive and legislative authorities of the states, and if they are found to be contrary to the constitution, may declare them to be of no legal validity. Surely the exercise of the same right over judicial tribunals is not a higher or more dangerous act of sovereign power.

Nor can such a right be deemed to impair the independence of state judges. It is assuming the very ground in controversy to assert that they possess an absolute independence of the United States. In respect to the powers granted to the United States, they are not independent; they are expressly bound to obedience by the letter of the constitution; and if they should unintentionally transcend their authority, or misconstrue the constitution, there is no more reason for giving their judgments an absolute and irresistible force, than for giving it to the acts of the other co-ordinate departments of state sovereignty.

The argument urged from the possibility of the abuse of the revising power, is equally unsatisfactory. It is always a doubtful course, to argue against the use or existence of a power, from the possibility of its abuse. It is still more difficult, by such an argument, to ingraft upon a general power a restriction which is not to be found in the terms in which it is given. From the very nature of things, the absolute right of decision, in the last resort, must rest somewhere—wherever it may be vested it is susceptible of abuse. In all questions of jurisdiction the inferior, or appellate court, must pronounce the final judgment; and common sense, as well as legal reasoning, has conferred it upon the latter.

It is further argued, that no great public mischief can result from a construction which shall limit the appellate power of the United States to cases in their own courts: first, because state judges are bound by an oath to support the constitution of the United States, and must be presumed to be men of learning and integrity; and, secondly, because congress must have an unquestionable right to remove all cases within the scope of the judicial power from the state courts to the courts of the United States, at any time before final judgment, thought not after final judgment. As to the first reason—admitting that the judges of the state courts are, and always will be, of as much learning, integrity, and wisdom, as those of the courts of the United States, (which we very cheerfully admit,) it does not aid the argument. It is manifest that the constitution has proceeded upon a theory of its own, and given or withheld powers according to the judgment of the American people, by whom it was adopted. [The] constitution has presumed (whether rightly or wrongly we do not inquire) that state attachments, state prejudices, state jealousies, and state interests, might some times obstruct, or control, or be supposed to obstruct or control, the regular administration of justice. Hence, in controversies between states; between citizens of different states; between citizens claiming grants under different states; between a state and its citizens, or foreigners, and between citizens and foreigners, it enables the parties, under the authority of congress, to have the controversies heard, tried, and determined before the national tribunals. No other reason than that which has been stated can be assigned, why some, at least, of those cases should not have been left to the cognizance of the state courts. In respect to the other enumerated cases—the cases arising under the constitution, laws, and treaties of the United States, cases affecting ambassadors and other public ministers, and cases of admiralty and maritime jurisdiction—reasons of a higher and more extensive nature, touching the safety, peace, and sovereignty of the nation, might well justify a grant of exclusive jurisdiction.

This is not all. A motive of another kind, perfectly compatible with the most sincere respect for state tribunals, might induce the grant of appellate power over their decisions. That motive is the importance, and even necessity of *uniformity* of decisions throughout the whole United States, upon all subjects within the purview of the constitution. Judges of equal learning and integrity, in different states, might differently interpret a statute, or a treaty of the United States, or even the constitution itself: If there were no revising authority to control these jarring and discordant judgments, and harmonize them into uniformity, the laws, the treaties, and the constitution of the United States would be different in different states, and might, perhaps, never have precisely the same construction, obligation, or efficacy, in any two states. The public mischiefs that would attend such a state of things would be truly deplorable; and it cannot be believed that they could have escaped the enlightened convention which formed the constitution. What, indeed, might then have been only prophecy, has now become fact; and the appellate jurisdiction must continue to be the only adequate remedy for such evils.

There is an additional consideration, which is entitled to great weight. The constitution of the United States was designed for the common and equal benefit of all the people of the United States. The judicial power was granted for the same benign and salutary purposes. It was not to be exercised exclusively for the benefit of parties who might be plaintiffs, and would elect the national forum, but also for the protection of defendants who might be entitled to try their rights, or assert their privileges, before the same forum. Yet, if the construction contended for be correct, it will follow, that as the plaintiff may always elect the state court, the defendant may be deprived of all the security which the constitution intended in aid of his rights. Such a state of things can, in no respect, be considered as giving equal rights. . . .

On the whole, the court are of opinion, that the appellate power of the United States does extend to cases pending in the state courts; and that the 25th section of the judiciary act, which authorizes the exercise of this jurisdiction in the specified cases, by a writ of error, is supported by the letter and spirit of the constitution. We find no clause in that instrument which limits this power; and we dare not interpose a limitation where the people have not been disposed to create one. . . .

[Reversed.]

Does it follow from these cases and from the institution of judicial review that inferior federal courts have the authority to declare federal legislation unconstitutional under the Constitution?[158] What about the authority to declare state and local governmental actions unconstitutional?[159] Finally, should state judges be able to invalidate their own state's legislation under the federal constitution?[160]

ii. The "Political Question" Doctrine

The Supreme Court has a great deal of discretion in deciding which cases it wants to hear. This discretion results principally from the employment by the Congress of its authority under Article III, section 2 to regulate the Supreme Court's appellate jurisdiction. Congress has by statute established two avenues of appellate review. The first, called "appeal," is mandatory. However, this avenue is extremely limited, for an appeal only lies from a decision of a three-judge district court panel (which is a rare animal in itself) that grants or denies injunctive relief.[161] All other review by the Supreme Court is by writ of certiorari, which is discretionary. For example, a party in any civil or criminal case that has been decided by a federal court of appeals can petition for certiorari whether or not constitutional issues are involved.[162] However, the Supreme Court will not grant the petition, and hear the case, unless it involves "special and important reasons,"[163] such as a conflict in the decisions of the various appellate courts, or when an important federal issue has not yet been decided.

The discretion to choose by writ of certiorari what cases to hear must be distinguished from another doctrine that seems to function like discretion, but is actually based on the theory and conviction that the Supreme Court lacks discretion to decide certain cases even though they arise under the Constitution and involve real controversies. The doctrine is referred to, somewhat misleadingly, as the political question doctrine. It holds that the Supreme Court is prohibited by principles of separation of powers from interfering in the fundamental workings of the other two "political" branches of government.

Because the political question doctrine works at a high level of abstraction, it is difficult to describe and predict its impact on everyday disputes. To help guide itself in deciding which cases it shall not decide, the Supreme Court has articulated four questions.[164] These are:

- Does the Constitution exhibit a "textually demonstrable" commitment of the issue to one of the political branches, that is, to the Congress or the president?

---

158   See 16 Am. Jur. 2d, Constitutional Law § 116.

159   See Chemerinsky, *Parity.*

160   E.g., Jackman v. Bodine, 43 N.J. 453(1964); see US Const. Art. VI, § 2 and Williams.

161   28 U.S.C. § 1253.

162   28 U.S.C. § 1254.

163   US Sup. Ct. Rule 17.

164   Baker v. Carr, 369 U.S. 186 (1962).

- Is there a lack of judicially manageable standards for resolving the issue?

- Is there a need for finality in the action of the political branch?

- Is it difficult or impossible to devise effective judicial remedies?

Applying the separation of powers policies embedded in these questions, the Supreme Court has refused to review procedures concerning constitutional amendments,[165] election to the Congress,[166] and impeachment,[167] although in the last case it suggested that "political" matters are reviewable if they exceed the textual limits of the Constitution. The area of foreign relations has also been one in which the Supreme Court has indicated that the Constitution forbids it from second-guessing the president, Senate, and Congress.[168]

Subpart B: The Governments of the States

Today it is sometimes difficult to fathom that thirteen of the states were in existence before the federal government, that the new federal government has eventually replaced them in major areas, that it has come to dominate them financially, but that it has still not subjugated them or relegated them to the status of federal agencies.

Federalism functions haphazardly in the United States. It shields state legislatures from most direct interference by the federal government, but does not protect them against federal preemption of traditional state matters, or allow them to violate federal constitutional rights or regulate interstate or foreign commerce.[169] While state executive branches cannot be forced to enforce federal law, they are subject to some federal control, such as when they are acting as employers, or when affecting federal constitutional rights. State judiciaries, unlike state executive officers, must enforce federal law directly, provided the law is constitutional.

Various prudential reasons have been advanced for federal structures like the one in the United States. The most frequent justification is roughly the same as the policy underlying the principle of separation of powers: division of the

---

165   Coleman v. Miller, 307 U.S. 422 (1939).

166   Roudebush v. Hartke, 405 U.S. 15 (1972).

167   Nixon v. United States, 506 U.S. 224 (1993).

168   E.g., Martin v. Mott, 25 U.S. 19 (1827), considering what the recognized government of a country is, and Goldwater v. Carter, 444 U.S. 996 (1979), where four justices opined that the question whether the president may unilaterally terminate a treaty is political and thus unreviewable.

169   This text does not treat the so-called "negative" or "dormant" commerce clause, that is, the implied prohibition against regulation by the states of interstate and international commerce. For a good recent summary see Lawrence. See generally Tribe at p. 401 *et seq.*

monopoly on governmental power to avoid tyranny, caprice, and oppression. Madison took issue with this argument. In discussing why the states should not be disbanded, he wrote:

> The great objection made [against] an abolition of State [governments] was that the [general government] could not extend its care to all the minute objects which fall under the cognizance of the local jurisdictions. The objection as stated lay not [against] the probable abuse of the general power but [against] the imperfect use that could be made of it throughout so great an extent of country, and over so great a variety of objects. . . .Were it practicable for the [general government] to extend its care to every requisite object without the cooperation of the State [governments] the people would not be less free as members of one great Republic than as members of thirteen small ones.[170]

A second reason advanced is experimentation. According to Justice Brandeis in dissent in *New State Ice Co. v. Liebman*:

> To stay experimentation in things social and economic is a grave responsibility. Denial of the right to experiment might be fraught with serious consequences to the Nation. It is one of the happy incidents of the federal system that a single courageous State may, if its citizens choose, serve as a laboratory; and try novel social and economic experiments without risk to the rest of the country.[171]

A third justification for federalism is plurality for its own sake, an appreciation for differing regional legislation that reflects various social, political, and other phenomena. A fourth argument is democratic involvement, which is more practical at the local or even state level than on the federal level. The chances for citizen involvement, and for accountability and a sense of responsibility felt by elected officials, are greater when geographic and other distances are reduced. Finally, overlapping jurisdictions are thought to encourage competition between federal and state officials for the approval of the populace.

In order to help the reader better appreciate the tension between the federal and state governments, the two positions—federalism vs. "states rights"—are polarized in the following discussion under two provisions of the Constitution, the Supremacy Clause[172] and the 10th Amendment. This part begins by looking at the text of the Constitution. It then sketches the historical rise of federal dominance and presents the present state of the law on "states rights." The part concludes with thoughts on whether or not the state governments should not be federalized, or if their continued existence does not serve public interests that might be collected under the term "subsidiarity" or "localism."

---

170   As quoted in Choper at p. 248.
171   285 U.S. 262, 322 (1932).
172   Art. VI, cl. 2.

1. The Supremacy Clause

> This Constitution, and the Laws of the United States which shall be made in Pursuance thereof; and all Treaties made, or which shall be made, under the Authority of the United States, shall be the supreme Law of the Land; and the Judges in every State shall be bound thereby, any Thing in the Constitution or Laws of any State to the Contrary notwithstanding.[173]

Unlike the federal government, the states enjoy general governmental powers, including what is generally referred to as the "police power," that is, the power to promote the health, morals, safety, and general welfare. The police power allows the states and their subdivisions to enact any law that is not repugnant to constitutional law. As a review of the catalogue of federal powers will reveal, the federal government enjoys no comparable power.

a. Concurrent Jurisdiction

In light of the expansive powers of the states, it is perhaps surprising that the states receive so little mention in the Constitution. This is undoubtedly because the Framers were confronted with designing a new federal government, not with designing state governments, which were already in existence and governed for the most part by their own constitutions.

As foreseen by the Constitution, the major role to be played by the states in influencing the affairs of the federal government, and in protecting state autonomy, was in the Senate. Regardless of the geographic size or population of a state, each state is entitled to two senators.[174] Originally, the senators were chosen by the state legislature, much as representatives are appointed to the Bundesrat in Germany. This practice came to mean that political parties, which are not mentioned in the Constitution, exerted substantial, indirect control on the federal government, for no law can take effect unless both houses of Congress approve. The practice of appointing senators in this fashion was abolished in 1913 on the ratification of the 17th Amendment. Ever since, senators, like members of the House of Representatives, are elected directly by the people. The senators' "district" is coincidental with the geographic boundaries of the state. Election and reelection to the Senate no longer mean responding to the political interests of an identifiable institution, but rather to diffuse popular interests and concerns. Thus, in a very real sense, the states as institutions were disenfranchised by the 17th Amendment.

The role of the states in the election of the president and vice-president is equally indirect. As mentioned above, these offices are filled via the electoral college. The electoral college in turn consists of electors in a number equal to the combined number of senators and representatives in the state. The electors are chosen

---

173   Art. VI, § 2.
174   Art. I, § 3.

by the legislature and are ordinarily bound by state law to vote for the candidates who received the highest numbers of votes in the popular election.

The only direct control that the states as institutions possess over the federal government is that exercised on amending the Constitution. According to Article V, in order for the Constitution to be amended, the amendment must be proposed by two-thirds of both house of Congress and ratified by three-fourths of the legislatures of the states. (No use has yet been made of the alternative procedure provided for in Article V, the constitutional convention.) The paucity of amendments to the Constitution testifies to the difficulty of this process, and to the corresponding insipidity of the states as institutions in directing federal policy.

On the other hand, the Constitution does significantly harness the states. Beginning in the first Article, the Constitution forbids the states, among other things, to enter into treaties, coin money, and grant any title of nobility.[175] The states are also forbidden, without the consent of the Congress, to tax imports or exports, except to the extent absolutely necessary to enforce their inspection laws.[176] Nor may states, without the consent of Congress, keep troops in time of peace, or engage in war unless actually invaded or in imminent danger of being invaded.[177] Further, each state must accord "Full Faith and Credit . . . to the public Acts, Records, and judicial Proceedings of every other State."[178] Each state has an obligation to extradite persons charged with crimes in another state.[179] And, more importantly, each state must accord citizens of other states the same "Privileges and Immunities" that automatically are accorded its own citizens.[180]

The most important limitations on the powers of the states are found in the amendments to the Constitution. Thus, slavery was abolished in the states which had it.[181] Former slaves were given the same rights as others to vote in federal and state elections.[182] The manufacture, sale, and transportation of intoxicating beverages were prohibited.[183] Women and 18-year-olds were given the franchise in all federal and state elections.[184] (Women's suffrage was begun on a limited level by Kentucky in 1838 and accorded on an equal basis with men in the Wyo-

---

175   Art. I, § 10, cl. 1.

176   Art. I, § 10, cl. 2.

177   Art. I, § 10, cl. 3.

178   Art. IV, § 1.

179   Art. IV, § 2, cl. 2.

180   Art. IV, § 2, cl. 1.

181   Amend. 13.

182   Amend. 15.

183   Amend. 18, repealed by Amend. 21.

184   Amends. 19 and 26.

ming Territory in 1869.) But the most profound limitations on the powers of the states are found in section 1 of the 14th Amendment:

> All persons born or naturalized in the United States and subject to the jurisdiction thereof, are citizens of the United States and of the State wherein they reside. No State shall make or enforce any law which shall abridge the privileges or immunities of citizens of the United States; nor shall any State deprive any person of life, liberty, or property, without due process of law; nor deny any person within its jurisdiction the equal protection of the laws.

As discussed in the second part of this book, the "due process" and "equal protection" clauses are the two most important fonts of constitutional rights in the US today. The "due process clause" of the 14th Amendment has been interpreted by the federal courts to forbid the states to violate most of the rights protected by the Bill of Rights, which were originally directed to the federal government alone.[185] This interpretation automatically brings disputes between people who feel their rights are being violated by the governments of the states within the "federal question" jurisdiction of the federal courts. The impact of this federalization of rights has been felt most acutely in the criminal arena, where the vast majority of prosecutions are for violations of state law. But few areas of public life have been left unaffected. The status of the states has waned in the wake of the recognition of federal rights.

In summary, the Constitution is not a document that defines the goals and institutions of American government. There are no catalogues, as there are in the German Constitution, that divide governmental powers between the state and federal governments. Rather, the US Constitution confines itself, with few exceptions, to delineating the powers of the federal government, on the one hand, and the rights of the citizens on the other. The governments of the states are sandwiched somewhere in between.

Nonetheless it is useful to think in terms of three groups of governmental powers: (1) those granted exclusively to the federal government or expressly denied to the states, (2) those exercised concurrently with the states, and (3) those reserved to the states exclusively, basically because they do not fall within the enumerated powers of the Congress. As we saw above, exclusive federal powers are very few in number. They include the powers over foreign affairs (e.g., naturalization and citizenship, declaration of war, national defense, treaties) and over the federal government's political agenda, budget, officials, institutions, and property. At the other end are those powers, also very few in number, that are reserved exclusively to the states. These are discussed below, after the discussion of preemption.

---

185   Duncan v. Louisiana, 391 U.S. 145 (1968).

b. Preemption

With the exception of those few cases in which exclusive legislative power has been bestowed on the federal government, and assuming the federal government has not legislated on the same subject, state governments are free to legislate on any subject they choose, providing, of course, that they do not contravene some particular constitutional impediment, for example, by violating the privileges and immunities clause[186] or by discriminating against interstate commerce.[187] Thus, it was held in any early case that states could enact bankruptcy laws because Congress had not made use of its authority to regulate bankruptcies.[188]

The complexion changes when Congress has legislated on the subject, whether or not the state legislation preceded or succeeded the federal. If Congress has legislated, the state law is not automatically void. Rather, it is void only if Congress clearly intended to preempt state law. The Supreme Court described the appropriate inquiry in *Gade v. National Solid Waste Management Association*:

> Preemption may be either express or implied, and is compelled whether Congress' command is explicitly stated in the statute's language or implicitly contained in its structure and purpose. Absent explicit preemptive language, we have recognized at least two types of implied preemption: field preemption, where the scheme of federal regulation is so pervasive as to make reasonable the inference that Congress left no room for the States to supplement it, and conflict preemption, where compliance with both federal and state regulations is a physical impossibility, or where state law stands as an obstacle to the accomplishment and execution of the full purposes and objectives of Congress.[189]

The Supreme Court frequently states that, where preemption is not express, it should not likely be implied. As stated in *Medtronic, Inc. v. Lohr*:

> [B]ecause the States are independent sovereigns in our federal system, we have long presumed that Congress does not cavalierly preempt state-law causes of action. In all preemption cases, and particularly in those in which Congress has legislated in a field which the States have traditionally occupied, we 'start with the presumption' that 'the historic police powers of the States were not to be superseded by the Federal Act unless that was the clear and manifest purpose of Congress.'[190]

Returning to our example of bankruptcy laws, the Supreme Court has invalidated a state law that denied a drivers license to one who had failed to satisfy a judgment arising out of an automobile accident, even if the debt had been discharged in bankruptcy. The court concluded that the purpose of the federal bankruptcy law was to provide uniform standards for determining when a debt was

---

186   Edwards v. California, 314 U.S. 160 (1941).

187   Welton v. Missouri, 91 U.S. 275 (1876).

188   Sturges v. Crowninshield, 17 U.S. 122 (1819).

189   505 U.S. 88, 98 (1992).

190   518 U.S. 470 (1996).

discharged, and that to allow states to regulate in this fashion would undermine this purpose.[191]

2. The Tenth Amendment

> The powers not delegated to the United States by the Constitution, nor prohibited by it to the States, are reserved to the States respectively, or to the people.

In Subpart A of Part One of this book, we saw that, although the federal government is textually a government of limited, enumerated powers, in fact these powers have been very widely construed, by the Congress and by the federal courts, to stretch those powers to envelop almost every conceivable field of human endeavor. In the foregoing subpart we saw that there is no need for a correspondingly wide interpretation of the original powers of the states, for these powers are considered plenary unless, which rarely happens, the Constitution expressly or impliedly confers exclusive jurisdiction on the federal government or unless, which quite often happens, the Congress legislates on a matters that are concurrently regulated by one or more states, and the congressional legislation expressly or impliedly preempts the state legislation.

In this subpart we consider what residual exclusive powers, if any, persist only with the states. This question is traditionally addressed in the context of the 10th Amendment, but it could also be addressed under the "guarantee clause"[192] or under the doctrine that the federal government is one of enumerated powers. In other words, the 10th Amendment is tautological.[193] In upholding sections of the Fair Labor Standards Act as within the scope of regulation of interstate commerce, Justice Stone, delivering the opinion of the court in *United States v. Darby*, wrote:

> Our conclusion is unaffected by the Tenth Amendment. . . . The amendment states but a truism that all is retained which has not been surrendered. There is nothing in the history of its adoption to suggest that it was more than declaratory of the relationship between the national and state governments as it had been established by the Constitution before the amendment or that its purpose was other than to allay fears that the new national government might seek to exercise powers not granted, and that the states might not be able to exercise fully their reserved powers.[194]

a. The Tenth Amendment in the Courts

We concluded in an earlier section that the federal government has exclusive jurisdiction over its political agenda, budget, officials, institutions, and property. The same cannot quite be said for state governments. The federal government

---

191   Perez v. Campbell, 402 U.S. 637 (1971).

192   Art. IV, § 4.

193   New York v. United States, 505 U.S. 144, 157 (1992) (O'Connor, J., concurring).

194   312 U.S. 100, 123-124 (1940).

may regulate conditions of state governmental employment, which, at least indirectly, regulates state budgets.[195] Concerning property, the Supreme Court has never held that Congress may regulate land in state ownership. Two cases, however, explicitly recognize congressional power under the commerce clause to regulate some economic uses of private land.[196]

In the areas of state political agendas and institutions the states fare better. Congress may not force the states to enact or enforce a federal regulatory program. In *New York v. United States*[197] the Supreme Court considered the constitutionality of the Low-Level Radioactive Waste Policy Amendments Act of 1985, by which Congress sought to require the states to provide for the safe disposal of radioactive wastes generated within their borders. The act even went so far as to provide that the states would "take title" to any wastes within their borders that were not properly disposed of by a certain date, and that they then would be liable for "all damages directly or indirectly incurred." The Supreme Court ruled the provision unconstitutional. If the federal government could "commandeer" the states, the court reasoned, it would undermine government accountability because Congress could make a decision, but the states would bear the political responsibility for a decision that was not theirs. The only direct encroachment on the political agenda of the states that has been upheld by the courts is the questionable decision upholding a federal law that compelled state utility commissions to consider adopting federal standards, but stopped short of trying to require them to adopt those standards.[198] In short, there is no American equivalent to German "framework laws," by which the federal government requires the German states (*Länder*) to legislate.[199]

In light of these cases, and the one that follows, how can state judges be required to enforce federal laws?[200]

The case that follows concerns the constitutionality of the Brady Handgun Violence Prevention Act.

---

195 See United States v. Darby, 312 U.S. 100 (1941) (minimum wage and maximum hours), Garcia v. San Antonio Metropolitan Transit Authority, 469 U.S. 528 (1985), United Transportation Union v. Long Island R.R. Co, 455 U.S. 678 (1982) (Railway Labor Act), Equal Opportunity Employment Commission v. Wyoming, 460 U.S. 226 (1983), and Gregory v. Ashcroft, 501 U.S. 452 (1991) (Age Discrimination in Employment Act).

196 See Hodel v. Virginia Surface Mining & Reclamation Assn., Inc., 452 U.S. 264 (1981), discussed above, and Wickard v. Filburn, 317 U.S. 111 (1942), involving home-grown wheat for home consumption grown on 23 acres—9 hectares—of land.

197 505 U.S. 157 (1992).

198 Federal Energy Regulatory Commission v. Mississippi, 456 U.S. 742 (1982).

199 Currie at pp. 50-52.

200 See also Testa v. Klatt, 330 U.S. 386 (1947).

CASE: Printz v. United States
521 U.S. 98 (1997)

JUSTICE SCALIA delivered the opinion of the Court.

The Brady Act required the Attorney General to establish a national system for instantly checking prospective handgun purchasers' backgrounds. It also commanded the "chief law enforcement officer" (CLEO) of each local jurisdiction to conduct checks and perform related tasks on an interim basis until the national system became operative. Petitioners, the CLEOs for counties in Montana and Arizona, filed separate actions challenging the interim provisions' constitutionality. In each case, the district court held that the background check provision was unconstitutional, but concluded that it was severable from the remainder of the act, effectively leaving a voluntary background check system in place. The Ninth Circuit reversed, finding all of the interim provisions constitutional.

The question presented in these cases is whether certain interim provisions of the Brady Handgun Violence Prevention Act . . . commanding state and local law enforcement officers to conduct background checks on prospective handgun purchasers and to perform certain related tasks, violate the Constitution.

. . .

From the description set forth above, it is apparent that the Brady Act purports to direct state law enforcement officers to participate, albeit only temporarily, in the administration of a federally enacted regulatory scheme. . . .

The petitioners here object to being pressed into federal service, and contend that congressional action compelling state officers to execute federal laws is unconstitutional. Because there is no constitutional text speaking to this precise question, the answer to the CLEOs' challenge must be sought in historical understanding and practice, in the structure of the Constitution, and in the jurisprudence of this Court. We treat those three sources, in that order, in this and the next two sections of this opinion.

Petitioners contend that compelled enlistment of state executive officers for the administration of federal programs is, until very recent years at least, unprecedented. The Government contends, to the contrary, that the earliest Congresses enacted statutes that required the participation of state officials in the implementation of federal laws. . . . The Government's contention demands our careful consideration, since early congressional enactments "provid[e] 'contemporaneous and weighty evidence' of the Constitution's meaning. . . ." Indeed, such "contemporaneous legislative exposition of the Constitution . . ., acquiesced in for a long term of years, fixes the construction to be given its provisions." . . . Conversely if, as petitioners contend, earlier Congresses avoided use of this highly attractive power, we would have reason to believe that the power was thought not to exist.

The Government observes that statutes enacted by the first Congresses required state courts to record applications for citizenship . . ., transmit abstracts of citizenship applications and other naturalization records to the Secretary of State . . ., and to register aliens seeking naturalization and issue certificates of registry. . . . It may well be, however, that these requirements applied only in States that authorized their courts to conduct naturalization proceedings. See . . . *Holmgren v. United States* . . . (explaining that the Act of March 26, 1790 "conferred authority upon state courts to admit aliens to citizenship" and refraining from addressing the question "whether the States can be required to enforce such naturalization laws against their consent"); *United States v. Jones* . . . (1883)(stating that these obligations were imposed "with the consent of the States" and "could not be enforced against the consent of the States"). Other statutes of that era apparently or at least arguably required state courts to perform functions unrelated to naturalization, such as resolving controversies between a captain and the crew of his ship concerning the seaworthiness of the vessel . . ., hearing the claims of slave owners who had apprehended fugitive slaves and issuing certificates authorizing the slave's forced removal to the State from which he had fled . . ., taking proof of the claims of Canadian refugees who had assisted the United States during the Revolutionary War . . ., and ordering the deportation of alien enemies in times of war. . . .

These early laws establish, at most, that the Constitution was originally understood to permit imposition of an obligation on state judges to enforce federal prescriptions, insofar as those prescriptions related to matters appropriate for the judicial power. That assumption was perhaps implicit in one of the provisions of the Constitution, and was explicit in another. In accord with the so called Madisonian Compromise, Article III, §1, established only a Supreme Court, and made the creation of lower federal courts optional with the Congress—even though it was obvious that the Supreme Court alone could not hear all federal cases throughout the United States. . . . And the Supremacy Clause, Art. VI, cl. 2, announced that "the Laws of the United States . . . shall be the supreme Law of the Land; and the Judges in every State shall be bound thereby." It is understandable why courts should have been viewed distinctively in this regard; unlike legislatures and executives, they applied the law of other sovereigns all the time. . . .

For these reasons, we do not think the early statutes imposing obligations on state courts imply a power of Congress to
impress the state executive into its service. Indeed, it can be
argued that the numerousness of these statutes, contrasted
with the utter lack of statutes imposing obligations on the
States' executive (notwithstanding the attractiveness of that
course to Congress), suggests an assumed absence of such
power. The only early federal law the Government has
brought to our attention that imposed duties on state executive officers is the Extradition Act of 1793, which required
the "executive authority" of a State to cause the arrest and
delivery of a fugitive from justice upon the request of the executive authority of the State from which the fugitive had
fled. . . . That was in direct implementation, however, of the
Extradition Clause of the Constitution itself, see Art. IV, §2.

Not only do the enactments of the early Congresses, as far as
we are aware, contain no evidence of an assumption that the
Federal Government may command the States' executive
power in the absence of a particularized constitutional authorization, they contain some indication of precisely the opposite assumption. On September 23, 1789—the day before its
proposal of the Bill of Rights . . .—the First Congress enacted a law aimed at obtaining state assistance of the most
rudimentary and necessary sort for the enforcement of the
new Government's laws: the holding of federal prisoners in
state jails at federal expense. Significantly, the law issued
not a command to the States' executive, but a recommendation to their legislatures. Congress "recommended to the
legislatures of the several States to pass laws, making it expressly the duty of the keepers of their gaols, to receive and
safe keep therein all prisoners committed under the authority
of the United States," and offered to pay 50 cents per month
for each prisoner. . . . Moreover, when Georgia refused to
comply with the request . . ., Congress's only reaction was a
law authorizing the marshal in any State that failed to comply with the Recommendation of September 23, 1789, to rent
a temporary jail until provision for a permanent one could be
made. . . .

. . .

To complete the historical record, we must note that there is
not only an absence of executive commandeering statutes in
the early Congresses, but there is an absence of them in our
later history as well, at least until very recent years. The
Government points to the Act of August 3, 1882 . . ., which
enlisted state officials "to take charge of the local affairs of
immigration in the ports within such State, and to provide for
the support and relief of such immigrants therein landing as
may fall into distress or need of public aid"; to inspect arriv-
ing immigrants and exclude any person found to be a "convict, lunatic, idiot," or indigent; and to send convicts back to

their country of origin "without compensation." The statute did not, however, mandate those duties, but merely empowered the Secretary of the Treasury "to enter into contracts with such State . . . officers as may be designated for that purpose by the governor of any State."

The Government cites the World War I selective draft law that authorized the President "to utilize the service of any or all departments and any or all officers or agents of the United States and of the several States, Territories, and the District of Columbia, and subdivisions thereof, in the execution of this Act," and made any person who refused to comply with the President's directions guilty of a misdemeanor. . . . However, it is far from clear that the authorization "to utilize the service" of state officers was an authorization to compel the service of state officers; and the misdemeanor provision surely applied only to refusal to comply with the President's authorized directions, which might not have included directions to officers of States whose governors had not volunteered their services. It is interesting that in implementing the Act President Wilson did not commandeer the services of state officers, but instead requested the assistance of the States' governors, see Proclamation of May 18, 1917, . . . ("call[ing] upon the Governor of each of the several States . . . and all officers and agents of the several States . . . to perform certain duties"); Registration Regulations Prescribed by the President Under the Act of Congress Approved May 18, 1917, Part I, §7 ("the governor [of each State] is *requested* to act under the regulations and rules prescribed by the President or under his direction") (emphasis added), obtained the consent of each of the governor . . ., and left it to the governors to issue orders to their subordinate state officers. . . . It is impressive that even with respect to a wartime measure the President should have been so solicitous of state independence.

The Government points to a number of federal statutes enacted within the past few decades that require the participation of state or local officials in implementing federal regulatory schemes. Some of these are connected to federal funding measures, and can perhaps be more accurately described as conditions upon the grant of federal funding than as mandates to the States; others, which require only the provision of information to the Federal Government, do not involve the precise issue before us here, which is the forced participation of the States' executive in the actual administration of a federal program. We of course do not address these or other currently operative enactments that are not before us; it will be time enough to do so if and when their validity is challenged in a proper case. For deciding the issue before us here, they are of little relevance. Even assuming they represent assertion of the very same congressional power challenged here, they are of such recent vintage that they are no more probative than the statute before us of a constitutional tradition that lends meaning to the text. Their persuasive force is far outweighed by almost two centuries of apparent congressional avoidance of the practice. Compare *INS v. Chadha* . . . , in which the legislative veto, though enshrined in perhaps hundreds of federal statutes, most of which were enacted in the 1970's and the earliest of which was enacted in 1932, . . . was nonetheless held unconstitutional.

The constitutional practice we have examined above tends to negate the existence of the congressional power asserted here, but is not conclusive. We turn next to consideration of the structure of the Constitution, to see if we can discern among its "essential postulate[s]" . . . a principle that controls the present cases.

It is incontestible that the Constitution established a system of "dual sovereignty." . . . Although the States surrendered many of their powers to the new Federal Government, they retained "a residuary and inviolable sovereignty," The Federalist No. 39, at 245 (J. Madison). This is reflected throughout the Constitution's text . . ., including (to mention only a few examples) the prohibition on any involuntary reduction or combination of a State's territory, Art. IV, §3; the Judicial Power Clause, Art. III, §2, and the Privileges and Immunities Clause, Art. IV, §2, which speak of the "Citizens" of the States; the amendment provision, Article V, which requires the votes of three fourths of the States to amend the Constitution; and the Guarantee Clause, Art. IV, §4, which "presupposes the continued existence of the states and . . . those means and instrumentalities which are the creation of their sovereign and reserved rights". . . . Residual state sovereignty was also implicit, of course, in the Constitution's conferral upon Congress of not all governmental powers, but only discrete, enumerated ones, Art. I, §8, which implication was rendered express by the Tenth Amendment's assertion that "[t]he powers not delegated to the United States by the Constitution, nor prohibited by it to the States, are reserved to the States respectively, or to the people."

The Framers' experience under the Articles of Confederation had persuaded them that using the States as the instruments of federal governance was both ineffectual and provocative of federal state conflict. . . . Preservation of the States as independent political entities being the price of union, and "[t]he practicality of making laws, with coercive sanctions, for the States as political bodies" having been, in Madison's words, "exploded on all hands," . . . the Framers rejected the concept of a central government that would act upon and through the States, and instead designed a system in which the state and federal governments would exercise concurrent authority over the people—who were, in Hamilton's words, "the only proper objects of government". . . .

. . .

Finally, and most conclusively in the present litigation, we turn to the prior jurisprudence of this Court. Federal commandeering of state governments is such a novel phenomenon that this Court's first experience with it did not occur until the 1970's, when the Environmental Protection Agency promulgated regulations requiring States to prescribe auto emissions testing, monitoring and retrofit programs, and to designate preferential bus and carpool lanes. The Courts of Appeals for the Fourth and Ninth Circuits invalidated the regulations on statutory grounds in order to avoid what they perceived to be grave constitutional issues . . .; and the District of Columbia Circuit invalidated the regulations on both constitutional and statutory grounds. . . . After we granted certiorari to review the statutory and constitutional validity of the regulations, the Government declined even to defend them, and instead rescinded some and conceded the invalidity of those that remained, leading us to vacate the opinions below and remand for consideration of mootness. . . .

. . .

We held in New York [v. United States] that Congress cannot compel the States to enact or enforce a federal regulatory program. Today we hold that Congress cannot circumvent that prohibition by conscripting the State's officers directly. The Federal Government may neither issue directives requiring the States to address particular problems, nor command the States' officers, or those of their political subdivisions, to administer or enforce a federal regulatory program. It matters not whether policymaking is involved, and no case by case weighing of the burdens or benefits is necessary; such commands are fundamentally incompatible with our constitutional system of dual sovereignty. Accordingly, the judgment of the Court of Appeals for the Ninth Circuit is reversed.

It is so ordered.

[Concurring and dissenting opinions omitted.]

b. A Principle of Localism or Subsidiarity?

The political and judicial struggle regarding states' rights in the United States seems destined, at least in the near future, to be dominated by the concepts and precepts of the commerce and the spending clauses. This is unfortunate, because the tradition, thinking, and terminology of commerce, spending, and economics do not lend themselves well to the present-day debate on federalism. For instance, the reason why school-ground guns do not seem to many to be an appropriate subject for federal regulation has nothing to do with commerce or the economy or federal spending but rather with the tradition of local supervision of education and with the conviction that local governance of education is democratically preferable to national governance.

Some commentators argue that education, land-use, law enforcement, courts, and private law, especially family law, should remain "localized" or that the federal concurrent powers, even that over interstate commerce, ought to be exercisable only where there is special justification.[201] Uniform federal environmental standards, for example, might be easy to justify, whereas uniform family law, educational, land-use, and law enforcement standards might not be. These and similar concerns could be subsumed under something akin to the European principle of subsidiarity, which is found in the texts of the Constitution of Germany and in the Treaty of Rome, the "constitution" of the European Union. In Germany, the principle of subsidiarity finds potential application to a long list of subject matter areas, such as civil law, criminal law, weapons legislation, and welfare, in which the federal and state governments have concurrent jurisdiction. In these areas, Article 72 of the German Basic Law circumscribes the federal legislative prerogative:

> (2) The federal government has legislative jurisdiction [in matters subject to concurrent jurisdiction] only to the extent that federal legislation is necessary because
>
> 1. a matter cannot be effectively regulated by legislation of individual states or
>
> 2. the regulation of a matter by state law could impair the interests of other states or of the whole [of the people] or
>
> 3. the protection of legal or economic uniformity . . . demands it.

The principle of subsidiarity enjoins institutions of the European Union to act in areas of concurrent jurisdiction only when local measures are inadequate. This new provision reads as follows:

> The Community shall act within the limits of the powers conferred upon it by this Treaty and of the objectives assigned to it therein.
>
> In areas which do not fall within its exclusive competence, the Community shall take action, in accordance with the principle of subsidiarity, only if and in so far as the objectives of the proposed action cannot be sufficiently achieved by the Member States and can therefore, by reason of the scale or effects of the proposed action, be better achieved by the Community.[202]

One potential constitutional anchor for a principle of localism or subsidiarity is the 10th Amendment. Alternatively, the "necessary and proper" clause[203] might be read to embody subsidiarity, as could the spending power (Art. I, §8, cl.1),

---

201   See Lundmark, *Guns* at p. 204.

202   Maastricht Treaty on European Union, Art. G(5).

203   Art. I, § 8, cl. 18.

which speaks of spending for the general, not local, welfare. Or subsidiarity might be held to belong to penumbral states' rights à la the privacy rights of individuals.[204] Or perhaps the Constitution will be amended, or the congressional mentality will so change in favor of local, democratic self-determination, accountability, and flexibility that no amendment will be necessary.

---

204 See Griswold v. Connecticut, 381 U.S. 479 (1965): The "specific guarantees in the Bill of Rights have penumbras, formed by emanations from those guarantees that help give them life and substance."

PART TWO: CONSTITUTIONAL RIGHTS

The remainder of this book centers on core principles of constitutional rights. Sometimes constitutional rights are referred to by the term "civil" rights, but that term is avoided in this text because it can include statutory as well as constitutional rights. "Right," as used in this text, means "constitutional right."

The coverage must necessarily be selective. This book gives scant mention to statutory rights, even though these rights may be far more important to citizen and non-citizens than the constitutional variety. The Age Discrimination in Employment Act,[206] the Americans with Disabilities Act of 1990,[207] and the Civil Rights Act of 1964, including Title VII,[208] are just three of the myriad federal statutes that protect individuals against governmental (and often private) actors. Rights recognized by the laws and constitutions of the states and their subdivisions are also beyond the purview of this book. For example, in *Robins v. Pruneyard Shopping Center*[209] the California Supreme Court refused to follow the United States Supreme Court's decision in *Lloyd v. Tanner*[210] on the ground that the California Constitution is more protective of free speech than the First Amendment.[211] To cite an example from statutory law, where more examples of divergencies from federal norms can be found: the Unruh Civil Rights Act in California[212] prohibits discrimination in housing against families with children.[213] In the equal protection area, courts have construed state constitutions to require the reform of school funding.[214] On the whole, however, state constitutional protection of rights is virtually identical to that of the federal constitution.[215]

Three major categories of constitutional rights are not covered by this book, although they are sometimes mentioned in passing. The first categorical exception from coverage is procedure. Procedural rights are generally the province of administrative law and civil procedure. The second exception covers all substantive and procedural rights that belong to the domain of criminal law and procedure. Property rights, the third exception, enjoy a unique status among liberty rights; but their constitutional protection heeds principles somewhat at odds with those of other liberty rights, making a brief summary for purposes of this volume infeasible. One significant issue shared by property and other liberty

---

206   29 U.S.C. §§ 621-634.
207   42 U.S.C. § 12101 *et seq.*
208   42 U.S.C. § 2000 *et seq.*
209   23 Cal. 3d 889, aff'd 447 U.S. 74 (1980).
210   407 U.S. 551 (1972).
211   See generally Kahn.
212   Cal. Civ. Code § 51.
213   Marina Pt., Ltd. v. Wolfson, 30 Cal. 3d 721 (1982); see generally Singer and 30 A.L.R. 4th 1187 (1998).
214   E.g., Serrano v. Priest, 5 Cal. 3d 584 (1971), which the United States Supreme Court declined to follow in San Antonio Indep. School Dist. v. Rodriguez, 411 U.S. 1 (1973).
215   See Solimine & Walker at p. 1467 and nn. 68-70.

rights, but which is not treated in this book, is the extent to which corporations and associations are entitled to invoke constitutional protection, and whether or not the equal treatment of natural and legal persons does not harm or at least dilute the rights of the former.

Finally, with few exceptions, the brevity of this book does not allow the handling of constitutional, statutory, and common law rights in purely private transactions, for that would mean treating virtually all private law topics, including the law of obligations (tort, contract, and unjust enrichment), property, and family law. Few areas of private law have escaped examination for constitutionality in recent decades under what is sometimes referred to as the "constitutionalization of private law." Some areas of private law, such as defamation and, to a lesser extent, the legitimacy of children, have been more or less co-opted by the Constitution and are included in the materials that follow. Their discussion in this book is not just unavoidable; it is indispensable to an appreciation of the role of the United States Constitution and the Supreme Court in American society.

Constitutional rights are viewed as either liberty or equality rights. Liberty rights shield persons as individuals against state action. Equality rights protect the individual as a member of a protected group, which is usually referred to as a "class." In order to accord with the language of the Fifth and 14th Amendments, liberty rights are referred to as "due process" rights. (Sometimes the adjective "substantive" is added to distinguish them from procedural due process rights.) Equality rights are ordinarily referred to as "equal protection" rights, which conforms more closely to the verbiage of the 14th Amendment.

As illuminated in the materials that follow, the boundary between liberty and equality is fluid. Indeed, liberty rights can be linguistically recast as equality rights, and *vice versa*: ultimately, the person claiming a liberty right can style herself a group of one, who is being "discriminated against" on the basis of some individualistic characteristic or behavior. She consequently can employ the jargon of both liberty and equality. If the particular governmental measure affects every person equally, it is said that only due process would be available to challenge the measure. However, examples to illustrate this last proposition are harder to find than might at first be thought. Would a statute requiring the donation of one kidney from each human being only violate due process? What if the statute were attacked by a group of persons who have but one kidney? Similarly, a law that denied everyone the right to travel interstate would not likely be challenged by those who do not intend to travel, or who are physically unable to do so.

Until the 1950s the equal protection clause remained largely dormant. Thinking in equal-protection terms began to take hold with the Great Society programs of the administration of President Lyndon B. Johnson and with the Civil Rights Movement, which sought to promote the interests of African-Americans as a group. Coincidentally, the Supreme Court had become shy of protecting due process rights because of the intense criticism it had suffered due to the unpopular recognition of economic rights. It was hoped that the methodology of equality would offer a value-neutral, or at least less conservative, way of protecting constitutional rights.

The expansion of the role of the federal and state legislatures as distributors of statutory privileges and benefits necessitated the "discrimination" between the groups or "classes" of persons to be benefited, and those who would not be. The equal protection clause also offered a conceptual advantage in that it lent itself readily to thinking in terms of groups, rather than of individuals, that were benefited by, or excluded from, the privileges accorded under the growing number of government programs. Thus, in large measure, the growth in equal protection analysis has coincided with the expansion of the welfare state.

The interplay between liberty and equality rights gives rise to any number of additional topics treated below in more detail. One such topic is the perceived conflict between liberty and equality, where the bestowal of more equality is said necessarily to reduce individual liberty.[216] Perhaps a better way to express this presumed conflict is to say that one man's liberty is another man's equality. For instance, extending the franchise to women in effect halved the voting rights (liberty) of each man and distributed his half to a woman, leaving the aggregate of societal liberty arguably the same. This image assumes that liberty is a zero-sum game. It does not admit of the possibility that a redistribution of rights can augment societal liberty.

Another topic is the emotional root of rights. Liberty respects greed and sloth, whereas equality legitimizes envy.[217] We find ourselves using the language of liberty when seeking respect, and that of equality when seeking pity. Yet another topic is the vertical, corrective quality of liberty and the horizontal, distributive justice of equality.

The themes of Part One of this book—separation of powers and federalism—reincarnate themselves in Part Two in the guise of rights. For the recognition of judicially enforceable rights does more or less directly what separation of powers and federalism do mediately: protect individual liberty. The tension between the legislative and judicial powers is experienced most intensely when a court invalidates a properly enacted law because it violates a constitutional right. Federalism accounts for the phenomena that not quite all of the federal rights listed in the Bill of Rights can be asserted against the state and local governments[218] and that not all of the rights that protect people from the state and local governments bind the federal government.[219]

---

216 See discussion at note 398 *et seq.*

217 Holmes at p. 942; see Plato at p. 301, discussed in Lundmark, *Forms* at p. 649.

218 E.g., Apodaca v. Oregon, 406 U.S. 404 (1972), jury protection of the 6th Amendment.

219 E.g., Hampton v. Mow Sun Wong, 426 U.S. 88 (1976), equal protection of the 14th Amendment; Ogden v. Saunders, 25 U.S. 213 (1827), contract clause of Art. I, § 10.

The coverage begins with two matters of primary concern to the judicial protection of constitutional rights. First is the question of the governmental nature of the impingement on constitutional rights, for constitutional rights generally accord protection only against acts of governmental actors, so-called "state action." Second is the methodology of striking a just balance between democratic, majoritarian interests on the one hand, and individual rights on the other. This methodology is discussed under the rubric "levels of scrutiny."

1. "State Action"

The "state action" doctrine is summarized at this juncture because of its primacy to the recognition and enforcement of all constitutional rights. The word "state" in "state action" is used in the sense of "governmental." Ordinarily this means that the person or persons who caused the alleged infringement of constitutional rights must have been acting on behalf of a public entity. For, according to the state action doctrine, federal constitutional rights do not protect against action by private people or organizations, but rather only against action by public actors.

The term "public actors" in this context embraces all local, state, and federal agencies, including some private-law businesses and organizations, and their agents and employees. For example, in *Lebron v. National Railroad Passenger Corporation*[220] the Supreme Court held the railway corporation Amtrak to be a public entity for purposes of the state action doctrine. In reaching its conclusion, the Supreme Court relied on the fact that the President of the United States appoints members to the board of directors of Amtrak. It was of no moment that the authorizing legislation specifically denied that Amtrak was a governmental agency.

The reasons, or at least the explanations, for the doctrine of state action are historical, prudential, and textual. Historically, the US Constitution is a product of Enlightenment thinking about natural law and liberalism, which was in large measure inspired by the felt irrationality and capriciousness of monarchial rule. The Founding Fathers were preoccupied with potential threats from the government they were creating, and not with wider social, religious, economic, and moral affairs. Further, it was thought that the common law adequately protected individual rights from other individuals so that constitutional protection was unnecessary.[221] Through the centuries, as legislative law replaced common law, this private-law protective task has passed more to the legislatures, or to cooperative efforts by judges and legislators.

The prudential justification for the state action requirement is basically that the federal judicial (and perhaps legislative) restraint encapsulated in the state action

---

220   513 U.S. 374 (1995).
221   Chemerinsky, Constitutional Law at p. 390.

doctrine means, alternatively, more sovereignty for the states (federalism) or more freedom from regulation (liberty). Most Americans would probably agree with the aphorism attributed to Jefferson: "That government is best that governs least." And the Supreme Court has held that the Constitution does not impose a general obligation on state, federal, or local government to protect people from each other.[222]

The textual explanation for the state action doctrine is the clearest and strongest: All of the rights articulated in the text of the Constitution (see Attach. D) and in all except one of the amendments are addressed to either the federal or to the state governments. For example, freedom of speech is enshrined in the First Amendment, which begins, "Congress shall make no law. . . ." Equality receives specific mention only in the second sentence of the 14th Amendment, which reads in part, "nor shall any State . . . deny to any person within its jurisdiction the equal protection of the laws."

The 13th Amendment is somewhat of an anomaly, for it is directed both at public and private conduct. It reads, "Neither slavery nor involuntary servitude, except as a punishment for crime whereof the party shall have been duly convicted, shall exist within the United States, or any place subject to their jurisdiction." While the 13th Amendment was intended to destroy private-law rights, it also binds the government.[223]

The state action doctrine is sometimes misunderstood to mean that private law is beyond the purview of the Constitution. This is most certainly not true. In the United States, private law, that is, the law that governs private actions between private persons, falls basically within the law making province of the states. Private law consists either of statutory law of common law (judge made law), or of a mixture of the two. In enacting statutes to regulate private transactions, or even public ones for that matter, state legislators engage in "state action" *per se* and are subject to constitutional restraints. State-court judges, in developing their common law and in interpreting legislation, fall squarely within the supremacy clause of Article VI, section 2, which states that "the Judges in every State shall be bound" by the Constitution.

Further, all American judges, state and federal and at every level, are bound not to follow (roughly said: "to declare unconstitutional") laws that they hold to be incompatible with constitutional rights. This creates a climate that is sensitive to the protection of constitutional values at every stage of judicial proceedings.

Does this then mean that the state action doctrine is a sham and that every aspect of human life, however private, is subject to constitutional scrutiny? Not quite. Business entities and commercial transactions are governed by federal, state, and

---

222   See DeShaney v. Winnebago County Department of Social Services, 489 U.S. 189 (1989).
223   See Bailey v. Alabama, 219 U.S. 219 (1911), holding imprisonment for failure to pay a debt unconstitutional.

local controls, and these incorporate—and sometimes augment—constitutional rights and extend them to cover otherwise private commercial transactions. For example, legislation routinely broadens the privacy rights of employees by preventing prospective employers from learning about sexual orientation, from demanding genetic testing, and from testing for AIDS. Legislation also forbids discrimination against customers. But, that being said, there are non-commercial private activities in daily life that do still remain outside the dominion of constitutional, statutory, and common law, where private actors can do things that would not be allowed by public actors and businesses.

Accordingly, you may use race, gender, age, religion, and national origin in choosing your friends; but, if you are a landlord or landlady, you may not consider these criteria in renting an apartment. You may prefer not to shop in a liquor store because it is owned by Arabs; but the Arabian owners may not refuse to sell to you because you are Jewish. You may wish to adopt only Asian children; but the adoption agency may not deny your application because you are Roman Catholic. You may vote for a candidate solely because she is female; but the candidate, once elected, cannot award you a lucrative contract simply because you were born in Berlin.

The Supreme Court has recognized two general exceptions to the state action requirement. These exceptions in effect extend the concept of state action to include some private action. The first exception, for public functions, encompasses activities, undertaken by purely private individuals or organizations, that traditionally belonged to the exclusive prerogative of the state. Voting in primary elections is an example. A political party, which is a private organization, cannot exclude blacks from voting in party primary or pre-primary elections that select the party's candidate for public office.[224] Another case illustrating the public function exception from the state action requirement concerned a "company town" whose streets and sidewalks, while privately owned, were the functional equivalent of public streets.[225] Private prison guards, private policemen, and others "acting under color of state law" for purposes of 42 United States Code section 1983 can also be viewed as falling within this exception.[226]

The other extension of the state action doctrine covers private action with significant state involvement. Adjudicated cases include the following: administration by the public administrator of a will containing a racially discriminatory condition;[227] joint public/private action to seize a debtor's assets in execution of a judgment;[228] judicial enforcement of a race-based restrictive covenant in a

---

224   Smith v. Allwright, 321 U.S. 649 (1944); Terry v. Adams, 345 U.S. 461 (1953).

225   Marsh v. Alabama, 326 U.S. 501 (1946).

226   See Richardson v. McKnight, 521 U.S. 399 (1997), where private prison guards were "found to have acted under color of state law."

227   Evans v. Abney, 396 U.S. 435 (1970).

228   Lugar v. Edmondson Oil Co., 457 U.S. 922 (1982).

deed;[229] use of race-based peremptory challenges in a civil trial;[230] and operating a restaurant on publicly owned property.[231]

2. Levels of Scrutiny

Every case concerning alleged violations of constitutional rights presents certain common questions of pedigree and magnitude of the intrusion, and of weightiness of the private right and countervailing public interest. The questions of pedigree include whether the action is based on a law, and whether that law is in turn based on the state or federal constitution. These questions arise in the subjects covered in Part One of this book. Questions of magnitude of the intrusion arise when an otherwise constitutional law comes into conflict with a constitutional right. More extensive incursions can be conceptually justified if the public interest is urgent, or the private right less weighty.

Following the practice of the Supreme Court, this book systemizes the methodology of judicial review ("scrutiny") of rights into a more or less unitary hierarchy that amalgamates questions of pedigree, intensity, and weight into four tests. In doing so, it attempts to reduce, but not completely avoid, discussions of the nuances or "glosses" placed on the various tests by the Justices of the Supreme Court when they are considering specific constitutional rights. Conceptually, at least, alleged violations of constitutional rights are judged within this formalized dogmatic structure, which employs a different constitutional yardstick depending on the importance level to which the right is assigned. Some commentators hold that this tiered approach is neither desirable nor practically possible.[232]

The first two tests are employed to judge the constitutionality of the ends and means of every governmental act. The ends of any such act must be lawful or "valid"; and the means chosen must rationally lead to the accomplishment of these ends. Conceptually at least, this level of review involves no balancing whatsoever: the ends are either lawful or unlawful; the means chosen are either aimed at reaching the ends, or they are not. The other two tests or "levels of review" do, however, involve balancing. These tests are invoked when the governmental act impinges upon certain constitutional rights.

The levels of review elaborated below are employed to judge the constitutionality of governmental actions "on their face," that is, without considering the particular factual predicament of the challenger. The other style of judicial review, that which considers the particular facts of the case, is called "as applied."

---

229 Shelley v. Kraemer, 334 U.S. 1 (1948).

230 Edmonson v. Leesville Concrete Co., 500 U.S. 614 (1991).

231 Burton v. Wilmington Parking Authority, 365 U.S. 715 (1961).

232 E.g., Shaman; Beal v. Doe, 432 U.S. 438, 461 n. 6 (1977), Marshall, J., dissenting, and advocating a sliding scale.

a. Lawful (Valid) Ends

Hearkening back to the Part One of this book, all governmental action must be based on a law which in turn is based on the state or federal constitution. Another way of expressing the same thing is that the (federal, state, or local) governmental goal must fall within the powers that the entity enjoys, or else it is *ultra vires* and void. For example, in *Pollock v. Farmers' Loan & Trust Co.*[233] the Supreme Court ruled that Congress lacked power to tax incomes from property, and in *Oregon v. Mitchell*[234] the Supreme Court held that Congress was powerless to set the voting age in state and local elections. Incidentally, these rulings led respectively to the 16th and 26th Amendments.

When judging the legitimacy of a statute of the Congress, the legislative goal must fall within the ambit of an enumerated power, such as the interstate commerce clause. As shown in Part One, various tests have been developed to judge the fundamental validity of legislation, depending on its alleged constitutional basis.[235]

When the legislation is obviously within the jurisdiction of the particular legislative body that enacted it, courts will sometimes gloss over this foundational issue. At other times, this first level of scrutiny will finally resolve the legal dispute.[236]

b. Rational Means ("Minimum Scrutiny")

What happens if the governmental goal is proper, but the means chosen to attain the goal are not calculated, or are poorly designed, to accomplish the goal? Said another way, what if the law is not "rational"? Ordinarily, courts show great deference to legislation, and will not interfere with legislative judgments unless they are "demonstrably arbitrary and irrational."[237] The burden of proof is on the person challenging the state action.[238] This level of review ("scrutiny") is usually termed the "rational basis" test.

The attitude of deference accorded even state legislators by the United States Supreme Court is summarized in *Williamson v. Lee Optical Co.*:

> [T]he Oklahoma law may exact a needless, wasteful requirement in many cases. But it is for the legislature, and not the courts, to balance the advantages and disadvantages of the new requirement. . . . [T]he law need not be in every respect logically consistent with its aims to be constitutional. It is enough that there is an evil at hand for

---

233   157 U.S. 429 (1895).

234   400 U.S. 112 (1970).

235   See, e.g., United States v. Lopez, 514 U.S. 549 (1995).

236   E.g., Williams v. Vermont, 472 U.S. 14 (1985), finding no valid reason to deny a tax credit to new residents.

237   Duke Power Co. v. Carolina Environmental Study Group, Inc., 438 U.S. 69 (1978).

238   United States v. Carolene Products Co., 304 U.S. 144 (1938).

correction, and that it might be thought that the particular legislative measure was a rational way to correct it. The day is gone when this Court uses the Due Process Clause [to] strike down state laws . . . because they may be unwise, improvident, or out of harmony with a particular school of [thought].[239]

It is rare that a law employs an irrational, arbitrary, or unreasonable means to accomplish a legitimate goal. One of the few governmental actions ruled unconstitutional by the Supreme Court on this basis was the practice of a county tax assessor in *Allegheny Pittsburgh Coal Co. v. County Commission*[240] not to reassess real property for tax purposes until the property was sold. The court ruled not only that the practice was arbitrary, but also that it was unsupported by state law and therefore *ultra vires*.

The common law is not immune from minimal constitutional scrutiny. Even jury awards of punitive damages in private actions can be challenged on constitutional grounds if they are "grossly excessive," that is, if the award bears no rational relationship to the state's interests in punishment and deterrence.[241]

c. "Strict Scrutiny" (Compelling Ends, Necessary Means)

"Rational basis" is the weakest mode of judicial review, where courts accord the most respect to the democratically declared interests of the majority. The highest level of review is termed "strict scrutiny." If a public action, usually a statute, is judged by this standard, it must satisfy two criteria: the ends must be compelling, and the means necessary. These two requirements are discussed in order.

Under strict scrutiny, it is not enough that the goal or purpose sought to be achieved by the government (termed "state interest") is merely lawful, as required for minimum scrutiny. Rather, to satisfy strict scrutiny, the governmental goal must be compelling.[242] Examples of interests judged "compelling" by the courts are difficult to find. Consequently, Professor Gerald Gunther at Stanford University has quipped that "strict scrutiny" is "strict in theory fatal in fact."[243] Two of the few cases upholding laws challenged under this test are in the area of voting. The Supreme Court has upheld state requirements that candidates of new political parties demonstrate public support before having their names placed on the ballot. The compelling state interest consisted of preserving the integrity of the electoral process, which would otherwise have become unmanageable and confusing.[244] Voter registration and 30-day residency requirements before voting

---

239   348 U.S. 483 (1955).

240   488 U.S. 336 (1989).

241   BMW of North America, Inc. v. Gore, 517 U.S. 559 (1996).

242   San Antonio Indep. School Dist. v. Rodriguez, 411 U.S. 1 (1973).

243   Gunther, *Foreword* at p. 8.

244   American Party of Texas v. White, 415 U.S. 767 (1974).

have similarly been justified by the compelling state interest in preserving the integrity of the electoral process.[245]

The second requirement under the standard of "strict scrutiny" is that the means must be necessary to attain the manifest goal. That is, "the means chosen to accomplish the State's asserted purpose must be specifically and narrowly tailored to accomplish that purpose."[246] Under this prong of strict scrutiny, the government must show (for it has the burden of proof) that the alternative that it has chosen is the least restrictive (due process) or least discriminatory (equal protection).[247] Staying with voting rights (and the right to travel), the Supreme Court has struck down as too restrictive durational residency requirement of one year in state elections and three months in county elections.[248] A similar fate befell residency requirements for public welfare benefits and free non-emergency medical care, since the private need is great and the administrative burden on the state slight.[249]

Strict scrutiny is used both for certain due process and certain equal protection rights. In the context of due process, strict scrutiny is employed for all rights explicitly guaranteed by the Constitution, and for many others which have been held to be implicitly guaranteed. Together the due process rights generally entitled to strict scrutiny are called "fundamental rights." Explicitly guaranteed rights include freedom of religion, freedom of speech, freedom of association, freedom to petition the government for a redress of grievances, all traceable to the First Amendment, and the right to vote, which is secured by various constitutional provisions and amendments. Implicit fundamental rights include the right to travel and the right of privacy. For equal protection purposes, courts utilize strict scrutiny to assess the constitutionality of measures that involve a "suspect class." Suspect classifications are those based on race, national origin, and sometimes foreign citizenship.

d. "Intermediate Scrutiny" ("Proportionality")

"Intermediate scrutiny," as one might suspect, is the name given to review that demands more than a lawful goal and minimal rationality but that is not quite rigorous enough to be called strict. Here the governmental purpose must be important, but not necessarily "compelling." And the means chosen must be substantially related to the purpose, but they need not be "necessary." The approach

---

245 Marston v. Lewis, 410 U.S. 679 (1973).

246 Wygant v. Jackson Board of Education, 476 U.S. 267, 280 (1986).

247 Miller v. Johnson, 515 U.S. 900 (1995).

248 Dunn v. Blumstein, 405 U.S. 330 (1972).

249 Shapiro v. Thompson, 394 U.S. 618 (1969); Memorial Hospital v. Maricopa County, 415 U.S. 250 (1974). See also Saenz v. Roe, 526 U.S. 489 (1999), reported below.

is similar to "proportionality" review in European law,[250] although it does not go by that name in the United States. As with strict scrutiny, the government bears the burden of proof under intermediate scrutiny.

An example of a law that failed the "substantially related" test can be found in *Rubin v. Coors Brewing Co.*,[251] which considered the constitutionality of a post-Prohibition federal law that prohibited brewers from reporting alcohol content on beer containers. The goal of the legislation was to discourage breweries from increasing sales by raising alcohol levels. The courts employed intermediate scrutiny because the law regulated commercial speech. They ruled the law unconstitutional because the government could have achieved its goal through less restrictive means.[252]

As with strict scrutiny, intermediate scrutiny is employed both under the due process clause and under the equal protection clause. Under equal protection analysis, intermediate scrutiny is exercised over governmental measures that discriminate against or penalize so-called quasi-suspect classes. To date, quasi-suspect classifications have been held to be those based on legitimacy[253] and gender.[254] Under due process, intermediate scrutiny is applied to the regulation of speech in public forums[255] and to commercial speech.[256]

Consider whether, in the following case, the Supreme Court is employing strict or intermediate scrutiny. Why does the court employ equal protection rather than due process analysis? Why does the court not use the privileges and immunities clause of Article IV, section 2?

CASE: Plyler v. Doe
457 U.S. 202 (1982)

JUSTICE BRENNAN delivered the opinion of the Court.

[A Texas statute authorized local school districts to deny free public education to children who had not been "legally admitted" into the United States. Pursuant to this statute, the Tyler Independent School District required "undocumented" children to pay a "tuition fee" in order to enroll.]

---

250 See authorities cited in Lundmark, *Systemizing* at p.33. The Supreme Court uses what it calls "proportionality review" to judge the constitutionality of fines under the 8th Amendment. This has the effect of subjecting fines to intermediate scrutiny. See United States v. Bajakajian, 524 U.S. 321 (1998)

251 515 U.S. 618 (1995).

252 See Lundmark, *Freiheit.*

253 Lehr v. Robertson, 463 U.S. 248 (1983).

254 Craig v. Boren, 429 U.S. 190 (1976).

255 Ward v. Rock Against Racism, 491 U.S. 781 (1989).

256 Central Hudson Gas & Electric Corp. v. Public Service Commission of New York, 447 U.S. 557, 566 (1980).

[In] applying the Equal Protection Clause to most forms of state action, we thus seek only the assurance that the classification at issue bears some fair relationship to a legitimate public purpose.

But we would not be faithful to our obligations under the Fourteenth Amendment if we applied so deferential a standard to every classification. [With] respect to [some] classifications, it is appropriate to enforce the mandate of equal protection by requiring the State to demonstrate that its classification has been precisely tailored to serve a compelling governmental interest. In addition, we have recognized that certain forms of legislative classification, while not facially invidious, nonetheless give rise to recurring constitutional difficulties; in these limited circumstances we have sought the assurance that the classification reflects a reasoned judgment consistent with the ideal of equal protection by inquiring whether it may fairly be viewed as furthering a substantial interest of the State. We turn to a consideration of the standard appropriate for the evaluation of [the challenged law].

Sheer incapability or lax enforcement of the laws barring entry into this country, [has] resulted in the creation of a substantial "shadow population" of illegal migrants—numbering in the millions—within our borders. This situation raises the specter of a permanent caste of undocumented resident aliens, encouraged by some to remain here as a source of cheap labor, but nevertheless denied the benefits that our society makes available to citizens and lawful residents. . . .

Congress has developed a complex scheme governing admission to our Nation and status within our borders. The obvious need for delicate policy judgments has counseled the Judicial Branch to avoid intrusion into this field. But this traditional caution does not persuade us that unusual deference must be shown the [challenged classification]. The States enjoy no power with respect to the classification of aliens. This power is "committed to the political branches of the Federal Government." [And although] the States do have some authority to act with respect to illegal aliens, at least where such action mirrors federal objectives and furthers a legitimate state [goal], there is no indication that the disability imposed [the challenged law]corresponds to any identifiable congressional policy. [We] discern three colorable state interests that might support [the classification].

First, [the State suggests that it may] protect itself from an influx of illegal immigrants. [But there] is no evidence in the record suggesting that illegal entrants impose any significant burden on the State's economy. To the contrary, the available evidence suggests that illegal aliens underutilize public services, while contributing their labor to the local economy and tax money to the state fisc.

Second [the State suggests] that undocumented children are appropriately singled out for exclusion because of the special burdens they impose on the State's ability to provide high-quality public education. But the record in no way supports the claim that exclusion of undocumented children is likely to improve the overall quality of education in the State. [Moreover], even if improvement in the quality of education were a likely result of barring some number of children from the schools of the State, the State must support its selection of this group as the appropriate target for exclusion. In terms of educational cost and need, however, undocumented children are "basically indistinguishable" from legally resident alien children.

Finally, [the State suggests] that undocumented children are appropriately singled out because their unlawful presence within the United States renders them less likely than other children to remain within the boundaries of the State, and to put their education to productive social or political use within the State. Even assuming that such an interest is legitimate, it is an interest that is most difficult to quantify. The State has no assurance that any child, citizen or not, will employ the education provided by the State within the confines of the State's borders. In any event, the record is clear that many of the undocumented children disabled by this classification will remain in this country indefinitely, and that some will become lawful residents or citizens of the United States. It is difficult to understand precisely what the State hopes to achieve by promoting the creation and perpetuation of a subclass of illiterates within our boundaries, surely adding to the problems and costs of unemployment, welfare, and crime. It is thus clear that whatever savings might be achieved by denying these children an education, they are wholly insubstantial in light of the costs involved to these children, the State, and the Nation.

If the State is to deny a discrete group of innocent children the free public education that it offers to other children residing within its borders, that denial must be justified by a showing that it furthers some substantial state interest. No such showing was made here. . . .

[Concurring and dissenting opinions omitted. In his dissent, Chief Justice Burger wrote disparangingly about what he called the "quasi-fundmental rights" analysis introduced by the majority. This terminology is now used to refer to due process rights that warrant intermediate scrutiny.]

Subpart A: Liberty (Due Process)

As seen in Attachment D, the original text of the Constitution only sporadically recognized individual rights. There was no list or "bill" of rights, even though most state constitutions that were adopted during the American Revolution contained a clear declaration of rights.[257]

Historians offer a number of explanations for this omission, including that the enumeration of powers was sufficient protection, and that an enumeration of rights would imply that other rights did not exist.[258] Whatever the historic reason for the original omission, ratification of the new Constitution to replace the Articles of Confederation followed in a number of states only after Federalists (those promoting the new constitution) promised to add a bill of rights.

The first Congress convened under the Constitution set to work immediately on the task of adding a bill of rights to the Constitution. James Madison drafted 15 proposed amendments. The Congress accepted 12 of the proposals pursuant to the amendment procedure in Article V. By December 15, 1791 enough states had ratified ten of these to make them a permanent part of the Constitution. (One of the remaining two proposed amendments was finally ratified on May 7, 1992 and became the 27th Amendment.) Although technically not part of the original text of the Constitution, the Bill of Rights (the first 10 amendments) has historically been considered part of the Constitution for all intents and purposes.

This subpart emphasizes fundamental constitutional rights, that is, those that are subsumable under the due process clauses of the Fourth and 14th Amendments and that are subject to "strict scrutiny." To be deemed fundamental, the right must be "explicitly or implicitly guaranteed by the Constitution."[259] This distinction between explicit and implicit rights is followed in the following discussion. The question of how fundamental rights become recognized as "implicit" is deferred until those rights are discussed below.

The fundamental rights discussed below must be distinguished from minor, implicit, non-fundamental constitutional rights which find application in judging whether one has been accorded procedural due process. These are lower echelon constitutional rights that exist over and above the explicit and implicit fundamental rights that are the subject of this subpart. Textually understood, these non-fundamental rights emanate from, or at least can be subsumed under, the triune "life, liberty, or property" of the 5th and 14th Amendments.

---

257 E.g., Virginia Declaration of Rights of 1776; see generally Hall.

258 Chemerinsky, Constitutional Law at p. 5, noting that it was to quiet such fears that the 9th Amendment was added.

259 San Antonio Indep. School Dist. v. Rodriguez, 411 U.S. 1 (1973).

Procedural due process rights play an indispensable role in the criminal arena, which is beyond the scope of this book. In the civil (i.e., non-criminal) context, if the courts determine that a right or interest enjoyed by an individual is embraced by the term "liberty" or "property," then the individual is constitutionally entitled to procedural safeguards before that right or interest can be impaired or denied. Outside the criminal context, the Supreme Court has recognized a constitutional "liberty interest" in being free from physical restraints,[260] in contracting and engaging in gainful employment,[261] and in continuing a developed parent-child relationship.[262] "Property" has been held to safeguard the following: public education when school attendance is required,[263] welfare benefits,[264] driving privileges,[265] utility service,[266] existing causes of action,[267] and public employment.[268]

1. Explicit Fundamental Rights

If one disregards the Ninth and Tenth Amendments, which do not guarantee specific rights, half of the remaining eight amendments catalogue rights that basically are intended to protect those suspected of crimes.[269] One amendment, the Seventh Amendment, recognizes a right to a jury trial in civil cases before the federal courts, and thus creates a procedural, rather than a substantive, right. Of the three remaining amendments, two of them[270] are antiquated, having virtually no currency.[271] That leaves the First Amendment:

> Congress shall make no law respecting an establishment of religion, or prohibiting the free exercise thereof; or abridging the freedom of speech, or of the press, or the right of the people peaceably to assemble, and to petition the Government for a redress of grievances.

A review of the amendments that do not belong to the Bill of Rights[272] similarly results in the reduction to a single amendment that has served as the repository of

---

260 Vitek v. Jones, 445 U.S. 480 (1980).

261 Board of Regents v. Roth, 408 U.S. 564 (1972).

262 Lehr v. Robertson, 463 U.S. 248 (1983).

263 Goss v. Lopez, 419 U.S. 565 (1975).

264 Goldberg v. Kelly, 397 U.S. 254 (1970).

265 Bell v. Burson, 402 U.S. 535 (1971).

266 Memphis Light, Gas & Water Division v. Craft, 436 U.S. 1 (1978).

267 Logan v. Zimmerman Brush Co., 455 U.S. 422 (1982).

268 Arnett v. Kennedy, 416 U.S. 134 (1974).

269 See 4th, 5th (also protecting property), 6th, and 8th Amends.

270 2nd and 3rd Amends.

271 Commentators are almost universal in opining that the right to bear arms is not a personal right, but rather a right enjoyed by each state to arm a militia. Lundmark, *Guns* at p. 188.

272 11th through 27th Amends.

the most expansive constitutional rights. That is the 14th Amendment, section 1 of which reads:

> All persons born or naturalized in the United States and subject to the jurisdiction thereof, are citizens of the United States and of the State wherein they reside. No State shall make or enforce any law which shall abridge the privileges or immunities of citizens of the United States; nor shall any State deprive any person of life, liberty, or property, without due process or law; nor deny to any person within its jurisdiction the equal protection of the laws.

Textually, the 14th Amendment contains three protections of constitutional rights, respectively referred to as the privileges and immunities clause, the due process clause,[273] and the equal protection clause.

The first of these three clauses has remained largely a dead letter in protecting individual rights since the Supreme Court held in 1873, in a questionable opinion, that the fundamental rights protected against federal action by the first eight amendments were not "privileges or immunities of citizens of the United States" so as to be protected from state action under the 14th Amendment.[274]

The due process clause of the 14th Amendment, on the other hand, has been construed to "incorporate" the First Amendment and make it enforceable against the states.[275] The same process of "selective incorporation" has been used to apply almost all protections of the Bill of Rights to the states by finding that they are "implicit in the concept of ordered liberty."[276] The Supreme Court has never ruled on whether the right not to have soldiers quartered in one's home (3rd Amend.) or the prohibition against excessive fines (8th Amend.) apply against the state and local governments.[277] According to the Supreme Court, the "right to bear arms" (2nd Amend.) does not apply to the states.[278] Nor do the right to a grand jury indictment[279] and the right to a jury trial in civil cases.[280] Similarly, but in reverse, the federal due process clause (Fifth Amend.) has been held to incorporate the equal protection clause of the 14th Amendment against the federal government.[281]

Thus, from a textual standpoint, the individual rights protected by the US Constitution can be reduced to or subsumed under two overarching principles: due process and equal protection. Freedom of speech, discussed immediately below, is perhaps the cardinal constitutional liberty or due process right.

---

273   Compare the federal counterpart in the 5th Amend.
274   Slaughterhouse Cases, 83 U.S. 36 (1873).
275   Gitlow v. New York, 268 U.S. 652 (1925).
276   Palko v. Connecticut, 302 U.S. 319 (1937).
277   Chemerinsky, Constitutional Law at pp. 383-384.
278   Presser v. Illinois, 116 U.S. 252 (1886).
279   Hutardo v. California, 110 U.S. 516 (1884).
280   Minneapolis & St. Louis R.R. Co. v. Bombolis, 241 U.S. 211 (1816).
281   Bolling v. Sharpe, 347 U.S. 483 (1954).

a. Speech

Because of the preeminent role played by free speech in the political life and government of the United States, the subject of free speech has been selected for more extensive coverage in this book. The articulated freedoms of press, assembly, and petition are treated peripherally, if at all.

Scholars resort to four major theories to justify freedom of speech.[282] These are that freedom of speech is necessary for self-governance, that speech serves the discovery of truth via the marketplace of ideas, that it protects and promotes individual autonomy, and that it fosters tolerance. Invoking the first two of these justifications, Justice Brandeis defended freedom of speech in his well-known concurring opinion in *Whitney v. California*:

> Those who won our independence . . . valued liberty both as an end and as a means. . . . They believed that freedom to think as you will and to speak as you think are means indispensable to the discovery and spread of political truth. . . . Discussion affords ordinarily adequate protection against the dissemination of noxious doctrine. . . . [T]he remedy to be applied is more speech, not enforced silence.[283]

Although the decisional matrix that structures the protection of all civil liberty rights is identical, the United States Supreme Court has created frequently complex approaches to First Amendment rights in general, and freedom of speech in particular. Practical questions about the scope of the First Amendment's protection of speech, as with questions about other constitutional rights, result from conflicts between private and public interests. These two rival interests are represented in the following discussion by the headings Protected Expressive Conduct (Private Rights) and Regulation of Expression (Public Interests).

i. Protected Expressive Conduct (Private Rights)

Through the centuries, the Supreme Court and other federal courts, not to mention state courts, have frequently been confronted with deciding what conduct is protected by the First Amendment in general, and by the free speech clause in particular.

The following discussion omits historical developments, and theoretical nuances, in favor of including more factual detail from decisions from the last 50 years. These decisions show a high degree of protection of speech and related conduct, even extending constitutional protection to fund-raising and to commercial advertising.

After summarizing a number of the major decisions protective of expression, the discussion below briefly treats the four main categories of expression that do not enjoy protection by the First Amendment: crimes involving speech, torts involving speech, "fighting words," and obscenity.

---

282   Chemerinsky, Constitutional Law at p. 751; see Tribe at pp. 785 *et seq.*
283   274 U.S. 357, 375 (1927).

aa. Protected Speech and Conduct

Although it probably goes without saying, free speech includes not only the freedom to hold political and other opinions and beliefs, but also to act in accordance with these opinions and beliefs.[284] Consequently, the Supreme Court has decided a number of cases brought by employees of federal, state, and local governments alleging violations of their First Amendment rights. Some representative cases are mentioned in the following paragraph.

While the government may require employees to take an oath to support the federal and state constitutions,[285] it may not demand that they pledge to "promote respect for the flag and . . . reverence for law and order."[286] The speech and association protections of the First Amendment forbid hiring, promotion, transfer, or firing of a public employee for party affiliation unless the hiring authority demonstrates that party affiliation is an appropriate requirement for the effective performance of the public office.[287] They similarly forbid retaliatory termination or non-renewal of a contract with an independent contractor on such grounds.[288] However, the government may constitutionally place some limitations on a public employee's rights of political speech and association if the limits are neutral and they are necessary to preserve efficient, nonpartisan public agencies, and to protect public employees from being forced to work for the election of their superiors.[289] This last protection can be extremely important in light of the fact that over half a million people hold elective office in the United States.[290]

Less obviously, the Supreme Court has ruled that the freedom to speak includes the freedom not to speak. For example, the Supreme Court upheld the right of a car owner in New Hampshire to block out the state's motto "Live Free or Die" on his state-issued license plate. The court wrote, "The right to speak and the right to refrain from speaking are complementary components of the broader concept of 'individual freedom of mind.'"[291] In the same vein the Supreme Court ruled unconstitutional a compulsory flag salute and compulsory recitation of the "Pledge of Allegiance" in *West Virginia State Board of Education v. Barnette*, holding:

> [T]he compulsory flag salute and pledge required affirmation of a belief and an attitude of mind. . . . If there is any fixed star in our constitutional constellation, it is that no official, high or petty, can prescribe what shall be orthodox in politics, nationalism,

---

284 Dawson v. Delaware, 503 U.S. 159 (1992).

285 Connell v. Higginbotham, 403 U.S. 207 (1971).

286 Baggett v. Bullitt, 377 U.S. 360 (1964).

287 Rutan v. Republican Party of Illinois, 497 U.S. 62 (1990).

288 O'Hare Truck Service, Inc. v. City of Northlake, 518 U.S. 712 (1996).

289 Broadrick v. Oklahoma, 413 U.S. 601 (1973).

290 U.S. Dept. of Commerce, vol. I, no. II.

291 Wooley v. Maynard, 430 U.S. 705, 714 (1977).

religion or other matters of opinion or force citizens to confess by word or act their faith therein.[292]

Perhaps more momentously, in *Talley v. California*[293] the Supreme Court declared a ban on anonymous handbills unconstitutional, saying:

> [The] obnoxious press licensing law of England, which was also enforced on the Colonies was due in part to the knowledge that exposure of the names of printers, writers and distributors would lessen the circulation of literature critical of the government. . . . Anonymous pamphlets, leaflets, brochures, and even books have played an important role in the progress of mankind.

In *McIntyre v. Ohio Elections Commission*[294] the Supreme Court invalidated a prohibition against the distribution of anonymous campaign literature, and in *DeBartolo Corp. v. Florida Gulf Coast Building and Construction Trades Council*[295] it held that union construction workers enjoyed a constitutional right to pass out leaflets to customers at a shopping mall, urging them not to shop at any of the stores in the mall until the owner of the mall (who did not own the stores) had reached an agreement with the union on a construction contract.

(1) Conduct Protected as Speech ("Symbolic Expression")

Free speech can embrace conduct. For example, the freedom to hold and disseminate one's views includes the right to solicit and accept funds.[296] Speech also includes writing, even if the writing does not fall within the traditional ambit of freedom of the press, such as wearing a jacket with the inscription "Fuck the Draft" in a courthouse corridor.[297] These and other doctrines and cases concerning conduct are usually grouped under the heading "symbolic expression."

Although the symbolic communication of an idea is basically protected by the First Amendment, the communication will not be protected if the method of communication has been made illegal for reasons that are independent of the speech. Thus, while protesting the draft (military conscription) is constitutionally protected, burning or mutilating a man's draft card can constitutionally be prohibited for the independent reason that the card facilitates the smooth functioning of the selective service system, and there is no less restrictive alternative.[298] Applying this distinction, a prohibition against pupils' wearing of black arm bands in school to protest the Vietnam War was held invalid.[299]

---

292   319 U.S. 624 (1943).

293   362 U.S. 60 (1960).

294   514 U.S. 334 (1995).

295   485 U.S. 568 (1988).

296   Village of Schaumburg v. Citizens for a Better Environment, 444 U.S. 620 (1980). The Supreme Court ruled laws limiting the amount of money that a person or group can contribute to a political candidate valid in Buckley v. Valeo 424 U.S. 1 (1976).

297   Cohen v. California, 403 U.S. 15 (1971). "Draft" refers to military conscription.

298   United States v. O'Brien, 391 U.S. 367 (1968).

299   Tinker v. Des Moines Indep. Community School Dist., 393 U.S. 503 (1969).

CASE: United States v. Eichman
496 U.S. 310 (1990)

JUSTICE BRENNAN delivered the opinion of the Court.

In these consolidated appeals, we consider whether appellees' prosecution for burning a United States flag in violation of the Flag Protection Act of 1989 is consistent with the First Amendment. Applying our recent decision in *Texas v. Johnson*, 491 U. S. 397 (1989), the District Courts held that the Act cannot constitutionally be applied to appellees. We affirm.

I

[T]he United States prosecuted certain appellees for violating the Flag Protection Act of 1989, by knowingly setting fire to several United States flags on the steps of the United States Capitol while protesting various aspects of the Government's domestic and foreign policy. [T]he United States prosecuted other appellees for violating the Act by knowingly setting fire to a United States flag in Seattle while protesting the Act's passage. In each case, the respective appellees moved to dismiss the flag-burning charge on the ground that the Act, both on its face and as applied, violates the First Amendment. Both the United States District Court for the Western District of Washington . . . and the United States District Court for the District of Columbia . . . following Johnson, supra, held the Act unconstitutional as applied to appellees and dismissed the charges. The United States appealed both decisions directly to this Court pursuant to 18 U.S.C. 700(d). . . . We noted probable jurisdiction and consolidated the two cases.

II

Last term in Johnson, we held a Texas statute criminalizing the desecration of venerated objects, including the United States flag, was unconstitutional as applied to an individual who had set such a flag on fire during a political demonstration. . . .

After our decision in Johnson, Congress passed the Flag Protection Act of 1989. The Act provides in relevant part:

(a)(1) Whoever knowingly mutilates, defaces, physically defiles, burns, maintains on the floor or ground, or tramples upon any flag of the United States shall be fined under this title or imprisoned for not more than one year, or both.

(2) This subsection does not prohibit any conduct consisting of the disposal of a flag when it has become worn or soiled.

(b) As used in this section, the term 'flag of the United States' means any flag of the United States, or any part thereof, made of any substance, of any size, in a form that is commonly displayed." . . .

. . .

The Government contends that the Flag Protection Act is constitutional because, unlike the statute addressed in Johnson, the Act does not target expressive conduct on the basis of the content of its message. The Government asserts an interest in "protect[ing] the physical integrity of the flag under all circumstances" in order to safeguard the flag's identity "as the unique and unalloyed symbol of the Nation." . . . The Act proscribes conduct (other than disposal) that damages or mistreats a flag, without regard to the actor's motive, his intended message, or the likely effects of his conduct on onlookers. By contrast, the Texas statute expressly prohibited only those acts of physical flag desecration "that the actor knows will seriously offend" onlookers, and the former federal statute prohibited only those acts of desecration that "cas[t] contempt upon" the flag.

. . .

[T]he precise language of the Act's prohibitions confirms Congress' interest in the communicative impact of flag destruction. The Act criminalizes the conduct of anyone who "knowingly mutilates, defaces, physically defiles, burns, maintains on the floor or ground, or tramples upon any flag." . . . Each of the specified terms—with the possible exception of "burns"—unmistakably connotes disrespectful treatment of the flag and suggests a focus on those acts likely to damage the flag's symbolic value. And the explicit exemption in 700(a)(2) for disposal of "worn or soiled" flags protects certain acts traditionally associated with patriotic respect for the flag.

As we explained in Johnson . . .: "[I]f we were to hold that a State may forbid flag burning wherever it is likely to endanger the flag's symbolic role, but allow it wherever burning a flag promotes that role—as where, for example, a person ceremoniously burns a dirty flag—we would be . . . permitting a State to 'prescribe what shall be orthodox' by saying that one may burn the flag to convey one's attitude toward it and its referents only if one does not endanger the flag's representation of nationhood and national unity." . . .

III

. . .

We are aware that desecration of the flag is deeply offensive to many. But the same might be said, for example, of virulent ethnic and religious epithets, see *Termimiello v. Chicago* . . . , vulgar repudiations of the draft, see *Cohen v. California* . . . , and scurrilous caricatures, see *Hustler Magazine, Inc. v. Falwell*. . . . "If there is a bedrock principle underlying the First Amendment, it is that the Government may not prohibit the expression of an idea simply because society finds the idea itself offensive or disagreeable." Johnson. . . . Punishing desecration of the flag dilutes the very freedom that makes this emblem so revered, and worth revering. The judgments of the District Courts are

Affirmed.

[Dissenting opinion omitted.]

(2) Commercial Speech (Right to Advertise)

In 1976 the Supreme Court held that pharmacists have a constitutional right to advertise the prices of prescription drugs,[300] because advertising is commercial speech that is protected by the Constitution. Commercial speech is defined as speech whose dominant theme simply proposes a commercial transaction.[301]

Beginning with *Central Hudson Gas & Electric Corp. v. Public Service Commission of New York*,[302] the Supreme Court has formulated and refined a test to judge when the government may constitutionally regulate commercial speech. This test, which essentially amounts to intermediate scrutiny, identifies four groups of regulations of advertising:

laws outlawing advertising of illegal activities (these are not prohibited),

prohibitions of false and misleading advertising (these too are not prohibited),

true advertising that inherently risks becoming false or deceptive (this can be regulated), and

laws that limit commercial advertising to achieve other goals. (It is in this last group that most of the litigation has arisen.[303])

bb. Unprotected Speech

There are four generally recognized categories of speech and expression that are not protected by the First Amendment. In the order treated below, these are (1) crimes involving speech, (2) defamation and other torts, (3) fighting words, and (4) obscenity.

(1) Crimes Involving Speech

The notion that, when speech forms part of an independent crime, it enjoys no constitutional protection, is perhaps so obvious that it need not be elaborated

---

300   Virginia State Board of Pharmacy v. Virginia Citizens Consumer Council, Inc., 425 U.S. 748 (1976).

301   Bolger v. Youngs Drug Products Corp., 463 U.S. 60 (1983). Commercial speech first received protection by the Supreme Court under the First Amendment in Bigelow v. Virginia, 421 U.S. 809 (1975).

302   447 U.S. 557 (1980).

303   See Chemerinsky, Constitutional Law at pp. 896-903.

upon. Examples include an illegal transaction, such as an agreement to monopolize in contravention of the antitrust laws,[304] telling a bank teller to hand over all the money in his cash drawer, and lying when one is under oath (the crime of perjury).

A number of decisions of the United States Supreme Court involve alleged conspiracies to overthrow the government.[305] The Supreme Court has distinguished between urging people to believe in the need for violent overthrow, on the one hand, and urging them to act on their belief, on the other. The former is absolutely protected by the First Amendment, but the latter can be made punishable.[306] However, advocacy of the use of force, or the violation of law, cannot constitutionally be punished unless it is "directed to inciting or producing imminent lawless action and is likely to incite or produce such action." See the following case.

CASE: Brandenburg v. Ohio
395 U.S. 444 (1969)

PER CURIAM.

The appellant, a leader of a Ku Klux Klan group, was convicted under the Ohio Criminal Syndicalism statute for "advocat[ing] . . . the duty, necessity, or propriety of crime, sabotage, violence, or unlawful methods of terrorism as a means of accomplishing industrial or political reform" and for "voluntarily assembl[ing] with any society, group, or assemblage of persons formed to teach or advocate the doctrines of criminal syndicalism." . . . He was fined $1,000 and sentenced to one to 10 years' imprisonment. . . .

The record shows that a man, identified at trial as the appellant, telephoned an announcer-reporter on the staff of a Cincinnati television station and invited him to come to a Ku Klux Klan "rally" to be held at a farm in Hamilton County. With the cooperation of the organizers, the reporter and a cameraman attended the meeting and filmed the events. Portions of the films were later broadcast on the local station and on a national network.

The prosecution's case rested on the films and on testimony identifying the appellant as the person who communicated with the reporter and who spoke at the rally. The State also introduced into evidence several articles appearing in the film, including a pistol, a rifle, a shotgun, ammunition, a Bible, and a red hood worn by the speaker in the films.

---

304   But calls for political boycotts are protected. See Lundmark, *Free Speech*.
305   E.g., Gitlow v. New York, 268 U.S. 652 (1925); Dennis v. United States, 341 U.S. 494 (1951).
306   Yates v. United States, 354 U.S. 298 (1957).

One film showed 12 hooded figures, some of whom carried firearms. They were gathered around a large wooden cross, which they burned. No one was present other than the participants and the newsmen who made the film. Most of the words uttered during the scene were incomprehensible when the film was projected, but scattered phrases could be understood that were derogatory of Negroes and, in one instance, of Jews. Another scene on the same film showed the appellant, in Klan regalia, making a speech. The speech, in full, was as follows:

> This is an organizers' meeting. We have had quite a few members here today which are—we have hundreds, hundreds of members throughout the State of Ohio. I can quote from a newspaper clipping from the Columbus, Ohio Dispatch, five weeks ago Sunday morning. The Klan has more members in the State of Ohio than does any other organization. We're not a revengent organization, but if our President, our Congress, our Supreme Court, continues to suppress the white, Caucasian race, it's possible that there might have to be some revengeance taken.

> We are marching on Congress July the Fourth, four hundred thousand strong. From there we are dividing into two groups, one group to march on St. Augustine, Florida, the other group to march into Mississippi. Thank you.

The second film showed six hooded figures one of whom, later identified as the appellant, repeated a speech very similar to that recorded on the first film. The reference to the possibility of "revengeance"[307] was omitted, and one sentence was added: "Personally, I believe the nigger should be returned to Africa, the Jew returned to Israel." Though some of the figures in the films carried weapons, the speaker did not.

[T]he constitutional guarantees of free speech and free press do not permit a State to forbid or proscribe advocacy of the use of force or of law violation except where such advocacy is directed to inciting or producing imminent lawless action and is likely to incite or produce such action. As we said in *Noto v. United States*, . . . "the mere abstract teaching . . . of the moral propriety or even moral necessity for a resort to force and violence, is not the same as preparing a group for violent action and steeling it to such action.". . . A statute which fails to draw this distinction impermissibly intrudes upon the freedoms guaranteed by the First and Fourteenth Amendments. It sweeps within its condemnation speech which our Constitution has immunized from governmental control. . . .

---

307 "Revengence" is not a recognised English word. Mr. Brandenburg has apparently confused "vengeance" and "revenge".

Measured by this test, Ohio's Criminal Syndicalism Act cannot be sustained. . . . Neither the indictment nor the trial judge's instructions to the jury in any way refined the statute's bald definition of the crime in terms of mere advocacy not distinguished from incitement to imminent lawless action.

Accordingly, we are here confronted with a statute which, by its own words and as applied, purports to punish mere advocacy and to forbid, on pain of criminal punishment, assembly with others merely to advocate the described type of action. Such a statute falls within the condemnation of the First and Fourteenth Amendments. The contrary teaching of *Whitney v. California, supra,* cannot be supported, and that decision is therefore overruled.

Reversed.

[Concurring opinions omitted.]

In 1950 Joseph Beauharnais passed out leaflets in Chicago charging the black population with destroying white neighborhoods, and calling upon the mayor and city council of Chicago to "Preserve and Protect White Neighborhoods! From the constant and continuous invasion, harrassment and encroachment by the negroes." This leaflet continued: "[I]f persuasion and the need to prevent the white race from becoming mongrelized by the Negroes will not unite us, then the aggressions, rapes, robberies, knives, guns and marijuana of the negro, surely will."

Beauharnais was convicted and fined $200 under a state statute that made it a crime to defame a class of people.[308] Should his conviction have been upheld, as it was, by the United States Supreme Court?[309]

(2) Defamation and Other Torts

Defamation is a tort, generally belonging to the uncodified common law of the state, that entitles one to damages (and sometimes an injunction) for the injury done to one's reputation by untruthful statements. According to the Supreme Court, state laws on defamation and other torts, such as violation of copyright[310] and infliction of emotional distress,[311] must meet certain minimal standards to ensure that First Amendment rights are not impinged upon.

---

308 Beauharnais v. Illinois, 353 U.S. 250 (1952). The statute, which has since been replaced, prohibited any publication that portrayed "depravity, criminality, unchastity, or lack of virtue of a class of citizens, of any race, color, creed or religion...which exposes the citizens of any race, color, creed or religion to contempt, derision, or obloquy".

309 See comments in Collin v. Smith, 578 F.2d 1197, 1204-1205 (7th Cir. 1978).

310 Harper & Row v. Nation Enterprises, 471 U.S. 539 (1985).

311 See Lundmark, Common Law at pp. 10-14, 65-68.

These minimal standards are that the defendant must at least have been negligent (no strict or "no-fault" liability); that the factual misstatement must have warned a reasonably prudent editor or broadcaster of its defamatory potential; that damages be limited to compensation for actual injury (including injury to reputation, personal humiliation, and mental suffering); that punitive damages be awarded only in matters of public concern and where the defendant acted with knowledge of falsity or reckless disregard for truth; and that, in matters of public concern, and contrary to the common law rule, the plaintiff must bear the burden of proving that the statements are false.[312]

The constitutional significance of defamation increases dramatically when one moves from the private into the public arena and one is dealing with matters of public interest. Here the courts and legislatures must resolve the conflict between the need to protect the reputation and privacy of individuals on the one hand and the public's want, need, or right to know on the other. This conflict has been resolved rather crudely in the United States by decisions of the United States Supreme Court beginning with *New York Times v. Sullivan.*[313]

Sullivan concerned a large civil libel (a form of defamation) judgment awarded in the Alabama courts in favor of a local elected official against certain African American clergymen and the New York Times for an advertisement in that newspaper that contained false statements about the official. The Supreme Court reversed the judgment. In doing so it held that,[314] before a public official can recover damages, she must prove by clear and convincing evidence that the statement was false and that the defendant had acted with actual malice, that is, that the defendant knew the statement to be false or else had acted with reckless disregard for the truth.

"Public official" has been expanded to include a candidate for public office.[315] *New York Times v. Sullivan* has also been extended to "public figures." One can become a public figure in two ways. One can achieve "general fame or notoriety in the community and pervasive involvement in the affairs of society" and become a public figure for all purposes, or one may "voluntarily inject himself or be drawn into a particular controversy, thus becoming a public figure for a limited range of issues."[316]

---

312   Philadelphia Newspaper, Inc. v. Hepps, 475 U.S. 767 (1986); Dun & Bradstreet, Inc. v. Greenmoss Builders, Inc., 472 U.S. 749 (1985); Gertz v. Robert Welch, Inc., 418 U.S. 323 (1974).

313   376 U.S. 254 (1964).

314   "Clear and convincing evidence" is a standard of proof requiring more convincing proof than merely the "weight of the evidence" employed in most civil cases, but it need not rise to the level of proof required by the "beyond a reasonable doubt" standard of the criminal law.

315   Rosenblatt v. Baer, 383 U.S. 75 (1966).

316   Gertz v. Robert Welch, Inc., 418 U.S. 323 (1974).

(3) Fighting Words

The Supreme Court ruled in 1942 that "fighting words" are not protected by the Constitution because their slight personal social value is outweighed by the public interest in preserving order.[317] In *Chaplinsky*, the Court wrote:

> [A]llowing the broadest scope to the language and purpose of the Fourteenth Amendment [that incorporates the First Amendment against the states], it is well understood that the right of free speech is not absolute at all times and under all circumstances. There are certain well-defined and narrowly limited classes of speech, the prevention and punishment of which have never been thought to raise any constitutional problem. These include the lewd and obscene, the profane, the libelous, and the insulting or fighting words—those which by their very utterance inflict injury or tend to incite an immediate breach of the peace. . . . [S]uch utterances are no essential part of any exposition of ideas, and are of such slight social value as a step to truth that any benefit that may be derived from them is clearly outweighed by the social interest in order and morality. "Resort to epithets or personal abuse is not in any proper sense communication of information or opinion safeguarded by the Constitution."[318]

Chaplinsky ends its list of exceptions to constitutional protection of speech with two different classes: "insulting . . . words . . . which by their very utterance inflict injury" and "fighting words . . . which by their very utterance . . . tend to incite an immediate breach of the peace." It is unclear whether the former class (insulting words) exists as an exception to the constitutional protection of speech, for the Supreme Court has yet to review a conviction for uttering "insulting words" as such. While "insult" may give rise to a cause of action for damages,[319] in general it is not a crime by itself, as it is in Germany.[320]

Convictions that reach the Supreme Court for review have been for violation of statutes and ordinances criminalizing "breach of the peace" or "disorderly conduct." For example, the defendant in *Gooding v. Wilson*[321] said to a police officer, "White son of a bitch, I'll kill you," and "You son of a bitch, I'll choke you to death." He was convicted under a Georgia statute that made it criminal to "use to or of another, and in his presence, opprobrious words or abusive language, tending to cause a breach of the peace." The Supreme Court found the statute overbroad, and emphasized that the Georgia courts (and presumably police and prosecutors) had a constitutional obligation to construe the statute narrowly so as only to prohibit unprotected fighting words.

In one case the Supreme Court overturned the conviction of a parent who had repeatedly referred to teachers and members of the school board as

---

317   Chaplinsky v. New Hampshire, 315 U.S. 568 (1942).

318   At pp. 571-572.

319   See, e.g., Cal. Civ. Code § 43.

320   § 192 Strafgesetzbuch (*Beleidigung*); see Eberle at p. 862.

321   405 U.S. 518 (1972).

"mother-fuckers" at a school board meeting.[322] In another case a woman told the police who were arresting her son that they were "god-damn-mother-fucker police." Her conviction for using "opprobrious language" was reversed.[323] In yet another case an individual holding a speech referred to police officers as "mother-fucking fascist pig cops" and singled out one officer whom he labelled a "black mother-fucking pig." This speaker's conviction was also reversed.[324]

One of the reasons for the reversals in the above cases was the conviction by the Supreme Court that the right of uninhibited debate on public issues is an essential ingredient of the American political system. Thinking back to the reasoning of *New York Times v. Sullivan*, one might argue that insults directed at police and other public officers and officials are protected by the Constitution because of the democratic need for uninhibited debate. In *New York Times v. Sullivan*, Justice Brennan identified a "profound national commitment to the principle that debate on public issues should be uninhibited, robust, and wide-open, and that it may well include vehement, caustic, and sometimes unpleasantly sharp attacks."[325]

Another conviction that was reversed by the Supreme Court was that of a man who had said, protesting military conscription, "If they ever make me carry a rifle the first man I want to get in my sights is L.B.J. [then president Johnson]. They are not going to make me kill my black brothers." The Supreme Court ruled that the man's statement was "political hyperbole," and thus could not be punished under a law making it a crime "knowingly and willfully [to threaten] to take the life of or to inflict bodily harm upon the President."[326]

(4) Obscenity

Obscene material is not protected by the First Amendment because, according to the Supreme Court, it is "utterly without social importance."[327] "Obscene material," the *Roth* court continued, "is material which deals with sex in a manner appealing to the prurient interest." Said another way it is "material having a tendency to excite lustful thoughts."

On several occasions after *Roth* the Supreme Court decided what material "had a tendency to excite lustful thoughts" and what did not. After a few years, frustrated by not having been able to articulate standards by which to identify obscenity, Justice Stewart wrote, "I shall not today attempt further to define the kinds of material I understand to be embraced within that shorthand description;

---

322   Rosenfeld v. New Jersey, 409 U.S. 901 (1972).

323   Lewis v. City of New Orleans, 408 U.S. 913 (1972).

324   Brown v. Oklahoma, 408 U.S. 914 (1972).

325   New York Times Co. v. Sullivan, 376 U.S. 254, 270 (1964).

326   Watts v. United States, 394 U.S. 705 (1969).

327   Roth v. United States, 354 U.S. 476, 484 (1957).

and perhaps I could never succeed in intelligibly doing so. But I know it when I see it."[328]

A more or less workable test for determining what is obscene and what is not was announced in 1973 in *Miller v. California*:

[T]he basic guidelines for the trier of fact must be: (a) whether 'the average person, applying contemporary community standards' would find that the work, taken as a whole, appeals to the prurient interest; (b) whether the work depicts or describes, in a patently offensive way, sexual conduct specifically defined by the applicable state's law; and (c) whether the work, taken as a whole, lacks serious literary, artistic, political or scientific value.[329]

Child pornography can constitutionally be prohibited in the interest of protecting children even if it does not meet the *Miller* criteria.[330]

Even if sale and distribution of obscene material may be criminally prohibited, possession in one's home may not be penalized because doing so would violate one's constitutional right of personal privacy.[331]

CASE: Reno v. American Civil Liberties Union
521 U.S. 844 (1997)

Justice Stevens delivered the opinion of the Court.

At issue is the constitutionality of two statutory provisions enacted to protect minors from "indecent" and "patently offensive" communications on the Internet. Notwithstanding the legitimacy and importance of the congressional goal of protecting children from harmful materials, we agree with the three judge District Court that the statute abridges "the freedom of speech" protected by the First Amendment.

. . .

The Telecommunications Act of 1996 . . . was an unusually important legislative enactment. As stated on the first of its 103 pages, its primary purpose was to reduce regulation and encourage "the rapid deployment of new telecommunications technologies." The major components of the statute have nothing to do with the Internet; they were designed to promote competition in the local telephone service market, the multichannel video market, and the market for over the air broadcasting. The Act includes seven Titles, six of which are the product of extensive committee hearings and the subject of discussion in Reports prepared by Committees of the Senate and the House of Representatives. By contrast, Title

---

328   Jacobellis v. Ohio, 378 U.S. 184, 197 (1964).
329   413 U.S. 15, 36 (1973).
330   New York v. Ferber, 456 U.S. 942 (1982).
331   Stanley v. Georgia, 394 U.S. 351 (1969).

V—known as the "Communications Decency Act of 1996" (CDA)—contains provisions that were either added in executive committee after the hearings were concluded or as amendments offered during floor debate on the legislation. An amendment offered in the Senate was the source of the two statutory provisions challenged in this case. They are informally described as the "indecent transmission" provision and the "patently offensive display" provision.

The first . . . prohibits the knowing transmission of obscene or indecent messages to any recipient under 18 years of age. It provides in pertinent part:

(a) Whoever—

(1) in interstate or foreign communications—. . .

(B) by means of a telecommunications device knowingly—

(i) makes, creates, or solicits, and

(ii) initiates the transmission of, any comment, request, suggestion, proposal, image, or other communication which is obscene or indecent, knowing that the recipient of the communication is under 18 years of age, regardless of whether the maker of such communication placed the call or initiated the communication; . . .

(2) knowingly permits any telecommunications facility under his control to be used for any activity prohibited by paragraph (1) with the intent that it be used for such activity,

shall be fined under Title 18, or imprisoned not more than two years, or both.

The second provision . . . prohibits the knowing sending or displaying of patently offensive messages in a manner that is available to a person under 18 years of age. It provides:

(d) Whoever—

(1) in interstate or foreign communications knowingly—

(A) uses an interactive computer service to send to a specific person or persons under 18 years of age, or

(B) uses any interactive computer service to display in a manner available to a person under 18 years of age,any comment, request, suggestion, proposal, image, or other communication that, in context, depicts or describes, in terms patently offensive asmeasured by contemporary community standards, sexual or excretory activities or organs, regardless of whether the user of such service placed the call or initiated the communication; or

(2) knowingly permits any telecommunications facility under such person's control to be used for an activity

prohibited by paragraph (1) with the intent that it be used for such activity,

shall be fined under Title 18, or imprisoned not more than two years, or both.

The breadth of these prohibitions is qualified by two affirmative defenses. . . . One covers those who take "good faith, reasonable, effective, and appropriate actions" to restrict access by minors to the prohibited communications. . . . The other covers those who restrict access to covered material by requiring certain designated forms of age proof, such as a verified credit card or an adult identification number or code. . . .

. . .

The Government argues that the statute is no more vague than the obscenity standard this Court established in *Miller v. California*. . . . But that is not so. In Miller, this Court reviewed a criminal conviction against a commercial vendor who mailed brochures containing pictures of sexually explicit activities to individuals who had not requested such materials. Having struggled for some time to establish a definition of obscenity, we set forth in Miller the test for obscenity that controls to this day:

(a) whether the average person, applying contemporary community standards would find that the work, taken as a whole, appeals to the prurient interest; (b) whether the work depicts or describes, in a patently offensive way, sexual conduct specifically defined by the applicable state law; and (c) whether the work, taken as a whole, lacks serious literary, artistic, political, or scientific value. . . .

Because the CDA's "patently offensive" standard (and, we assume arguendo, its synonymous "indecent" standard) is one part of the three prong Miller test, the Government reasons, it cannot be unconstitutionally vague.

The Government's assertion is incorrect as a matter of fact. The second prong of the Miller test—the purportedly analogous standard—contains a critical requirement that is omitted from the CDA: that the proscribed material be "specifically defined by the applicable state law." This requirement reduces the vagueness inherent in the open ended term "patently offensive" as used in the CDA. Moreover, the Miller definition is limited to "sexual conduct," whereas the CDA extends also to include (1) "excretory activities" as well as (2) "organs" of both a sexual and excretory nature.

The Government's reasoning is also flawed. Just because a definition including three limitations is not vague, it does not follow that one of those limitations, standing by itself, is not vague. Each of Miller's additional two prongs—(1) that, taken as a whole, the material appeal to the "prurient" interest, and (2) that it "lac[k] serious literary, artistic, political, or scientific value"—critically limits the uncertain sweep of the obscenity definition. . . .

. . .

The breadth of the CDA's coverage is wholly unprecedented. Unlike the regulations upheld in Ginsberg and Pacifica, the scope of the CDA is not limited to commercial speech or commercial entities. Its open ended prohibitions embrace all nonprofit entities and individuals posting indecent messages or displaying them on their own computers in the presence of minors. The general, undefined terms "indecent" and "patently offensive" cover large amounts of non pornographic material with serious educational or other value. Moreover, the "community standards" criterion as applied to the Internet means that any communication available to a nation wide audience will be judged by the standards of the community most likely to be offended by the message. The regulated subject matter includes any of the seven "dirty words" used in the Pacifica monologue [a radio performance by comedian George Carlin which was the subject of the case *F.C.C. v. Pacifica Foundation* . . .], the use of which the Government's expert acknowledged could constitute a felony. . . . It may also extend to discussions about prison rape or safe sexual practices, artistic images that include nude subjects, and arguably the card catalogue of the Carnegie Library.

. . .

In an attempt to curtail the CDA's facial overbreadth, the Government advances three additional arguments for sustaining the Act's affirmative prohibitions: (1) that the CDA is constitutional because it leaves open ample "alternative channels" of communication; (2) that the plain meaning of the Act's "knowledge" and "specific person" requirement significantly restricts its permissible applications; and (3) that the Act's prohibitions are "almost always" limited to material lacking redeeming social value.

The Government first contends that, even though the CDA effectively censors discourse on many of the Internet's modalities—such as chat groups, newsgroups, and mail exploders—it is nonetheless constitutional because it provides a "reasonable opportunity" for speakers to engage in the restricted speech on the World Wide Web. . . . This argument is unpersuasive because the CDA regulates speech on the basis of its content. A "time, place, and manner" analysis is therefore inapplicable. . . .

We agree with the District Court's conclusion that the CDA places an unacceptably heavy burden on protected speech, and that the defenses do not constitute the sort of "narrow tailoring" that will save an otherwise patently invalid unconstitutional provision. In Sable, . . . we remarked that the speech restriction at issue there amounted to " 'burn[ing] the house to roast the pig.' " The CDA, casting a far darker shadow over free speech, threatens to torch a large segment of the Internet community.

At oral argument, the Government relied heavily on its ultimate fall back position: If this Court should conclude that the CDA is insufficiently tailored, it urged, we should save the statute's constitutionality by honoring the severability clause, . . . and construing nonseverable terms narrowly. In only one respect is this argument acceptable.

A severability clause requires textual provisions that can be severed. We will follow §608's guidance by leaving constitutional textual elements of the statute intact in the one place where they are, in fact, severable. The "indecency" provision . . . applies to "any comment, request, suggestion, proposal, image, or other communication which is obscene or indecent.". . . Appellees do not challenge the application of the statute to obscene speech, which, they acknowledge, can be banned totally because it enjoys no First Amendment protection. . . . As set forth by the statute, the restriction of "obscene" material enjoys a textual manifestation separate from that for "indecent" material, which we have held unconstitutional. Therefore, we will sever the term "or indecent" from the statute, leaving the rest of §223(a) standing. In no other respect, however, can §223(a) or §223(d) be saved by such a textual surgery.

. . .

This case is therefore unlike those in which we have construed a statute narrowly because the text or other source of congressional intent identified a clear line that this Court could draw. [Decisions.] Rather, our decision in *United States v. Treasury Employees* . . . is applicable. In that case, we declined to "dra[w] one or more lines between categories of speech covered by an overly broad statute, when Congress has sent inconsistent signals as to where the new line or lines should be drawn" because doing so "involves a far more serious invasion of the legislative domain." This Court "will not rewrite a . . . law to conform it to constitutional requirements." . . .

In this Court, though not in the District Court, the Government asserts that—in addition to its interest in protecting children—its "[e]qually significant" interest in fostering the growth of the Internet provides an independent basis for upholding the constitutionality of the CDA. . . . The Government apparently assumes that the unregulated availability of "indecent" and "patently offensive" material on the Internet is driving countless citizens away from the medium because of the risk of exposing themselves or their children to harmful material.

We find this argument singularly unpersuasive. The dramatic expansion of this new marketplace of ideas contradicts the factual basis of this contention. The record demonstrates that the growth of the Internet has been and continues to be phenomenal. As a matter of constitutional tradition, in the absence of evidence to the contrary, we presume that governmental regulation of the content of speech is more likely to interfere with the free exchange of ideas than to encourage it. The interest in encouraging freedom of expression in a democratic society outweighs any theoretical but unproven benefit of censorship.

For the foregoing reasons, the judgment of the district court is affirmed.

It is so ordered.

[Concurring and dissenting opinions omitted.]

---

ii. Regulation of Expression (Public Interests)

The rights of private individuals collide with the interests of the public through the medium of statutory and common law, such as the law of defamation. This subsection concerns statutory law that explicitly regulates expressive conduct. It addresses how these laws are judged in the abstract or "on their face." Notice the similarities of the *Heffron* test to intermediate level scrutiny.

aa. Time, Place, and Manner

According to *Heffron v. International Society for Krishna Consciousness*, a measure may constitutionally impose reasonable limitations on the time, place, and manner of exercising free speech rights if four criteria are satisfied:

- The measure must be content-neutral;

- It must be narrowly tailored;

- It must serve a significant governmental interest; and

- It must leave ample alternative forums or channels of communication of protected expression.[332]

A violation of the first criterion (content-neutrality) might independently invalidate the law under the equal protection clause.[333] "Narrowly tailored," the second criterion, means that the law must be neither overbroad nor vague. A law is overbroad when it regulates substantially more speech than is necessary to

---

332   Heffron v. International Society for Krishna Consciousness, 452 U.S. 640 (1981).
333   Chicago Police Department v. Mosley, 408 U.S. 92 (1972).

further the significant governmental interest.[334] The vagueness doctrine "requires that a penal statute define the criminal offense with sufficient definiteness that ordinary people can understand what conduct is prohibited and in a manner that does not encourage arbitrary and discriminatory enforcement."[335]

By requiring in the third criterion that the public interests be "significant," the courts are saying that not just any public interest will do. Public safety, specifically, the orderly and safe movement of crowds at a state fair, has been held sufficiently significant to justify a requirement that the distribution of literature and solicitation of funds be restricted to booths available on a first-come, first-served basis.[336] Public safety and personal privacy are sufficiently significant to require that door-to-door solicitors and canvassers first identify themselves to local authorities.[337] Traffic safety and aesthetics may support restrictions on billboards.[338] Personal privacy, aesthetics, and orderly land-use planning can also warrant restrictions on noise[339] and on the siting of "adult" movie theaters.[340] But the aesthetic interest in avoiding litter does not warrant requiring that handbills carry the name and address of their author.[341] Nor can it justify a near-total ban on residential signs.[342]

Concerning the fourth criterion, ample alternative forums, some public property is so historically associated with the exercise of First Amendment rights that it cannot be totally closed to protected speech, such as speeches, meetings, parades, and demonstrations. Examples of such "public forums" include streets, sidewalks, and parks,[343] including the public sidewalks abutting the Supreme Court's building and grounds,[344] the grounds around a statehouse,[345] and the sidewalks outside foreign embassies.[346] Further, other public property that is not historically associated with the exercise of First Amendment rights may be deemed a public forum if the state opens it "by policy or by practice" as a place for expressive activity.[347]

---

334   Schad v. Borough of Mt. Ephraim, 452 U.S. 61 (1981).

335   Kolender v. Lawson, 461 U.S. 352, 357 (1983).

336   Heffron v. International Society for Krishna Consciousness, 452 U.S. 640 (1981).

337   See Hynes v. Mayor of Oradell, 425 U.S. 610 (1976), where the ordinance was nonetheless ruled void for vagueness.

338   Metromedia, Inc. v. City of San Diego, 453 U.S. 490 (1981).

339   Kovacs v. Cooper, 336 U.S. 77 (1949).

340   City of Renton v. Playtime Theatres, Inc., 475 U.S. 41 (1986).

341   Schneider v. State, 308 U.S. 147 (1939).

342   City of Ladue v. Gilleo, 512 U.S. 43 (1994).

343   Hague v. CIO, 307 U.S. 496 (1939).

344   United States v. Grace, 461 U.S. 171 (1983).

345   Edwards v. South Carolina, 372 U.S. 229 (1963).

346   See Boos v. Barry, 485 U.S. 312 (1988).

347   Perry Education Association v. Perry Local Educators' Association, 460 U.S. 37 (1983), concerning the internal mail system of a public school.

Because of the constitutional prestige of First Amendment rights, it should come as no surprise that laws impinging, or potentially impinging, upon constitutionally protected free speech are judged by the exacting standards of strict scrutiny. What may be surprising is that the strict scrutiny test is also employed to judge the abstract constitutionality of laws that impinge upon rights given intermediate protection (commercial speech, for example). As illustrated in the following case, even laws directed at the lowest echelon of non-protected speech must survive strict scrutiny analysis. Notice the court's use of equal protection discourse. And ask yourselves what other crimes the young man might have been charged with committing.

By way of background to the following case, a teenager had allegedly erected and set fire to a cross on a black family's lawn. He was charged under the St. Paul, Minnesota, Bias-Motivated Crime Ordinance. This ordinance prohibited the display of a burning cross, a swastika, or other symbol that one knows or has reason to know "arouses anger, alarm or resentment in others" on the basis of race, color, creed, religion, or gender. The state supreme court had construed the phrase "arouses anger, alarm or resentment in others" to limit the ordinance's reach to fighting words within the meaning of *Chaplinsky*. It upheld the ordinance because it was narrowly tailored to serve a compelling governmental interest.

CASE: R.A.V.[348] v. City of St. Paul
505 U. S. 377 (1992)

JUSTICE SCALIA delivered the opinion of the Court.

[We] accept the Minnesota Supreme Court's authoritative statement that the ordinance reaches only those expressions that constitute "fighting words" within the meaning of Chaplinsky. Petitioner [urges] us to modify the scope of the *Chaplinsky* formulation, thereby invalidating the ordinance as "substantially overbroad." We find it unnecessary to consider this issue. Assuming, arguendo, that all of the expression reached by the ordinance is proscribable under the "fighting words" doctrine, we nonetheless conclude that the ordinance is facially unconstitutional in that it [prohibits] speech solely on the basis of the subjects the speech addresses.

I

. . .

The First Amendment generally prevents government from proscribing speech [because] of disapproval of the ideas expressed. Content-based regulations are presumptively invalid. From 1791 to the present, however, our society [has] permitted restrictions upon the content of speech in a few

---

348   The petitioner's initials are used instead of his name because the petitioner was a minor.

limited areas, which are "of such slight social value as a step to truth that any benefit that may be derived from them is clearly outweighed by the social interest in order and morality." [*Chaplinsky.*] [We] have sometimes said that these categories of expression are "not within the area of constitutionally protected speech." [Such] statements must be taken in context, however. [What] they mean is that these areas of speech can, consistently with the First Amendment, be regulated because of their constitutionally proscribable content (obscenity, defamation, etc.)—not that they are categories of speech entirely invisible to the Constitution, so that they may be made the vehicles for content discrimination unrelated to their distinctively proscribable content. Thus, the government may proscribe libel; but it may not make the further content discrimination of proscribing only libel critical of the government, [and although a city may proscribe obscenity, it may not prohibit] only those legally obscene works that contain criticism of the city government. . . .

When the basis for the content discrimination consists entirely of the very reason the entire class of speech at issue is proscribable, no significant danger of idea or viewpoint discrimination exists. Such a reason, having been adjudged neutral enough to support exclusion of the entire class of speech from First Amendment protection, is also neutral enough to form the basis of distinction within the class. To illustrate: a State might choose to prohibit only that obscenity which is the most patently offensive in its prurience—i.e., that which involves the most lascivious displays of sexual activity. But it may not prohibit, for example, only that obscenity which includes offensive political messages. And the Federal Government can criminalize only those threats of violence that are directed against the President—since the reasons why threats of violence are outside the First Amendment (protecting individuals from the fear of violence, from the disruption that fear engenders, and from the possibility that the threatened violence will occur) have special force when applied to the person of the President. But the Federal Government may not criminalize only those threats against the President that mention his policy on aid to inner cities. And to take a final example, [a] State may choose to regulate price advertising in one industry, but not in others, because the risk of fraud (one of the characteristics of commercial speech that justifies depriving it of full First Amendment protection) is in its view greater there. But a State may not prohibit only that commercial advertising that depicts men in a demeaning fashion.

Another valid basis for according differential treatment to even a content-defined subclass of proscribable speech is [that] words can in some circumstances violate laws directed not against speech, but against conduct (a law against treason, for example, is violated by telling the enemy the Nation's defense secrets), [and] a particular content-based subcategory of a proscribable class of speech can be swept up incidentally within the reach of a statute directed at conduct, rather than speech. Thus, for example, sexually derogatory "fighting words," among other words, may produce a violation of Title VII's general prohibition against sexual discrimination in employment practices. Where the government does not target conduct on the basis of its expressive content, acts are not shielded from regulation merely because they express a discriminatory idea or philosophy. [Indeed], to validate such selectivity (where totally proscribable speech is at issue), it may not even be necessary to identify any particular "neutral" basis, so long as the nature of the content discrimination is such that there is no realistic possibility that official suppression of ideas is afoot. (We cannot think of any First Amendment interest that would stand in the way of a State's prohibiting only those obscene motion pictures with blue-eyed actresses.) Save for that limitation, the regulation of "fighting words," like the regulation of noisy speech, may address some offensive instances and leave other, equally offensive, instances alone.

II

Applying these principles to the St. Paul ordinance, we conclude that, even as narrowly construed by the Minnesota Supreme Court, the ordinance is facially unconstitutional. Although the phrase in the ordinance, "arouses anger, alarm or resentment in others," has been limited by the Minnesota Supreme Court's construction to reach only those symbols or displays that amount to "fighting words," the remaining, unmodified terms make clear that the ordinance applies only to "fighting words" that insult, or provoke violence, "on the basis of race, color, creed, religion or gender." Displays containing abusive invective, no matter how vicious or severe, are permissible unless they are addressed to one of the specified disfavored topics. Those who wish to use "fighting words" in connection with other ideas—to express hostility, for example, on the basis of political affiliation, union membership, or homosexuality—are not covered. The First Amendment does not permit St. Paul to impose special prohibitions on those speakers who express views on disfavored subjects.

In its practical operation, moreover, the ordinance goes even beyond mere content discrimination to actual viewpoint discrimination. Displays containing some words—odious racial epithets, for example—would be prohibited to proponents of all views. But "fighting words" that do not themselves invoke race, color, creed, religion, or gender—aspersions upon a person's mother, for example—would seemingly be usable ad libitum in the placards of those arguing in favor of racial, color, etc., tolerance and equality, but could not be used by those speakers' opponents. One could hold up a sign saying, for example, that all "anti-Catholic bigots" are misbegotten; but not that all "papists" are, for that would insult and provoke violence "on the basis of religion." St. Paul has no such authority to license one side of a debate to fight freestyle, while requiring the other to follow Marquis of Queensberry rules.

What we have here, it must be emphasized, is not a prohibition of fighting words that are directed at certain persons or groups (which would be facially valid if it met the requirements of the Equal Protection Clause); but rather, a prohibition of fighting words that contain (as the Minnesota Supreme Court repeatedly emphasized) messages of "bias-motivated" hatred and, in particular, as applied to this case, messages "based on virulent notions of racial supremacy." . . . One must wholeheartedly agree with the Minnesota Supreme Court that "[i]t is the responsibility, even the obligation, of diverse communities to confront such notions in whatever form they appear," but the manner of that confrontation cannot consist of selective limitations upon speech. St. Paul's brief asserts that a general "fighting words" law would not meet the city's needs, because only a content-specific measure can communicate to minority groups that the "group hatred" aspect of such speech "is not condoned by the majority." The point of the First Amendment is that majority preferences must be expressed in some fashion other than silencing speech on the basis of its content.

. . .

Finally, St. Paul [argues] that, even if the ordinance regulates expression based on hostility towards its protected ideological content, this discrimination is nonetheless justified because it is narrowly tailored to serve compelling state interests. Specifically, [it asserts] that the ordinance helps to ensure the basic human rights of members of groups that have historically been subjected to discrimination, including the right of such group members to live in peace where they wish. We do not doubt that these interests are compelling, and that the ordinance can be said to promote them. But the "danger of censorship" presented by a facially content-based statute, requires that that weapon be employed only where it is "necessary to serve the asserted [compelling] interest." The existence of adequate content-neutral alternatives thus "undercut[s] significantly" any defense of such a statute, casting considerable doubt on the government's protestations that "the asserted justification is in fact an accurate description of the purpose and effect of the law." The dispositive question in this case, therefore, is whether content discrimination is reasonably necessary to achieve St. Paul's compelling interests; it plainly is not. An ordinance not limited to the favored topics, for example, would have precisely the same beneficial effect. In fact, the only interest distinctively served by the content limitation is that of displaying the city council's special hostility towards the particular biases thus singled out. That is precisely what the First Amendment forbids. . . .

Let there be no mistake about our belief that burning a cross in someone's front yard is reprehensible. But St. Paul has sufficient means at its disposal to prevent such behavior without adding the First Amendment to the fire.

The judgment of the Minnesota Supreme Court is reversed. . . .

[Concurring opinions omitted.]

bb. Licensing and Prior Restraints

Licensing ordinances are often the medium through which First Amendment rights come into conflict with alleged "significant public interests" such as public safety, personal privacy, traffic safety, aesthetics, and orderly land-use planning. Because licensing ordinances restrict the "time, place, and manner" of exercising free speech rights, they are judged by the *Heffron* criteria of content-neutrality, narrowly tailored, significant governmental interest, and ample alternatives.

Licensing of public property for expressive uses is common, and generally constitutional. The Supreme Court has ruled that permit fees can be charged to cover the administrative costs of the permitting and of the event itself.[349] However, remembering the *Heffron* criteria (content-neutrality, narrowly tailored, significant governmental interest, and ample alternatives), any attempt to employ content-based criteria in the granting of the license (as opposed to imposing a condition on the license) will fail unless the distinction in content is "necessary to serve a compelling state interest and [the ordinance] is narrowly drawn to achieve that end."[350] The courts are laxer when it comes to certain types of public property that is not describable as a public forum. For example, in *Cornelius v. NAACP Legal Defense & Education Fund*[351] the Supreme Court allowed organizers of a charity drive for government employees to limit participation to traditional health and welfare charities.

---

349   Cox v. New Hampshire, 312 U.S. 569 (1941).

350   Perry Education Association v. Perry Local Educators' Association, 460 U.S. 37 (1983); e.g., Erznoznik v. City of Jacksonville, 422 U.S. 205 (1975), unsuccessfully attempting to single out nudity in regulating films shown by drive-in theaters whose screens are visible from highways.

351   473 U.S. 788 (1985).

Licensing ordinances which do not directly relate to the use of public property are extremely difficult to justify under the *Heffron* criteria, even if they relate to unprotected speech. The seminal case on this topic of "prior restraints" is *Near v. Minnesota*,[352] in which the Supreme Court reversed an injunction, granted pursuant to a state statute, against a newspaper that had published a series of articles that made defamatory and anti-Semitic accusations, preventing it from publishing any malicious, scandalous, or defamatory material. The court wrote:

> [I]t has been generally, if not universally, considered that it is the chief purpose of the guaranty to prevent previous restraints upon publication. . . .
>
> . . .
>
> The fact that for approximately one hundred and fifty years there has been almost an entire absence of attempts to impose previous restraints upon publications . . . is significant of the deep-seated conviction that such restraints would violate constitutional right.
>
> . . .
>
> [The] fact that liberty of the press may be abused by miscreant purveyors of scandal does not make any the less necessary the immunity of the press from previous restraint in dealing with official misconduct. Subsequent punishment for such abuses as may exist is the appropriate remedy.[353]

Following *Near*, the Supreme Court in *Lovell v. City of Griffin*[354] invalidated an ordinance that prohibited the distribution of "literature of any kind" without first obtaining a license. In *Freeman v. Maryland*[355] the court invalidated a similar ordinance that applied to motion pictures. Licensing of motion pictures has largely, if not totally, disappeared in the United States. Indeed, the well-advertised ratings of films as "G," "R," etc. are entirely voluntary for film makers and theaters.[356] If there is still a film licensing ordinance on the books, it would have to meet the procedural safeguards announced in *Freeman* to be valid. Specifically, the standards for denial of a license under the ordinance would have to be "narrowly drawn, reasonable, and definite," the ordinance would have to provide that the censoring agency (and not the applicant) must promptly seek a judicial injunction in case of controversy, the censoring agency would have to bear the burden of demonstrating that the speech is not protected, and the judicial determination would have to be prompt. Criteria similar to these are used for government seizures of allegedly obscene materials. The government may not seize such materials unless there is a prior judicial determination in an adversary hearing that the materials are not protected by the First Amendment.[357]

---

352   283 U.S. 697 (1931).
353   At pp. 713, 718, and 720.
354   303 U.S. 444 (1938).
355   380 U.S. 51 (1965).
356   Mosk at p. 137.
357   Marcus v. Search Warrant, 367 U.S. 717 (1961).

Near recognized that prior restraints could be constitutional in exceptional cases, such as to prevent the publication of obscenity, the sailing dates of ships in wartime, and incitements to acts of violence and the overthrow by force of orderly governments.[358] The reference to the sailing dates of ships was cited unsuccessfully to prevent the publication of excerpts from the "Pentagon Papers," a top secret, 47-volume report on the Vietnam war prepared by the Department of Defense.[359] Each of the nine justices who heard the case wrote an opinion. The per curiam opinion, signed by the six who voted to lift the injunction granted by the court of appeals, concluded that the government had failed to prove that any of the materials must be kept secret to protect national security.

b. Religion

The First Amendment contains two protections of religious rights, the "establishment clause" and the "free exercise [of religion] clause."[360] Some of the most fascinating (and baffling) questions confronted under the First Amendment concern the "establishment clause," which holds the honor of being the first clause of the First Amendment, treated in the following section.

i. Establishment of Religion

Professor Tribe identifies three different attitudes among the drafters of the Bill of Rights on the need to cleave religion from the state.[361] The evangelical view feared corruption of the churches by a worldly sovereign. Thomas Jefferson espoused the opposing view, that secular interests must be walled off from ecclesiastical incursions. A third view favored free competition among the various sects.

The Jeffersonian view has come to dominate modern thinking on the subject, although it can also be combined with the first approach under a "strict separation" theory.[362] Professor Chemerinsky also identifies a "neutralist theory" that is quite similar to the third theory recognized by Professor Tribe. According to the neutralist theory, government may not favor religion over secularism or one religion over another. Those adhering to this theory have in recent years advanced the test that the government runs afoul of the establishment clause if it "symbolically endorses" a particular religion or generally endorses either religion or secularism.[363] "Accommodation theorists" arguably subscribe to a fourth attitude. They would have government recognize the importance of religion in society and

---

358   283 U.S. at p. 716.

359   New York Times v. United States, 403 U.S. 713 (1971).

360   Consider also the protection of religious belief inherent in Art. VI, cl. 3.

361   Tribe at pp. 1158-1160.

362   Chemerinsky, Constitutional Law at pp. 977-984.

363   E.g., Lynch v. Donnelly, 465 U.S. 668, 694 (1984).

therefore accommodate its presence in government.[364] Under the accommodation theory, violation of the establishment clause would occur only if the state established a religion or coerced religious participation.[365]

Without formally adopting any particular theory, the Supreme Court has developed a three-pronged first articulated in *Lemon v. Kurtzmann*[366] test to judge challenges under the establishment clause: Is there a secular purpose; Does the measure have a principal or primary effect that neither advances nor inhibits religion; and Does it not foster excessive government entanglement with religion.[367]

Setting aside a time of silence in public schools for "mediation or voluntary prayer" was held to violate the first prong because it has no secular purpose.[368] The same fate befell a program to post the Ten Commandments on the walls of public school classrooms.[369] However, excusing children from public school to attend religious services does not offend the establishment clause, despite its religious purpose.[370]

Laws requiring businesses or government offices to close on Sundays are valid, even though they originally were enacted to aid religion.[371] Invocation and benediction prayers at meetings of public bodies have been upheld,[372] but the same practice has been ruled unconstitutional at public school graduations.[373] Christmas Nativity scenes on public property have often faced judicial challenge on grounds that they establish religion. A creche with "Gloria in Excelsis Deo" in a courthouse violates the establishment clause even if paid for by private funds, but a Chanukah menorah displayed with a Christmas tree does not.[374]

---

364   Chemerinsky, Constitutional Law at p. 981.

365   See Lee v. Weisman, 505 U.S. 577, 587 (1992).

366   403 U.S. 602 (1971)

367   Lemon v. Kurtzman, 403 U.S. 602 (1971).

368   Wallace v. Jaffree, 472 U.S. 38 (1985).

369   Stone v. Graham, 449 U.S. 39 (1980).

370   Zorach v. Clauson, 343 U.S. 306 (1952).

371   McGowan v. Maryland, 366 U.S. 420 (1961).

372   Marsh v. Chambers, 463 U.S. 783 (1983).

373   Lee v. Weisman, 505 U.S. 830 (1992).

374   County of Allegheny v. American Civil Liberties Union Greater Pittsburgh Chapter, 492 U.S. 573 (1989).

CASE: Rosenberger v. Rector and Visitors of
the University of Virginia
515 U.S. 819 (1995)

JUSTICE KENNEDY delivered the opinion of the Court.

I

. . .

The University of Virginia, an instrumentality of the Commonwealth for which it is named and thus bound by the First
and Fourteenth Amendments, authorizes the payment of outside contractors for the printing costs of a variety of student
publications. It withheld any authorization for payments on
behalf of petitioners for the sole reason that their student paper "primarily promotes or manifests a particular belie[f] in
or about a deity or an ultimate reality." That the paper did
promote or manifest views within the defined exclusion
seems plain enough. The challenge is to the University's regulation and its denial of authorization, the case raising issues
under the Speech and Establishment Clauses of the First
Amendment.

. . .

Having no further recourse within the University structure,
[Wide Awake Productions (WAP)], Wide Awake, and three
of its editors and members filed suit in the United States District Court for the Western District of Virginia, challenging
the [Student Activities Fund's (SAF's)] action as violative of
. . . 42 U.S.C. 1983. They alleged that refusal to authorize
payment of the printing costs of the publication, solely on
the basis of its religious editorial viewpoint, violated their
rights to freedom of speech and press, to the free exercise of
religion, and to equal protection of the law. They relied also
upon Article I of the Virginia Constitution and the Virginia
Act for Religious Freedom, Va. Code Ann. 57-1, 57-2 (1986
and Supp. 1994), but did not pursue those theories on appeal.
The suit sought damages for the costs of printing the paper,
injunctive and declaratory relief, and attorney's fees.

. . .

The United States Court of Appeals for the Fourth Circuit, in
disagreement with the District Court, held that the Guidelines did discriminate on the basis of content. It ruled that,
while the State need not underwrite speech, there was a
presumptive violation of the Speech Clause when viewpoint
discrimination was invoked to deny third-party payment
otherwise available to [Contracted Independent Organizations (CIOs)]. . . . The Court of Appeals affirmed the judgment of the District Court nonetheless, concluding that
the discrimination by the University was justified by the

"compelling interest in maintaining strict separation of church and state." . . .

II

It is axiomatic that the government may not regulate speech based on its substantive content or the message it conveys. . . . Other principles follow from this precept. In the realm of private speech or expression, government regulation may not favor one speaker over another. . . . Discrimination against speech because of its message is presumed to be unconstitutional. . . . These rules informed our determination that the government offends the First Amendment when it imposes financial burdens on certain speakers based on the content of their expression. . . . When the government targets not subject matter but particular views taken by speakers on a subject, the violation of the First Amendment is all the more blatant. See *R.A.V. v. St. Paul.* . . . Viewpoint discrimination is thus an egregious form of content discrimination. The government must abstain from regulating speech when the specific motivating ideology or the opinion or perspective of the speaker is the rationale for the restriction.

These principles provide the framework forbidding the State from exercising viewpoint discrimination, even when the limited public forum is one of its own creation. In a case involving a school district's provision of school facilities for private uses, we declared that "[t]here is no question that the District, like the private owner of property, may legally preserve the property under its control for the use to which it is dedicated." . . . The necessities of confining a forum to the limited and legitimate purposes for which it was created may justify the State in reserving it for certain groups or for the discussion of certain topics. . . . Once it has opened a limited forum, however, the State must respect the lawful boundaries it has itself set. The State may not exclude speech where its distinction is not "reasonable in light of the purpose served by the forum" . . ., nor may it discriminate against speech on the basis of its viewpoint. . . . Thus, in determining whether the State is acting to preserve the limits of the forum it has created so that the exclusion of a class of speech is legitimate, we have observed a distinction between, on the one hand, content discrimination, which may be permissible if it preserves the purposes of that limited forum, and, on the other hand, viewpoint discrimination, which is presumed impermissible when directed against speech otherwise within the forum's limitations. . . .

. . .

Based on the principles we have discussed, we hold that the regulation invoked to deny SAF support, both in its terms and in its application to these petitioners, is a denial of their right of free speech guaranteed by the First Amendment. It remains to be considered whether the violation following from the University's action is excused by the necessity of complying with the Constitution's prohibition against state establishment of religion. We turn to that question.

III

. . .

It does not violate the Establishment Clause for a public university to grant access to its facilities on a religion-neutral basis to a wide spectrum of student groups, including groups which use meeting rooms for sectarian activities, accompanied by some devotional exercises. . . . This is so even where the upkeep, maintenance, and repair of the facilities attributed to those uses is paid from a student activities fund to which students are required to contribute. . . . The government usually acts by spending money. Even the provision of a meeting room, as in Mergens, and Widmar, involved governmental expenditure, if only in the form of electricity and heating or cooling costs. The error made by the Court of Appeals, as well as by the dissent, lies in focusing on the money that is undoubtedly expended by the government, rather than on the nature of the benefit received by the recipient. If the expenditure of governmental funds is prohibited whenever those funds pay for a service that is, pursuant to a religion-neutral program, used by a group for sectarian purposes, then Widmar, Mergens and Lamb's Chapel would have to be overruled. Given our holdings in these cases, it follows that a public university may maintain its own computer facility and give student groups access to that facility, including the use of the printers, on a religion neutral, say first-come-first-served, basis. If a religious student organization obtained access on that religion-neutral basis and used a computer to compose or a printer or copy machine to print speech with a religious content or viewpoint, the State's action in providing the group with access would no more violate the Establishment Clause than would giving those groups access to an assembly hall. . . . There is no difference in logic or principle, and no difference of constitutional significance, between a school using its funds to operate a facility to which students have access, and a school paying a third-party contractor to operate the facility on its behalf. The latter occurs here. The University provides printing services to a broad spectrum of student newspapers qualified as CIOs by reason of their officers and membership. Any benefit to religion is incidental to the government's provision of secular services for secular purposes on a religion-neutral basis. Printing is a routine, secular, and recurring attribute of student life.

. . .

> To obey the Establishment Clause, it was not necessary for the University to deny eligibility to student publications because of their viewpoint. The neutrality commanded of the State by the separate Clauses of the First Amendment was compromised by the University's course of action. The viewpoint discrimination inherent in the University's regulation required public officials to scan and interpret student publications to discern their underlying philosophic assumptions respecting religious theory and belief. That course of action was a denial of the right of free speech and would risk fostering a pervasive bias or hostility to religion, which could undermine the very neutrality the Establishment Clause requires. There is no Establishment Clause violation in the University's honoring its duties under the Free Speech Clause.
>
> The judgment of the Court of Appeals must be, and is, reversed.
>
> *It is so ordered.*
>
> [Concurring and dissenting opinions omitted.]

ii. Free Exercise of Religion

Applying the free exercise (of religion) clause, courts will invalidate public action that singles out religion for adverse treatment, or hinders or discriminates against a particular religion.[375] However, the free exercise clause affords no right to a religious exemption from a neutral law that happens to impose a substantial burden on religious practices.[376]

Controversies surrounding the free exercise clause basically break into two halves: What is a religion, and Which religious practices ("exercises") are entitled to constitutional protection? The closest that the Supreme Court has come to defining "religion" has been in the context of construing the Universal Military Training and Selective Service Act, which exempted those "who by reason of their religious training and belief are conscientiously opposed to participation in war in any form."[377] The now defunct law defined "religious training and belief" as "an individual's belief in relation to a Supreme Being involving duties superior to those arising from any human relation, [as opposed to] essentially political, sociological, or philosophical views or a merely personal moral code." In

---

375 Church of the Lukumi Babalu Aye, Inc. v. City of Hialeah, 508 U.S. 520 (1993), declaring unconstitutional a city ordinance that barred ritual sacrifice of animals.

376 Employment Division v. Smith, 494 U.S. 872 (1990), refusing to recognize a constitutional right in the sacramental use of peyote.

377 451 U.S.C. app. § 456.

United States v. Seeger[378] the Supreme Court held that "religious . . . belief" for purposes of this act includes non-theistic beliefs: "We believe that . . . the test of belief 'in a relation to a Supreme Being' is whether a given belief that is sincere and meaningful occupies a place in the life of the possessor parallel to that filled by the orthodox belief in God of one who clearly qualifies for the exemption."[379] The reference to a supreme being in the Selective Service Act was deleted in 1967.

While the following case actually presents the issue as to which religious practices are entitled to constitutional protection, it also contains a fruitful discussion on the issue of what constitutes a religion.

CASE: Wisconsin v. Yoder
406 U.S. 205 (1972)

MR. CHIEF JUSTICE BURGER delivered the opinion of the Court.

. . .

Respondents Jonas Yoder and Wallace Miller are members of the Old Order Amish religion, and respondent Adin Yutzy is a member of the Conservative Amish Mennonite Church. They and their families are residents of Green County, Wisconsin. Wisconsin's compulsory school-attendance law required them to cause their children to attend public or private school until reaching age 16 but the respondents declined to send their children, ages 14 and 15, to public school after they completed the eighth grade. The children were not enrolled in any private school, or within any recognized exception to the compulsory-attendance law, and they are conceded to be subject to the Wisconsin statute.

On complaint of the school district administrator for the public schools, respondents were charged, tried, and convicted of violating the compulsory-attendance law in Green Country Court and were fined the sum of $5 each. Respondents defended on the ground that the application of the compulsory-attendance law violated their rights under the First and Fourteenth Amendments. The trial testimony showed that respondents believed, in accordance with the tenets of Old Order Amish communities generally, that their children's attendance at high school, public or private, was contrary to the Amish religion and way of life. They believed that by sending their children to high school, they would not only expose themselves to the danger of the censure of the church community, but, as found by the county court, also endanger

---

378   380 U.S. 163 (1965).

379   The concurring opinion by Justice Douglas also makes an equal protection argument.

their own salvation and that of their children. The State stipulated that respondents' religious beliefs were sincere.

In support of their position, respondents presented as expert witnesses scholars on religion and education whose testimony is uncontradicted. They expressed their opinions on the relationship of the Amish belief concerning school attendance to the more general tenets of their religion, and described the impact that compulsory high school attendance could have on the continued survival of Amish communities as they exist in the United States today. The history of the Amish sect was given in some detail, beginning with the Swiss Anabaptists of the 16th century who rejected institutionalized churches and sought to return to the early, simple, Christian life de-emphasizing material success, rejecting the competitive spirit, and seeking to insulate themselves from the modern world. As a result of their common heritage, Old Order Amish communities today are characterized by a fundamental belief that salvation requires life in a church community separate and apart from the world and worldly influence. This concept of life aloof from the world and its values is central to their faith.

. . .

I

There is no doubt as to the power of a State, having a high responsibility for education of its citizens, to impose reasonable regulations for the control and duration of basic education. See, e. g., *Pierce v. Society of Sisters*. . . . Providing public schools ranks at the very apex of the function of a State. Yet even this paramount responsibility was, in Pierce, made to yield to the right of parents to provide an equivalent education in a privately operated system. There the Court held that Oregon's statute compelling attendance in a public school from age eight to age 16 unreasonably interfered with the interest of parents in directing the rearing of their offspring, including their education in church-operated schools. As that case suggests, the values of parental direction of the religious upbringing and education of their children in their early and formative years have a high place in our society. . . . Thus, a State's interest in universal education, however highly we rank it, is not totally free from a balancing process when it impinges on fundamental rights and interests, such as those specifically protected by the Free Exercise Clause of the First Amendment, and the traditional interest of parents with respect to the religious upbringing of their children so long as they, in the words of Pierce, "prepare [them] for additional obligations." . . .

. . .

II

We come then to the quality of the claims of the respondents concerning the alleged encroachment of Wisconsin's compulsory school-attendance statute on their rights and the rights of their children to the free exercise of the religious beliefs they and their forebears have adhered to for almost three centuries. In evaluating those claims we must be careful to determine whether the Amish religious faith and their mode of life are, as they claim, inseparable and interdependent. A way of life, however virtuous and admirable, may not be interposed as a barrier to reasonable state regulation of education if it is based on purely secular considerations; to have the protection of the Religion Clauses, the claims must be rooted in religious belief. Although a determination of what is a "religious" belief or practice entitled to constitutional protection may present a most delicate question, the very concept of ordered liberty precludes allowing every person to make his own standards on matters of conduct in which society as a whole has important interests. Thus, if the Amish asserted their claims because of their subjective evaluation and rejection of the contemporary secular values accepted by the majority, much as Thoreau rejected the social values of his time and isolated himself at Walden Pond, their claims would not rest on a religious basis. Thoreau's choice was philosophical and personal rather than religious, and such belief does not rise to the demands of the Religion Clauses.

. . .

In sum, the unchallenged testimony of acknowledged experts in education and religious history, almost 300 years of consistent practice, and strong evidence of a sustained faith pervading and regulating respondents' entire mode of life support the claim that enforcement of the State's requirement of compulsory formal education after the eighth grade would gravely endanger if not destroy the free exercise of respondents' religious beliefs.

III

. . .

We turn, then, to the State's broader contention that its interest in its system of compulsory education is so compelling that even the established religious practices of the Amish must give way. Where fundamental claims of religious freedom are at stake, however, we cannot accept such a sweeping claim; despite its admitted validity in the generality of cases, we must searchingly examine the interests that the State seeks to promote by its requirement for compulsory education to age 16, and the impediment to those objectives that would flow from recognizing the claimed Amish exemption. . . .

The State advances two primary arguments in support of its system of compulsory education. It notes, as Thomas Jefferson pointed out early in our history, that some degree of education is necessary to prepare citizens to participate effectively and intelligently in our open political system if we are to preserve freedom and independence. Further, education prepares individuals to be self-reliant and self-sufficient participants in society. We accept these propositions.

However, the evidence adduced by the Amish in this case is persuasively to the effect that an additional one or two years of formal high school for Amish children in place of their long-established program of informal vocational education would do little to serve those interests. Respondents' experts testified at trial, without challenge, that the value of all education must be assessed in terms of its capacity to prepare the child for life. It is one thing to say that compulsory education for a year or two beyond the eighth grade may be necessary when its goal is the preparation of the child for life in modern society as the majority live, but it is quite another if the goal of education be viewed as the preparation of the child for life in the separated agrarian community that is the keystone of the Amish faith. See *Meyer v. Nebraska*,. . . .

. . .

Affirmed.

[Concurring and dissenting opinions omitted.]

2. Implicit Fundamental Rights

In addition to the rights of speech, press, religion, etc. that are explicitly recognized in the Constitution and its amendments, courts have recognized a whole host of rights that are not directly traceable to a provision in the Constitution. The right to travel is one such right. Another previously mentioned is the right of children of undocumented (illegal) aliens to an education.[380]

Before addressing the question of which implicit rights have been recognized, the discussion will first address the theoretical questions of how and whether they should be recognized.

---

380   See Plyler, 457 U.S. 202 (1982), abstracted above.

a. The Judicial Recognition of Fundamental Rights

The more specific questions of how and whether fundamental rights should be recognized, and more general questions of how the Constitution should be interpreted, have been the subject of an ongoing debate that spanned the 20th century. These debates are summarized below.[381] Note parallels to the debates surrounding "selective incorporation."

Many theories have been advanced for how the constitution *should* be interpreted in general, and how, if at all, fundamental rights should be inferred in particular. At one pole are the originalists.[382] The originalists voice great respect for separation of powers, for federalism, and for democratic institutions. Accordingly, they are more willing than some to tolerate individual cases of apparent injustice. After all, such cases are necessary to ignite public opinion and mobilize the somewhat cumbersome democratic political processes of legislation and of amendment of state and federal constitutions. Originalists abhor abrupt changes in the law. They tend not to recognize implicit constitutional rights unless these were clearly intended by the Framers of the Constitution.

References to the intentions of the Framers of the Constitution are ridiculed by the anti-originalists. The anti-originalists accuse the originalists of wanting to calibrate the present meaning of the Constitution to conform with the intent of the Framers.[383] They point out that the amendment process is not merely cumbersome but positively anti-progressive. They insinuate that the originalists, by advocating democratic amendment of the Constitution, are really just opting for the conservative *status quo*. Anti-originalists want justice now. They are not content to wait for legislators and constitutional amendments. And, as for separation of powers, doesn't that principle exist to promote liberty? And aren't judges the final interpreters of liberty anyway?

While the anti-originalists reach ready consensus when criticizing the originalists, they are not so reliably harmonious when it comes to describing under what circumstances implicit rights can or should be recognized. Some advocate the importation of natural law principles.[384] Others look to moral consensus.[385] Still another would limit the judicial expansion of rights to the subject matter areas of procedure and equal protection.[386] No one seems willing openly to defend the position at the polar extreme of the originalists', that is, that an implicit fundamental right is anything that a majority of the Supreme Court says it is on any certain day. Consider the following statement of Supreme Court Justice Charles Evans Hughes: "We are under a Constitution, but the Constitution is what the

---

381   See generally Chemerinsky, Constitutional Law at pp. 15-25.

382   See, e.g., Bork.

383   See, e.g., Ely at p. 18.

384   E.g., Jaffa.

385   E.g., Simon.

386   See Ely at p. 87.

judges say it is, and the judiciary is the safeguard of our liberty and of our property under the Constitution."[387]

Despite the protestations and warnings of the originalists, courts have continued to "find" new fundamental rights in the Constitution without having a coherent theory for doing so. These rights are summarized in the following discussion.

b. Privacy and Other Implicit Rights

In the first third of the last century, the Supreme Court deemed economic rights, such as the right to contract, to be fundamental. As a consequence, much social welfare legislation was ruled unconstitutional. The most infamous of these rulings is *Lochner v. New York*,[388] which held that a law regulating the working hours of bakers unreasonably interfered with "the freedom of master and employee to contract in relation to their employment." The shift away from protecting economic rights coincided with President Roosevelt's announcement of his "Court Packing Plan."[389] *Lochner* was abandoned in *West Coast Hotel v. Parrish*,[390] which upheld a state minimum wage law for women.

For decades after the demise of *Lochner*, courts took a back seat to state and federal legislators on economic, social, and personal matters that did not impinge upon explicit constitutional rights. But in the mid 1960s, judges again felt the responsibility to protect implicit constitutional rights. This time, however, they eschewed economic rights for the most part (commercial speech is an exception) and embraced the protection of the rights of the criminally accused (not discussed in this book) and certain "personal" rights.

In *Griswold v. Connecticut*[391] the Supreme Court recognized a fundamental right to privacy, to date the most expansive of the personal, fundamental rights recognized by the Supreme Court. The Supreme Court's opinion in *Griswold*, which was penned by Justice Douglas, expressly rejected relegation of privacy to the discredited concept of "liberty." Rather, Justice Douglas found that privacy was implicit in the First, Third, Fourth, and Fifth Amendments:

> [S]pecific guarantees in the Bill of Rights have penumbras, formed by emanations from those guarantees that help give them life and substance. Various guarantees create zones of privacy. . . . We have had many controversies over these penumbral rights of privacy and repose. These cases bear witness that the right of privacy which presses for recognition here is a legitimate one.[392]

---

387   Hughes at pp. 139-140

388   198 U.S. 45 (1905).

389   See United States v. Carolene Products Co., 304 U.S. 144, 152 at n. 4 (1938), which inaugurated the age of multi-level review.

390   300 U.S. 379 (1937).

391   381 U.S. 479 (1965).

392   At pp. 484-485.

The list of implicit fundamental due process rights is a fairly long one, and the list appears to be growing. It includes the right to be a candidate for elective office,[393] the right to abort a pregnancy,[394] the right to procreate,[395] the right to purchase and use contraceptives,[396] the right to view pornography in one's own home,[397] the right to marry,[398] the right to reject medical treatment,[399] the right to keep one's family together,[400] the right to educate one's children as one chooses,[401] including the right to send one's children to a German-language school,[402] and the right of access to courts,[403] although this last right might be subsumed under the explicit First Amendment right to petition government for a redress of grievances.

The above list of implicit fundamental rights is not exhaustive. It should also be augmented by fundamental rights guaranteed to those suspected, accused, and convicted of crimes, although sometimes these find textual support in the Constitution,[404] and therefore belong in the list of explicit fundamental rights.

CASE: Roe v. Wade
410 U.S. 113 (1973)

MR. JUSTICE BLACKMUN delivered the opinion of the Court.

This [appeal presents] constitutional challenges to state criminal abortion legislation. The Texas statutes under attack here [make procuring an abortion a crime except "by medical advice for the purpose of saving the life of the mother." These statutes] are typical of those that have been in effect in many States for approximately a century. . . .

We forthwith acknowledge our awareness of the sensitive and emotional nature of the abortion controversy, of the vigorous opposing views, even among physicians, and of the deep and seemingly absolute convictions that the subject inspires. . . .

---

393   Lubin v. Parrish, 415 U.S. 709 (1974).

394   Roe v. Wade, 410 U.S. 113 (1973).

395   Skinner v. Oklahoma, 316 U.S. 535 (1942).

396   Griswold v. Connecticut, 381 U.S. 479 (1965).

397   Stanley v. Georgia, 394 U.S. 557 (1969).

398   Loving v. Virginia, 388 U.S. 1 (1976).

399   Cruzan v. Director, 497 U.S. 261 (1990).

400   Moore v. City of East Cleveland, 431 U.S. 494 (1977).

401   Pierce v. Society of Sisters, 268 U.S. 510 (1925).

402   Meyer v. Nebraska, 262 U.S. 390 (1923).

403   Bounds v. Smith, 430 U.S. 817 (1977).

404   E.g., In re Winship, 397 U.S. 358 (1970), requiring proof beyond a reasonable doubt.

Our task, of course, is to resolve the issue by constitutional measurement, free of emotion and of predilection. We seek earnestly to do this, and, because we do, we have inquired into, and in this opinion place some emphasis upon, medical and medical-legal history and what that history reveals about man's attitudes toward the abortion procedure over the centuries. . . .

[The] restrictive criminal abortion laws in effect in a majority of States today are of relatively recent vintage. [They] derive from statutory changes effected, for the most part, in the latter half of the 19th century.

[Abortion] was practiced in Greek times as well as in the Roman Era. [Most] Greek thinkers [commended] abortion, at least prior to viability. [At] common law, abortion performed *before* "quickening"—the first recognizable movement of the fetus in utero, appearing usually from the 16th to the 18th week of pregnancy—was not an indictable offense. [It] was not until [the] middle and late 19th century [that] the quickening distinction [was abandoned] and the degree of the offense [increased]. [Thus,] at common law, at the time of the adoption of our Constitution, and throughout the major portion of the 19th century, [a] woman enjoyed a substantially broader right to terminate a pregnancy than she does in most States today. . . .

Three reasons have been advanced to explain historically the enactment of criminal abortion laws in the 19th century and to justify their continued existence.

It has been argued occasionally that these laws were [designed] to discourage illicit sexual conduct. Texas, however, does not advance this justification in the present case. . . .

A second reason is concerned with abortion as a medical procedure. When most criminal abortion laws were first enacted, the procedure was [hazardous]. [Thus,] it has been argued that a State's real concern in enacting a criminal abortion law was to protect the pregnant woman. [Modern] medical techniques have altered this situation. [Mortality] rates for women undergoing early abortions, where the procedure is legal, appear to be as low as or lower than the rates for normal childbirth. [Of] course, important state interests in the areas of health and medical standards do remain. The State has a legitimate interest in seeing to it that abortion, like any other medical procedure, is performed under circumstances that insure maximum safety for the patient [and] the State retains a definite interest in protecting the woman's own health and safety when an abortion is proposed at a late stage of pregnancy.

The third reason is the State's interest [in] protecting prenatal life. Some of the argument for this justification rests on the theory that a new human life is present from the moment of conception. [But in] assessing the State's interest, recognition may [also] be given to the less rigid claim that [at] least *potential* life is involved. . . .

The Constitution does not explicitly mention any right of privacy. [But] the Court has recognized that a right of personal privacy, or a guarantee of certain areas or zones of privacy, does exist under the Constitution. In varying contexts, the Court or individual Justices have, indeed, found at least the roots of that right in the First Amendment, *Stanley v. Georgia* . . . ; in the Fourth and Fifth Amendments; in the penumbras of the Bill of Rights [Griswold]; in the Ninth Amendment, id., (Goldberg, J., concurring); or in the concept of liberty guaranteed by the first section of the Fourteenth Amendment, see *Meyer v. Nebraska*. These decisions make it clear that only personal rights that can be deemed "fundamental" or "implicit in the concept of ordered liberty," are included in this guarantee of personal privacy. They also make it clear that the right has some extension to activities relating to marriage, *Loving v. Virginia* . . . ; procreation, [Skinner]; contraception, [Eisenstadt]; family relationships, *Prince v. Massachusetts* . . . ; and child rearing and education [Pierce; Meyer].

This right of privacy, whether it be founded in the Fourteenth Amendment's concept of personal liberty [as] we feel it is, or [in] the Ninth [Amendment,] is broad enough to encompass a woman's decision whether or not to terminate her pregnancy. The detriment that the State would impose upon the pregnant woman by denying this choice altogether is apparent. Specific and direct harm medically diagnosable even in early pregnancy may be involved. Maternity, or additional offspring, may force upon the woman a distressful life and future. Psychological harm may be imminent. Mental and physical health may be taxed by child care. There is also the distress, for all concerned, associated with the unwanted child, and there is the problem of bringing a child into a family already unable, psychologically and otherwise, to care for it. In other cases, as in this one, the additional difficulties and continuing stigma of unwed motherhood may be involved. All these are factors the woman and her responsible physician necessarily will consider in consultation.

On the basis of elements such as these, appellant [argues] that the woman's right is absolute and that she is entitled to terminate her pregnancy at whatever time, in whatever way, and for whatever reason she alone chooses. With this we do not agree. [The] Court's decisions recognizing a right of privacy also acknowledge that some state regulation in areas protected by that right is appropriate. . . .

Where certain "fundamental rights" are involved, the Court has held that regulation limiting these rights may be justified only by a "compelling state interest," and that legislative enactments must be narrowly drawn to express only the legitimate state interests at stake. . . .

The appellee [argues] that the fetus is a "person" within the language and meaning of the Fourteenth Amendment. [If] this suggestion of personhood is established, the appellant's case, of course, collapses, for the fetus' right to life would then be guaranteed specifically by the Amendment. . . .

The Constitution does not define "person" in so many words. Section 1 of the Fourteenth Amendment contains three references to "person." ["Person"] is used in other places in the Constitution: in the listing of qualifications for Representatives and Senators, Art. I, § 2, cl. 2, and § 3, cl. 3; in the Apportionment Clause, Art. I, § 2, cl. 3; in the Migration and Importation provision, Art. I, § 9, cl. 1; in the Emolument Clause, Art. I, § 9, cl. 8; in the Electors provisions, Art. II, § 1, cl. 2, and the superseded cl. 3; in the provision outlining qualifications for the office of President, Art. II, § 1, cl. 5; in the Extradition provisions, Art. IV, § 2, cl. 2, and the superseded Fugitive Slave Clause 3; and in the Fifth, Twelfth, and Twenty-second Amendments, as well as in §§ 2 and 3 of the Fourteenth Amendment. But in nearly all these instances, the use of the word is such that it has application only post-natally. None indicates, with any assurance, that it has any possible pre-natal application. . . .

Texas urges that, apart from the Fourteenth Amendment, life begins at conception and is present throughout pregnancy, and that, therefore, the State has a compelling interest in protecting that life from and after conception. We need not resolve the difficult question of when life begins. When those trained [in] medicine, philosophy, and theology are unable to arrive at any consensus, the judiciary, at this point in the development of man's knowledge, is not in a position to speculate as to the answer.

It should be sufficient to note briefly the wide divergence of thinking on this most sensitive and difficult question. There has always been strong support for the view that life does not begin until live birth. This was the belief of the Stoics. It appears to be the predominant, though not the unanimous, attitude of the Jewish faith. It may be taken to represent also the position of a large segment of the Protestant community. [The] common law found greater significance in quickening. Physicians and their scientific colleagues [tended] to focus either upon conception, upon live birth, or upon the interim point at which the fetus becomes "viable," that is, potentially able to live outside the mother's womb, albeit with artificial aid. Viability is usually placed at about seven months (28 weeks) but may occur earlier, even at 24 weeks. [The Catholic church recognizes] the existence of life from the moment of conception. . . .

In areas other than criminal abortion [such as torts and inheritance], the law has been reluctant to endorse any theory that life, as we recognize it, begins before live birth or to accord legal rights to the unborn except in narrowly defined situations and except when the rights are contingent upon live birth. . . .

In view of all this, we do not agree that, by adopting one theory of life, Texas may override the rights of the pregnant woman that are at stake. We repeat, however, that the State does have an important and legitimate interest in preserving and protecting the health of the pregnant woman [and] that it has still *another* important and legitimate interest in protecting the potentiality of human life. These interests are separate and distinct. Each grows in substantiality as the woman approaches term and, at a point during pregnancy, each becomes "compelling."

With respect to [the] interest in the health of the mother, the "compelling" point, in the light of present medical knowledge, is at approximately the end of the first trimester. This is so because of the now-established medical fact [that] until the end of the first trimester mortality in abortion may be less than mortality in normal childbirth. It follows that, from and after this point, a State may regulate the abortion procedure to the extent that the regulation reasonably relates to the preservation and protection of maternal health. Examples of permissible state regulation in this area are requirements as to the qualifications of the person who is to perform the abortion; [as] to the facility in which the procedure is to be performed; [and] the like.

This means, on the other hand, that, for the period of pregnancy prior to this "compelling" point, the attending physician, in consultation with his patient, is free to determine, without regulation by the State, that, in his medical judgment, the patient's pregnancy should be terminated. If that decision is reached, the judgment may be effectuated by an abortion free of interference by the State.

With respect to [the] interest in potential life, the "compelling" point is at viability. This is so because the fetus then presumably has the capability of meaningful life outside the mother's womb. State regulation protective of fetal life after viability thus has both logical and biological justifications. If the State is interested in protecting fetal life after viability, it may go so far as to proscribe abortion during that period, except when it is necessary to preserve the life or health of the mother.

Measured against these standards, [the Texas statute] sweeps too broadly [and] therefore, cannot survive the constitutional attack made upon it here. . . .

To summarize and to repeat: . . .

(a) For the stage prior to approximately the end of the first trimester, the abortion decision and its effectuation must be left to the medical judgment of the pregnant woman's attending physician.

(b) For the stage subsequent to approximately the end of the first trimester, the State, in promoting its interest in the health of the mother, may, if it chooses, regulate the abortion procedure in ways that are reasonably related to maternal health.

(c) For the stage subsequent to viability, the State in promoting its interest in the potentiality of human life may, if it chooses, regulate, and even proscribe, abortion except where it is necessary, in appropriate medical judgment, for the preservation of the life or health of the mother. . . .

This holding, we feel, is consistent with the relative weights of the respective interests involved, with the lessons and examples of medical and legal history, with the lenity of the common law, and with the demands of the profound problems of the present day. . . .

[Concurring and dissenting opinions omitted.]

Subpart B: Equality (Equal Protection)

Like due process, equal protection is about rights. In the context of due process, the interests of the state, which represents the majority, are seen as conflicting with the rights of individuals. Under equal protection, on the other hand, the individual claims rights as a member of a group. Both liberty and equality rights are anti-democratic in the sense that they curb what the majority may do.

Equality in a literal sense is not articulated in the original Constitution, nor in the Bill of Rights. Commentators are fond of attributing this apparent inadequacy to the racism and sexism of the Founding Fathers. Yet all those who fathered the Constitution also backed the Declaration of Independence (Attach. A), and this document lauds equality before liberty:

We hold these truths to be self-evident: That all men are created equal. That they are endowed by their Creator with certain unalienable rights.

Further, while the Constitution and the Bill of Rights do not contain a sweeping declaration of equal protection, it is not true that the original Constitution turns a deaf ear to equality. The privileges and immunities clause, for example, ensures that states will not discriminate against citizens of other states.[405] Article IV, section 2 also contains the now superseded prohibition against depriving the class of slave owners of their property in slaves. The Constitution prevents the anti-egalitarian practice of granting titles of nobility.[406] And there are numerous protections of the equality of the states, including the only provision of the Constitution that, by its terms, cannot be amended without consent: the equal representation of each state in the Senate.[407]

This is not to deny that the social milieu and prejudices of the people had no impact on the Framers. On the contrary, the Framers undoubtedly thought of themselves as a fairly homogeneous lot, joined in their opposition to imperial domination. Their factions were geographical, political, and ecclesiastical. Not surprisingly, rights protecting state citizenship and political and religious beliefs found their way into the Bill of Rights. The Framers would have protested mightily had they been "discriminated against" on the basis of religious beliefs. The American Colonists certainly objected that their voting rights were marginalized in the English Parliament ("No taxation without representation"). In other words, if the American society of the 18th century had valued, for example, homosexuality, then homosexuality could, and perhaps would, have been explicitly protected by the Bill of Rights.

The reverse side of the same historical coin is that, had the Bill of Rights contained a guaranty of equality, this guaranty would not automatically have rendered unconstitutional classifications based on race, status, gender, sexual orientation, age, foreign citizenship, place of birth, wealth, intelligence, health, disability, etc. For example, the Constitution makes explicit distinctions based on race,[408] status as slave,[409] national citizenship,[410] place of birth,[411] and age.[412] (There is no comparable textual disability based on gender or sexual orientation.) In addition, statutory, administrative, and common law necessarily make hundreds of thousands of distinctions between people, rewarding some, and burdening or "discriminating against" others. To cite just a few examples, laws allow or require unequal treatment based on wealth (progressive income tax), intelligence, height, and disability (exemption from military conscription), and mental and bodily health (institutionalization and quarantine). Penal and other laws regulating behavior "discriminate" against those who behave contrary to

---

405   Art. IV, § 2, cl. 1.
406   Art. I, § 9, cl. 8 and § 10, cl. 1.
407   Art. V.
408   Art. I, § 2, cl. 3.
409   Art. I, § 2, cl. 3.
410   Art. I, § 3, cl. 3.
411   Art. II, § 1, cl. 5.
412   Art. I, § 2, cl. 2.

majoritarian will. Even non-volitional behavior can be subject to sanction, as in tort liability for negligence or, more pointedly, for strict liability. In other words, an equal protection clause does not tell politicians, bureaucrats, and judges what factors may, what factors shall, and what factors shall not be considered in making differentiations between people. Even discrimination based on race is not necessarily incompatible with an equal protection clause: the Virginia Declaration of Rights of 1776 contained an equal protection clause, and Virginia was a slave-owning state.[413]

There is probably a fundamental philosophical reason why neither the Bill of Rights nor the Constitution explicitly protects equality under the law. As was seen in Part One of this book, the Framers were concerned with constructing a new superstate. Their leitmotif was to bridle this new state, to check its powers, to limit intrusions into liberty. Separating powers horizontally and vertically serves this goal. So does the explicit recognition of fundamental rights. Equality rights, on the other hand, do not conceptually reduce the power of the state to interfere with liberty. Rather, equality rights act to diffuse the governmental intrusion, to spread it over more people. Said crassly, equality does not demand that government leave us alone. That's the mission of liberty. Equality insists that government leave me alone unless it also picks on you. When the government will not or cannot do this, invalidation results. But invalidation is the incidental effect, not the theoretical purpose, of equality.

This essential dispersing aspect of equality means that equality functions as private law in the sense that it adjusts private rights and obligations *inter se*. The most obvious examples arise out of the direct application of the equal protection clause to private conduct, such as the invalidation of the race-based covenant in *Shelley v. Kraemer.*[414] But examples are by no means confined to this small sphere. If laws impose burdens only on particular groups, then the lifting of those burdens through the medium of equal protection restores equilibrium among private rights. Similarly, if a government program denies benefits to particular groups, the judicial extension of the program to include those groups in effect conforms the distribution of those benefits to the expectations of those private actors who consider themselves constitutionally identical (equal) to those who initially received benefits.

Friedrich Hayek[415] championed the recognition that equality and liberty are at odds with each other. The more society insists on equal treatment, the less people are free to do what they want to do.[416] This observation is not as profound as it first might sound, for in effect it is defining "equality" as state regulation of conduct heretofore considered private, and defining "liberty" as the freedom to

---

413   Hall at pp. 69-70.
414   334 U.S. 1 (1948).
415   Hayek at p. 84.
416   Fletcher at p. 126.

discriminate in private transactions. But this is just one small part of liberty. Further, the alleged conflict between liberty and equality does not necessarily make the protection of equality undesirable. Almost every private law diminishes liberty in the sense that Hayek is talking about.[417] Laws that regulate the landlord-tenant relationship diminish landlords' choices. Laws prescribing that certain actions be in writing, such as wills, diminish freedom in the same sense. Traffic laws impose limitations on freedom. To repeat, liberty is not synonymous with "good" any more than equality is. Neither liberty nor equality enjoys a monopoly on justice.[418]

Government has undergone a dramatic change in function in the last half century or more. In earlier times the federal, state, and local governments provided only essential public services. National defense, uniform currency, etc. were guaranteed by the federal government. State governments supplied regional services, such as justice systems, water projects, and highways. Local governments funded schools, streets, and utilities, to name just a few. As the United States grew wealthy, governments assumed the role of redistributing wealth and of bestowing social benefits far and above those historically possible. This expansion of government caused a metamorphosis in the importance of rights, leading to immense growth in the prominence of equal protection. Whereas traditionally the government was an institution which could, for the most part, only take, in recent years it has become an institution which gives more and more. This extraordinary transformation has, more than anything else, accounted for the ascendancy of equality over liberty in the popular and legal mind.

1. Discrimination

A number of theories have been advanced to help recognize factors relevant to equal protection. These typically attempt to identify what factors cannot constitutionally be considered by law makers, since the opposite approach—the articulation of all factors that might constitutionally be considered—is hopelessly multifarious. Thus, for this very practical reason, equal protection has come to mean the absence of illegal discrimination.

Some theorists build on Justice Stone's famous footnote four in *United States v. Carolene Products Co.*[419] that decries "prejudice against discrete and insular minorities . . . which tends . . . to curtail the operation of those political processes

---

417 .Hayek is championing *laissez faire*, which he terms "liberty." As the beginning of The Constitution of Liberty exclaims: "We are concerned in this book with that condition of men in which coercion of some by others is reduced as much as is possible in society. This state we shall describe throughout as a state of liberty or freedom." Hayek at p. 11.

418 As developed and illustrated below, all liberty rights can be recast as equality rights; and, as such, their recognition too must, according to the alleged zero-sumness of liberty versus equality, be reducing liberty.

419 304 U.S. 144, 152-153 (1938).

ordinarily to be relied upon to protect minorities."[420] Other theorists endorse a nebulous "anti-subjugation principle," also called the "group-disadvantaging principle."[421] This principle holds that governmental rules, policies, and practices are unconstitutional if they perennially reinforce the subordinate status of any group.[422] Poetic support for the anti-subjugation principle is found in Justice Brennan's observation in *Zobel v. Williams*[423] that the "citizenship clause of the fourteenth amendment . . . does not allow for degrees of citizenship." (Does this mean that mentally retarded citizens must be allowed to vote, sit on juries, procreate, etc. to the same degree as others?)

Equal protection is difficult to distinguish from due process. Part of the confusion is due to the Supreme Court's avoidance of due process terminology ("rights talk"), which is perceived as having been discredited since *Lochner*.[424] Perhaps as a consequence of this perception, the Supreme Court employed equal protection rather than due process in *Loving v. Virginia*[425] to strike down a law prohibiting interracial marriage. Another reason why equality confounds with liberty is that due process rights can be analyzed from an equality standpoint, and *vice versa*. For example, Eichman, who burned an American flag, can be thought to have been "discriminated against" because those who burned flags of other countries were not punished.[426] Brandenburg, who made disparaging remarks about blacks and Jews, was singled out for prosecution, while those who made supportive remarks were not.[427] Yoder was discriminated against, one might say, for not sending his child to school.[428] Conversely, the issue in equal protection cases can be rephrased in terms of rights talk. The J.A. Croson Company enjoyed a right, one could say, to bid on contracts with the City of Richmond,[429] and this right was unconstitutionally impinged by requiring Croson to subcontract 30 percent of the contract to minorities. Yick Wo can be said to have had a right to exercise his profession as a laundry operator and consequently enjoyed a right to an exemption from the requirement that laundries operate only in brick buildings.[430]

---

420   E.g., Ely.

421   E.g., Tribe at pp. 1515-1516.

422   Fiss at pp. 148-156.

423   457 U.S. 66, 69 (1982).

424   See, e.g., Williamson v. Lee Optical Co., 348 U.S. 483 (1955).

425   388 U.S. 1 (1967).

426   United States v. Eichman, 496 U.S. 310 (1990). See Nowack & Rotunda, § 16.11 at p.956, noting that a violation of the First Amendment may also violate equal protection.

427   Brandenburg v. Ohio, 395 U.S. 444 (1969).

428   Wisconsin v. Yoder, 406 U.S. 205 (1972).

429   City of Richmond v. J.A. Croson Co., 488 U.S. 469 (1989), abstracted below.

430   Yick Wo v. Hopkins, 118 U.S. 356 (1886).

Luckily for lawyers and judges (and students), the Supreme Court employs the same decisional matrix for alleged violations of equal protection as it does for alleged violations of due process rights. Accordingly, almost all "discriminations" are judged by the rational basis standard. As a practical matter, it makes no difference whether the plaintiff's argument is couched in terms of liberty or equality. As a result, challenges to governmental actions are increasingly being brought on both equal protection and due process grounds.[431]

Perhaps a few additional examples are in order to illustrate this point. In *Kelley v. Johnson*,[432] the Supreme Court heard a complaint from a policeman who claimed a right to grow his hair as long as he wanted. He might just as well have argued that he was being discriminated against as a member of a group of men who belonged to a long-haired counterculture. Either way the courts would subject his claim to "minimal scrutiny." In *Bowers v. Hardwick*[433] the petitioner challenged a state law that made sodomy illegal. He claimed that he had a constitutional right to sodomize his boyfriend in the privacy of his home. He might as well have argued, but did not, that the law discriminated against him as a homosexual male because he engaged in this behavior. Either way, minimum scrutiny would still be used to judge his challenge.

The equal protection clause is found in the last clause of section 1 of the 14th Amendment:

> No State shall . . . deny any person within its jurisdiction the equal protection of the laws.

The equal protection clause of the 14th Amendment is thus textually directed to the states, not to the federal government. The historical reason for this is that the 14th Amendment, like the other Civil War Amendments (13th and 15th), was aimed at eradicating the institution of slavery, which only existed in state law. The 13th Amendment specifically abolished slavery. The 14th and 15th Amendments dealt with the anticipated reluctance of the former slave states to submit to the will of the vast majority of Americans. Thus, the 14th Amendment makes "[a]ll persons born in the United States . . . citizens of the United States and of the State wherein they reside." The 15th Amendment adds the arguably superfluous provision that "the right of citizens of the United States to vote shall not be denied or abridged by the United States or by any State on account of race, color, or previous condition of servitude."

The Supreme Court has interpreted the due process clause of the Fifth Amendment to contain an equal protection clause directed at the federal government.[434]

---

431   E.g., Washington v. Glucksberg, 521 U.S. 702 n. 3 (1997), City of Chicago v. Int'l College of Surgeons, 522 U.S. 156 (1997), and Campbell v. Louisiana, 523 U.S. 392 (1998).

432   425 U.S. 238 (1976).

433   478 U.S. 573 (1986).

434   See Bolling v. Sharpe, 347 U.S. 497 (1954).

The content of the federal and state protections are not necessarily identical, however.[435]

a. *De jure* Discrimination

The reigning doctrine of the Supreme Court looks not to the discriminatory effect of governmental action, but to its purpose, and asks if the purpose is to discriminate "invidiously."[436] According to the Supreme Court, intentional or "*de jure*" discrimination can be explicit in the governmental action (discriminatory "on its face"), or it may be implicit in the action if its enactment or enforcement is tainted by an invidious purpose. The discussion below follows this distinction.

i. Explicit Discriminations

Explicit discriminations are relatively easy to spot. Consider, for example, the following case.

On March 21, 1942, Congress enacted legislation making it a crime to violate an order issued by a military commander pursuant to specific authority. Three days later, the military commander of the western defense command ordered imposition of a curfew on all persons of Japanese ancestry living on the West Coast.

On May 3, 1942, the same military commander issued an exclusion order, requiring persons of Japanese descent, whether or not they were United States citizens, to leave their homes on the West Coast and report to "Assembly Centers." While some detainees were released from these centers on condition that they remain outside the prohibited zone, others were shipped to "Relocation Centers," which they were not allowed to leave without permission of the military commander.

Korematsu, a US citizen of Japanese descent, was tried and convicted of remaining in his home contrary to the exclusion order.

CASE: Korematsu v. United States
323 U.S. 214 (1944)

MR. JUSTICE BLACK delivered the opinion of the Court.

. . .

It should be noted, to begin with, that all legal restrictions which curtail the civil rights of a single racial group are immediately suspect. That is not to say that all such restrictions are unconstitutional. It is to say that courts must subject them to the most rigid scrutiny. Pressing public necessity may sometimes justify the existence of such restrictions; racial antagonism never can. . . .

---

435 Hampton v. Mow Sun Wong, 426 U.S. 88 (1976).
436 Washington v. Davis, 426 U.S. 229 (1976).

In the light of the principles we announced in the Hirabayashi case, we are unable to conclude that it was beyond the war power of Congress and the Executive to exclude those of Japanese ancestry from the West Coast war area at the time they did. True, exclusion from the area in which one's home is located is a far greater deprivation than constant confinement to the home from 8 p.m. to 6 a.m. [as in Hirabayashi]. Nothing short of apprehension by the proper military authorities of the gravest imminent danger to the public safety can constitutionally justify either. But exclusion from a threatened area, no less than curfew, has a definite and close relationship to the prevention of espionage and sabotage. The military authorities, charged with the primary responsibility of defending our shores, concluded that curfew provided inadequate protection and ordered exclusion. . . .

Here, as in the Hirabayashi case,

> . . . we cannot reject as unfounded the judgment of the military authorities and of Congress that there were disloyal members of that population, whose number and strength could not be precisely and quickly ascertained. We cannot say that the war-making branches of the Government did not have ground for believing that in a critical hour such persons could not readily be isolated and separately dealt with, and constituted a menace to the national defense and safety, which demanded that prompt and adequate measures be taken to guard against it.

Like curfew, exclusion of those of Japanese origin was deemed necessary because of the presence of an unascertained number of disloyal members of the group, most of whom we have no doubt were loyal to this country. It was because we could not reject the finding of the military authorities that it was impossible to bring about an immediate segregation of the disloyal from the loyal that we sustained the validity of the curfew order as applying to the whole group. In the instant case, temporary exclusion of the entire group was rested by the military on the same ground. The judgment that exclusion of the whole group was for the same reason a military imperative answers the contention that the exclusion was in the nature of group punishment based on antagonism to those of Japanese origin. That there were members of the group who retained loyalties to Japan has been confirmed by investigations made subsequent to the exclusion. Approximately five thousand American citizens of Japanese ancestry refused to swear unqualified allegiance to the United States and to renounce allegiance to the Japanese Emperor, and several thousand evacuees requested repatriation to Japan.

We uphold the exclusion order as of the time it was made and when the petitioner violated it. [In] doing so, we are not unmindful of the hardships imposed by it upon a large group of

American citizens. But hardships are part of war, and war is an aggregation of hardships. All citizens alike, both in and out of uniform, feel the impact of war in greater or lesser measure. Citizenship has its responsibilities as well as its privileges, and in time of war the burden is always heavier. Compulsory exclusion of large groups of citizens from their homes, except under circumstances of direst emergency and peril, is inconsistent with our basic governmental institutions. But when under conditions of modern warfare our shores are threatened by hostile forces, the power to protect must be commensurate with the threatened danger. . . .

It is said that we are dealing here with the case of imprisonment of a citizen in a concentration camp solely because of his ancestry, without evidence or inquiry concerning his loyalty and good disposition towards the United States. Our task would be simple, our duty clear, were this a case involving the imprisonment of a loyal citizen in a concentration camp because of racial prejudice. Regardless of the true nature of the assembly and relocation centers—and we deem it unjustifiable to call them concentration camps with all the ugly connotations that term implies—we are dealing specifically with nothing but an exclusion order. To cast this case into outlines of racial prejudice, without reference to the real military dangers which were presented, merely confuses the issue. Korematsu was not excluded from the Military Area because of hostility to him or his race. He was excluded because we are at war with the Japanese Empire, because the properly constituted military authorities feared an invasion of our West Coast and felt constrained to take proper security measures, because they decided that the military urgency of the situation demanded that all citizens of Japanese ancestry be segregated from the West Coast temporarily, and finally, because Congress, reposing its confidence in this time of war in our military leaders—as inevitably it must—determined that they should have the power to do just this. There was evidence of disloyalty on the part of some, the military authorities considered that the need for action was great, and time was short. We cannot—by availing ourselves of the calm perspective of hindsight—now say that at that time these actions were unjustified.

Affirmed.

Mr. Justice Jackson, dissenting. . . .

It would be impracticable and dangerous idealism to expect or insist that each specific military command in an area of probable operations will conform to conventional tests of constitutionality. When an area is so beset that it must be put under military control at all, the paramount consideration is that its measures be successful, rather than legal. . . .

But if we cannot confine military expedients by the Constitution, neither would I distort the Constitution to approve all that the military may deem expedient. This is what the Court appears to be doing, whether consciously or not. . . .

. . .

Much is said of the danger to liberty from the Army program for deporting and detaining these citizens of Japanese extraction. But a judicial construction of the due process clause that will sustain this order is a far more subtle blow to liberty than the promulgation of the order itself. A military order, however unconstitutional, is not apt to last longer than the military emergency. Even during that period a succeeding commander may revoke it all. But once a judicial opinion rationalizes such an order to show that it conforms to the Constitution, or rather rationalizes the Constitution to show that the Constitution sanctions such an order, the Court for all time has validated the principle of racial discrimination in criminal procedure and of transplanting American citizens. The principle then lies about like a loaded weapon ready for the hand of any authority that can bring forward a plausible claim of an urgent need. Every repetition imbeds that principle more deeply in our law and thinking and expands it to new purposes. . . .

I should hold that a civil court cannot be made to enforce an order which violates constitutional limitations even if it is a reasonable exercise of military authority. The courts can exercise only the judicial power, can apply only law, and must abide by the Constitution, or they cease to be civil courts and become instruments of military policy.

Of course the existence of a military power resting on force, so vagrant, so centralized, so necessarily heedless of the individual, is an inherent threat to liberty. But I would not lead people to rely on this Court for a review that seems to me wholly delusive. The military reasonableness of these orders can only be determined by military superiors. If the people ever let command of the war power fall into irresponsible and unscrupulous hands, the courts wield no power equal to its restraint. The chief restraint upon those who command the physical forces of the country, in the future as in the past, must be their responsibility to the political judgments of their contemporaries and to the moral judgments of history.

My duties as a justice as I see them do not require me to make a military judgment as to whether General DeWitt's evacuation and detention program was a reasonable military necessity. I do not suggest that the courts should have attempted to interfere with the Army in carrying out its task. But I do not think they may be asked to execute a military expedient that has no place in law under the Constitution I would reverse the judgment and discharge the prisoner.

[A concurring opinion and two dissenting opinions are omitted.]

Both the Japanese evacuation and the decision in *Korematsu* have been roundly criticized.[437] In 1984 a federal judge overturned Korematsu's conviction on the ground that the government had knowingly withheld information from the courts.[438] Four years later Congress acknowledged "the fundamental injustice" of the evacuation, and provided restitution.[439] *Korematsu* was the last occasion on which the Supreme Court upheld a measure intentionally disadvantaging a racial minority.

To this point the discussion has mostly talked about state action that "penalizes" or "discriminates against" members of groups. But what of legislation that confers benefits? What of government programs that grant scholarships only to good students, confer tax exemptions on parents, and reserve welfare to the truly needy? (Incidentally, these can also be seen as penalizing poor students, non-parents, and the wealthy, respectively.) As should be clear from the discussion so far, each of these governmental actions will be judged under minimum scrutiny because they do not penalize a suspect or quasi-suspect class. That means, assuming the action is not *ultra vires*, that the program will be upheld if it "reasonably" or "rationally" furthers the relevant governmental goal.

What of programs that benefit only members of suspect classes? How about a state scholarship program limited to African Americans, or a statute exempting Japanese or Roman Catholic Americans from capital punishment, or providing that Jews need only work 20 hour weeks in federal jobs for the same pay? (Incidentally, these can also be seen as penalizing non-African Americans, non-Japanese, non-Roman Catholics, and non-Jews, respectively.) Must they too withstand strict scrutiny? That was the question before the Supreme Court in the following case.

CASE: City of Richmond v. J.A. Croson Co.
488 U.S. 469 (1989)

JUSTICE O'CONNOR announced the judgment of the Court and delivered the opinion of the Court with respect to Parts I, III-B, and IV, an opinion with respect to Part II, in which THE CHIEF JUSTICE [REHNQUIST] and JUSTICE WHITE join, and an opinion with respect to Parts III-A and V, in which THE CHIEF JUSTICE [REHNQUIST], JUSTICE WHITE, and JUSTICE KENNEDY join. . . .

---

437   E.g., Daniels.

438   Korematsu v. United States, 584 F.Supp. 1406 (N.D. Cal. 1984).

439   102 Stat. 903 (1988).

I

[The Minority Business Enterprise] Plan[440] was adopted by the Richmond City Council after a public hearing. . . . Seven members of the public spoke to the merits of the ordinance: five were in opposition, two in favor. Proponents of the set-aside provision relied on a study which indicated that, while the general population of Richmond was 50% black, only 0.67% of the city's prime construction contracts had been awarded to minority businesses in the 5-year period from 1978 to 1983. It was also established that a variety of contractors' associations [had] virtually no minority businesses within their membership. The city's legal counsel indicated his view that the ordinance was constitutional under this Court's decision in *Fullilove v. Klutznick*. . . . Councilperson Marsh, a proponent of the ordinance, made the following statement:

> "There is some information, however, that I want to make sure that we put in the record. [I] can say without equivocation, that the general conduct of the construction industry in this area, and the State, and around the nation, is one in which race discrimination and exclusion on the basis of race is widespread."

There was no direct evidence of race discrimination on the part of the city in letting contracts or any evidence that the city's prime contractors had discriminated against minority-owned subcontractors. [The case was brought by a contractor whose low bid on a city project was not accepted because of failure to comply with the Plan's requirements. The District Court upheld the Plan, but the Court of Appeals struck it down as violating both prongs of equal protection scrutiny.] We affirm. . . .

II

. . .

[That] Congress may identify and redress the effects of society-wide discrimination does not mean that, a fortiori, the States and their political subdivisions are free to decide that

---

440   The Richmond City Council adopted its program in 1983, modeled on the federal one upheld in Fullilove. It required prime contractors on city projects to subcontract at least 30% of the dollar amount of the contract to one or more Minority Business Enterprises (MBEs). Borrowing the definition used by Congress in Fullilove, the Richmond Plan defined an MBE as "[a] business at least [51%] of which is owned and controlled [by] minority group members" and identified eligible minority groups as "Blacks, Spanish-speaking, Orientals, Indians, Eskimos, or Aleuts." There was no geographic limit to the Plan; an otherwise qualified MBE from anywhere in the nation could avail itself of the 30% set-aside. Regulations under the Plan provided that waivers would be granted "in exceptional circumstances," when "every feasible attempt has been made to comply, and it [has been] demonstrated that sufficient, relevant, qualified [MBEs] are unavailable or unwilling to participate in the contract to enable meeting the 30% MBE goal."

such remedies are appropriate. Section 1 of the Fourteenth Amendment is an explicit constraint on state power, and the States must undertake any remedial efforts in accordance with that provision. To hold otherwise would be to cede control over the content of the Equal Protection Clause to the 50 state legislatures and their myriad political subdivisions. The mere recitation of a benign or compensatory purpose for the use of a racial classification would essentially entitle the States to exercise the full power of Congress under § 5 of the Fourteenth Amendment and insulate any racial classification from judicial scrutiny under § 1. We believe that such a result would be contrary to the intentions of the Framers of the Fourteenth Amendment, who desired to place clear limits on the States' use of race as a criterion for legislative action. . . . As a matter of state law, the city of Richmond has legislative authority over its procurement policies, and can use its spending powers to remedy private discrimination, if it identifies that discrimination with the particularity required by the Fourteenth Amendment. Thus, if the city could show that it had essentially become a "passive participant" in a system of racial exclusion practiced by elements of the local construction industry, we think it clear that the city could take affirmative steps to dismantle such a system. It is beyond dispute that any public entity, state or federal, has a compelling interest in assuring that public dollars, drawn from the tax contributions of all citizens, do not serve to finance the evil of private prejudice.

III

A

The Richmond Plan denies certain citizens the opportunity to compete for a fixed percentage of public contracts based solely upon their race. To whatever racial group these citizens belong, their "personal rights" to be treated with equal dignity and respect are implicated by a rigid rule erecting race as the sole criterion in an aspect of public decision-making. Absent searching judicial inquiry into the justification for such race-based measures, there is simply no way of determining what classifications are "benign" or "remedial" and what classifications are in fact motivated by illegitimate notions of racial inferiority or simple racial politics. Indeed, the purpose of strict scrutiny is to "smoke out" illegitimate uses of race by assuring that the legislative body is pursuing a goal important enough to warrant use of a highly suspect tool. The test also ensures that the means chosen "fit" this compelling goal so closely that there is little or no possibility that the motive for the classification was illegitimate racial prejudice or stereotype. Classification based on race carry a danger of stigmatic harm. Unless they are strictly reserved for remedial settings, they may in fact promote notions of racial inferiority and lead to a politics of racial hostility. We thus reaffirm the view expressed by the plurality in Wygant that the standard of review under the Equal Protection Clause is not dependent on the race of those burdened or benefited by a particular classification. . . . In this case, blacks constitute approximately 50% of the population of the city of Richmond. Five of the nine seats on the city council are held by blacks. The concern that a political majority will more easily act to the disadvantage of a minority based on unwarranted assumptions or incomplete facts would seem to militate for, not against, the application of heightened judicial scrutiny in this case.

B

The District Court found the city council's "findings sufficient to ensure that, in adopting the Plan, it was remedying the present effects of past discrimination in the construction industry." Like the "role model" theory employed in Wygant, a generalized assertion that there has been past discrimination in an entire industry provides no guidance for a legislative body to determine the precise scope of the injury it seeks to remedy. It "has no logical stopping point." Wygant, supra, at 275 (plurality opinion). "Relief" for such an ill-defined wrong could extend until the percentage of public contracts awarded to MBE's in Richmond mirrored the percentage of minorities in the population as a whole. Appellant argues that it is attempting to remedy various forms of past discrimination that are alleged to be responsible for the small number of minority businesses in the local contracting industry. Among these the city cites the exclusion of blacks from skilled construction trade unions and training programs. The city also lists a host of nonracial factors which would seem to face a member of any racial group attempting to establish a new business enterprise, such as deficiencies in working capital, inability to meet bonding requirements, unfamiliarity with bidding procedures, and disability caused by an inadequate track record. While there is no doubt that the sorry history of both private and public discrimination in this country has contributed to a lack of opportunities for black entrepreneurs, this observation, standing alone, cannot justify a rigid racial quota in the awarding of public contracts in Richmond, Virginia. It is sheer speculation how many minority firms there would be in Richmond absent past societal discrimination, just as it was sheer speculation how many minority medical students would have been admitted to the medical school at Davis absent past discrimination in educational opportunities. Defining these sorts of injuries as "identified discrimination" would give local governments license to create a patchwork of racial preferences based on statistical generalizations about any particular field of endeavor. These defects are readily apparent in this case. The 30% quota cannot in any realistic sense be tied to any injury suffered by anyone. . . .

The District Court accorded great weight to the fact that the city council designated the Plan as "remedial." But the mere recitation of a "benign" or legitimate purpose for a racial classification is entitled to little or no weight. Racial classifications are suspect, and that means that simple legislative assurances of good intention cannot suffice. The District Court also relied on the highly conclusionary statement of a proponent of the Plan that there was racial discrimination in the construction industry "in this area, and the State, and around the nation." [Such] statements are of little probative value in establishing identified discrimination in the Richmond construction industry. [W]hen a legislative body chooses to employ a suspect classification, it cannot rest upon a generalized assertion as to the classification's relevance to its goals. The history of racial classifications in this country suggests that blind judicial deference to legislative or executive pronouncements of necessity has no place in equal protection analysis. See *Korematsu v. United States* . . . (Murphy, J., dissenting). Reliance on the disparity between the number of prime contracts awarded to minority firms and the minority population of the city of Richmond is similarly misplaced. In this case, the city does not even know how many MBE's in the relevant market are qualified to undertake prime or sub-contracting work in public construction projects. . . . Without any information on minority participation in subcontracting, it is quite simply impossible to evaluate overall minority representation in the city's construction expenditures.

. . .

In sum, none of the evidence presented by the city points to any identified discrimination in the Richmond construction industry. We, therefore, hold that the city has failed to demonstrate a compelling interest in apportioning public contracting opportunities on the basis of race. To accept Richmond's claim that past societal discrimination alone can serve as the basis for rigid racial preferences would be to open the door to competing claims for "remedial relief" for every disadvantaged group. The dream of a Nation of equal citizens in a society where race is irrelevant to personal opportunity and achievement would be lost in a mosaic of shifting preferences based on inherently unmeasurable claims of past wrongs. [See Bakke (Powell, J.).] We think such a result would be contrary to both the letter and spirit of [equal protection]. The foregoing analysis applies only to the inclusion of blacks within the Richmond set-aside program. There is absolutely no evidence of past discrimination against Spanish-speaking, Oriental, Indian, Eskimo, or Aleut persons in any aspect of the Richmond construction industry. [It] may well be that Richmond has never had an Aleut or Eskimo citizen. The random inclusion of racial groups that, as a practical matter, may never have suffered from discrimination in the construction industry in Richmond suggests that perhaps the city's purpose was not in fact to remedy past discrimination. If a 30% set-aside was "narrowly tailored" to compensate black contractors for past discrimination, one may legitimately ask why they are forced to share this "remedial relief" with an Aleut citizen who moves to Richmond tomorrow? The gross overinclusiveness of Richmond's racial preference strongly impugns the city's claim of remedial motivation.

IV

. . .

V

Nothing we say today precludes a state or local entity from taking action to rectify the effects of identified discrimination within its jurisdiction. If the city of Richmond had evidence before it that nonminority contractors were systematically excluding minority businesses from subcontracting opportunities, it could take action to end the discriminatory exclusion. Where there is a significant statistical disparity between the number of qualified minority contractors willing and able to perform a particular service and the number of such contractors actually engaged by the locality or the locality's prime contractors, an inference of discriminatory exclusion could arise.

. . .

The city points to no evidence that qualified minority contractors have been passed over for city contracts or subcontracts, either as a group or in any individual case.

. . .

Proper findings in this regard are necessary to define both the scope of the injury and the extent of the remedy necessary to cure its effects. Such findings also serve to assure all citizens that the deviation from the norm of equal treatment of all racial and ethnic groups is a temporary matter, a measure taken in the service of the goal of equality itself. Absent such findings, there is a danger that a racial classification is merely the product of unthinking stereotypes or a form of racial politics. [Because Richmond] has failed to identify the need for remedial action in the awarding of its public construction contracts, its treatment of its citizens on a racial basis violates the dictates of [equal protection].

[Affirmed.]

[Concurring and dissenting opinions omitted.]

ii. Implicit Discriminations

Laws that are racially neutral on their face may nevertheless constitute *de jure* discriminations in violation of the equal protection clause if their enactment or enforcement is motivated by racial discrimination. The leading case for the former proposition (discriminatorily motivated enactment) is *Gomillion v. Lightfoot*.[441] There city boundaries were changed with the effect that nearly all black voters were removed from the city. Although the challengers found no "smoking gun," the city was unable to offer any constitutional explanation for its suspicious action, and the re-districting was declared unconstitutional.

The leading case for the second proposition (discriminatory enforcement) is *Yick Wo v. Hopkins*,[442] where ordinances of the City and County of San Francisco required that, to avoid fire, laundries must be located in brick buildings. The ordinances allowed the board of supervisors to grant exemptions. Tellingly, the board granted exemptions to all but one of the non-Chinese applicants, but denied over 200 applications filed by Chinese persons. The Supreme Court unanimously reversed Yick Wo's conviction for operating a laundry without a license, holding:

> [T]he facts shown establish an administration directed so exclusively against a particular class of persons as to warrant and require the conclusion, that, whatever may have been the intent of the ordinances as adopted, they are applied by the public authorities charged with the administration, and thus representing the State itself, with a mind so unequal and oppressive as to amount to a practical denial by the State of equal protection of the laws.[443]

Over the course of the century since *Yick Wo* was decided, the Supreme Court has refined its enquiry somewhat. Nowadays, if a challenger proves a substantial disproportionate racial impact in the administration of a racially neutral law, the burden shifts to the state to show that the impact is due to lawful, constitutional factors.[444] This approach has led to a prohibition against use of peremptory challenges on the basis of jurors' race and gender.[445]

b. *De facto* Discrimination

What of laws and practices that are racially neutral on their face, in their motivation, and in their administration, but that still have a racially disproportionate impact? For example, what of college admissions criteria and maximum heights in the military that disfavor a disproportionately large percentage of American blacks?

---

441   364 U.S. 339 (1960). Drawing boundaries so as to benefit blacks was held constitutional where the legislature's use of race was not the "predominant factor." Hunt v. Cromartie, 121 S.Ct. 1452 (2001).

442   118 U.S. 356 (1886).

443   At p. 373.

444   Castaneda v. Partida, 430 U.S. 482 (1977).

445   Batson v. Kentucky, 476 U.S. 79 (1986); J.E.B. v. Alabama, 511 U.S. 127 (1994).

In the following case, unsuccessful black applicants for positions on the police force claimed that a test measuring verbal activity, vocabulary, and reading comprehension unconstitutionally discriminated against them. According to the district court, respondents' evidence supported the conclusion that a higher percentage of blacks than whites failed the test, but the test had not been validated to establish its reliability for measuring subsequent job performance. There was no claim that administration of the test constituted an "intentional" or "purposeful" act of discrimination.

CASE: Washington v. Davis
426 U.S. 229 (1976)

MR. JUSTICE WHITE delivered the opinion of the Court.

This case involves the validity of a qualifying test administered to applicants for positions as police officers in the District of Columbia Metropolitan Police Department. The test was sustained by the District Court but invalidated by the Court of Appeals. We are in agreement with the District Court and hence reverse the judgment of the Court of Appeals. . . .

The central purpose of the Equal Protection Clause of the Fourteenth Amendment is the prevention of official conduct discriminating on the basis of race. It is also true that the Due Process Clause of the Fifth Amendment contains an equal protection component prohibiting the United States from invidiously discriminating between individuals or groups. *Bolling v. Sharpe*. . . . But our cases have not embraced the proposition that a law or other official act, without regard to whether it reflects a racially discriminatory purpose, is unconstitutional solely because it has a racially disproportionate impact.

Almost 100 years ago, *Strauder v. West Virginia* . . . , established that the exclusion of Negroes from grand and petit juries in criminal proceedings violated the Equal Protection Clause, but the fact that a particular jury or a series of juries does not statistically reflect the racial composition of the community does not in itself make out an invidious discrimination forbidden by the Clause. . . .

The rule is the same in other contexts. *Wright v. Rockefeller* . . . , upheld a New York congressional apportionment statute against claims that district lines had been racially gerrymandered. The challenged districts were made up predominantly of whites or of minority races, and their boundaries were irregularly drawn. The challengers did not prevail because they failed to prove that the New York Legislature "was either motivated by racial considerations or in fact drew the districts on racial lines"; the plaintiffs had not shown that the statute "was the product of a state contrivance to segregate on the basis of race or place of origin." . . .

The school desegregation cases have also adhered to the basic equal protection principle that the invidious quality of a law claimed to be racially discriminatory must ultimately be traced to a racially discriminatory purpose. That there are both predominantly black and predominantly white schools in a community is not alone violative of the Equal Protection Clause. The essential element of de jure segregation is "a current condition of segregation resulting from intentional state action." *Keyes v. School Dist. No. 1*. . . .

This is not to say that the necessary discriminatory racial purpose must be express or appear on the face of the statute, or that a law's disproportionate impact is irrelevant in cases involving Constitution-based claims of racial discrimination. A statute, otherwise neutral on its face, must not be applied so as invidiously to discriminate on the basis of race. *Yick Wo v. Hopkins*. . . .

Nor on the facts of the case before us would the disproportionate impact of [the test] warrant the conclusion that it is a purposeful device to discriminate against Negroes and hence an infringement of the constitutional rights of respondents as well as other black applicants. As we have said, the test is neutral on its face and rationally may be said to serve a purpose the Government is constitutionally empowered to pursue. Even agreeing with the District Court that the differential racial effect of [the test] called for further inquiry, we think the District Court correctly held that the affirmative efforts of the Metropolitan Police Department to recruit black officers, the changing racial composition of the recruit classes and of the force in general, and the relationship of the test to the training program negated any inference that the Department discriminated on the basis of race or that "a police officer qualifies on the color of his skin rather than ability." . . .

A rule that a statute designed to serve neutral ends is nevertheless invalid, absent compelling justification, if in practice it benefits or burdens one race more than another would be far reaching and would raise serious questions about, and perhaps invalidate, a whole range of tax, welfare, public service, regulatory, and licensing statutes that may be more burdensome to the poor and to the average black than to the more affluent white. . . .

[Concurring and dissenting opinions omitted.]

2. Protected Groups

Every external act at any level of government might theoretically be challenged by a person who claims unfair, discriminatory, that is, unconstitutional treatment. Providing that the person meets "standing" and other procedural prerequisites, the judicial constitutional enquiry will remain at the level of minimum scrutiny unless the treatment being challenged implicates certain rights that the claimant enjoys as an individual or as a member of a group. Rights enjoyed by persons who do not claim membership in a protected group are treated above under due process. There, as was shown, higher scrutiny can be triggered by the invocation of fundamental rights (strict scrutiny) or of certain other, quasi-fundamental rights (intermediate scrutiny).

When group rights are involved, the same matrix of levels of review is employed. Strict scrutiny has been reserved for challenges involving so-called suspect classes. Race, national origin, and non-American citizenship have been held by the Supreme Court to be suspect classes, although, for reasons noted below, non-American citizenship ("alienage") is not employed as a suspect class when judging the constitutionality of federal measures. As detailed in the preceding section, *de jure* classifications in these instances (both negative and "benign" discrimination) are judged under strict scrutiny.

As with cases involving due process rights, equal protection has its own intermediate review. In the due process context, intermediate review is employed when quasi-fundamental rights are invoked. In the equal protection context, intermediate review is employed to judge the constitutionality of *de jure* classifications pertaining to quasi-suspect groups. Gender and illegitimacy are the only classifications presently entitled to intermediate review under the equal protection clause.

The discussion below begins with suspect classifications before turning to the quasi-suspect variety.

a. Suspect Classifications

The Supreme Court employs strict scrutiny when the government[446] discriminates against a "suspect class." Although the 14th Amendment provides few textual clues as to what classifications or discriminations were intended to be prohibited, the 15th Amendment does: race, color, or previous condition of servitude. As a historical matter, the "race" referred to meant the Negro race. "Color" meant the color of Negroes' skin. Discriminations against African American blacks are therefore particularly suspect from a historical standpoint. Courts have held almost all discriminations based on race or "ethnicity" (the currently

---

446   See discussion of "state action" above.

preferred term) to be inherently suspect.[447] One of very few exceptions to this practice was made in *Morton v. Mancari*,[448] which upheld job preferences for American Indians.

Perhaps the most profound use of strict scrutiny in the equal protection context has been in cases involving education. *Missouri ex rel. Gaines v. Canada*[449] redressed the refusal of the University of Missouri for racial reasons to admit Lloyd Gaines to the state's public law school, offering instead to provide for his matriculation in an adjoining state. Missouri tried unsuccessfully to invoke the "separate but equal" doctrine of *Plessy v. Ferguson*.[450] That doctrine was expressly overruled in the following decision, which ruled that separate public facilities, especially schools, are inherently unequal.

CASE: Brown v. Board of Education [Brown I]
347 U.S. 483 (1954)

MR. CHIEF JUSTICE WARREN delivered the [unanimous] opinion of the Court.

These cases come to us from the States of Kansas, South Carolina, Virginia, and Delaware. [In] each of the cases, minors of the Negro race [seek] the aid of the courts in obtaining admission to the public schools of their community on a nonsegregated basis. In each instance, they had been denied admission to schools attended by white children under laws requiring or permitting segregation according to race. [In most of the cases, the courts below denied relief, relying on] the so-called "separate but equal" doctrine announced by this Court in Plessy v. Ferguson. . . . [The] plaintiffs contend that segregated public schools are not "equal" and cannot be made "equal," and that hence they are deprived of the equal protection of the laws. . . .

In the first cases in this Court construing the Fourteenth Amendment, decided shortly after its adoption, the Court interpreted it as proscribing all state-imposed discriminations against the Negro race. The doctrine of "separate but equal" did not make its appearance in this Court until 1896 in [Plessy] involving not education but transportation. . . .

In approaching this problem, we cannot turn the clock back to 1868 when the Amendment was adopted, or even to 1896 when Plessy was written. We must consider public education in the light of its full development and its present place in American life throughout the Nation. Only in this way can it

---

447   E.g., Hernandez v. Texas, 347 U.S. 475 (1954).

448   417 U.S. 535 (1974).

449   305 U.S. 337 (1938).

450   163 U.S. 537 (1896).

be determined if segregation in public schools deprives these plaintiffs of [equal protection]. Today, education is perhaps the most important function of state and local governments. Compulsory school attendance laws and the great expenditures for education both demonstrate our recognition of the importance of education to our democratic society. It is required in the performance of our most basic public responsibilities, even service in the armed forces. It is the very foundation of good citizenship. Today it is a principal instrument in awakening the child to cultural values, in preparing him for later professional training, and in helping him to adjust normally to his environment. In these days, it is doubtful that any child may reasonably be expected to succeed in life if he is denied the opportunity of an education. Such an opportunity, where the state has undertaken to provide it, is a right which must be made available to all on equal terms.

We come then to the question presented: Does segregation of children in public schools solely on the basis of race, even though the physical facilities and other "tangible" factors may be equal, deprive the children of the minority group of equal educational opportunities? We believe that it does. In [Sweatt] this Court relied in large part on "those qualities which are incapable of objective measurement but which make for greatness in a law school." In McLaurin, the Court [again] resorted to intangible considerations: "[the] ability to study, to engage in discussions and exchange views with other students, and, in general, to learn [the] profession." Such considerations apply with added force to children in grade and high schools. To separate them from others of similar age and qualifications solely because of their race generates a feeling of inferiority as to their status in the community that may affect their hearts and minds in a way unlikely ever to be undone. The effect of this separation on their educational opportunities was well stated by a finding in the Kansas case by a court which nevertheless felt compelled to rule against the Negro plaintiffs: "Segregation of white and colored children in public schools has a detrimental effect upon the colored children. The impact is greater when it has the sanction of the law; for the policy of separating the races is usually interpreted as denoting the inferiority of the negro group. A sense of inferiority affects the motivation of a child to learn. Segregation with the sanction of law, therefore, has a tendency to [retard] the educational and mental development of negro children and to deprive them of some of the benefits they would receive in a [racially] integrated school system." Whatever may have been the extent of psychological knowledge at the time of [Plessy], this finding is amply supported by modern authority. Any language in [Plessy] contrary to this finding is rejected.

We conclude that in the field of public education the doctrine of "separate but equal" has no place. Separate educational facilities are inherently unequal. Therefore, we hold that the plaintiffs and others similarly situated for whom the actions have been brought are, by reason of the segregation complained of, deprived of [equal protection]. This disposition makes unnecessary any discussion whether such segregation also violates [due process]. Because these are class actions, because of the wide applicability of this decision, and because of the great variety of local conditions, the formulation of decrees in these cases presents problems of considerable complexity. On reargument, the consideration of appropriate relief was necessarily subordinated to the primary question—the constitutionality of segregation in public education. We have now announced that such segregation is a denial of [equal protection]. In order that we may have the full assistance of the parties in formulating decrees, the cases will be restored to the docket, and the parties are requested to present further argument on Questions 4 and 5 previously propounded by the Court for [reargument].

It is so ordered.

CASE: Brown v. Board of Education [Brown II]
349 U. S. 294 (1955)

MR. CHIEF JUSTICE WARREN delivered the [unanimous] opinion of the Court.

These cases were decided on May 17, 1954. The [unanimous] opinions of that date, declaring the fundamental principle that racial discrimination in public education is unconstitutional, are incorporated herein by reference. All provisions of federal, state, or local law requiring or permitting such discrimination must yield to this principle. There remains for consideration the manner in which relief is to be accorded. . . .

Full implementation of these constitutional principles may require solution of varied local school problems. School authorities have the primary responsibility for elucidating, assessing, and solving these problems; courts will have to consider whether the action of school authorities constitutes good faith implementation of the governing constitutional principles. Because of their proximity to local conditions and the possible need for further hearings, the courts which originally heard these cases can best perform this judicial appraisal. Accordingly, we believe it appropriate to remand the cases to those courts. In fashioning and effectuating the decrees, the courts will be guided by equitable principles. Traditionally, equity has been characterized by a practical flexibility in shaping its remedies and by a facility for adjusting and reconciling public and private needs. These cases call for the exercise of these traditional attributes of equity power. At stake is the personal interest of the plaintiffs in admission to public schools as soon as practicable on a nondiscriminatory basis. To effectuate this interest may call for elimination of a variety of obstacles in making the transition to school systems operated in accordance with the constitutional principles set forth in [Brown I]. Courts of equity may properly take into account the public interest in the elimination of such obstacles in a systematic and effective manner. But it should go without saying that the vitality of these constitutional principles cannot be allowed to yield simply because of disagreement with them.

While giving weight to these public and private considerations, the courts will require that the defendants make a prompt and reasonable start toward full compliance with [Brown I]. Once such a start has been made, the courts may find that additional time is necessary to carry out the ruling in an effective manner. The burden rests upon the defendants to establish that such time is necessary in the public interest and is consistent with good faith compliance at the earliest practicable date. To that end, the courts may consider problems related to administration, arising from the physical condition of the school plant, the school transportation system, personnel, revision of school districts and attendance areas into compact units to achieve a system of determining admission to the public schools on a nonracial basis, and revision of local laws and regulations which may be necessary in solving the foregoing problems. They will also consider the adequacy of any plans the defendants may propose to meet these problems and to effectuate a transition to a racially nondiscriminatory school system. During this period of transition, the courts will retain jurisdiction of these cases. The [cases are accordingly remanded to the lower courts to take such proceedings and enter such orders and decrees consistent with this opinion as are necessary and proper to admit to public schools on a racially nondiscriminatory basis with all deliberate speed the parties to these cases]. . . .

In response to *Brown*, school districts launched campaigns to integrate segregated schools. Sometimes school desegregation has been voluntarily. More often than not it has been court ordered. As a practical matter, desegregation of public schools has involved the bussing of pupils away from neighborhood schools. The Supreme Court has never ruled that schools have an affirmative duty to remedy *de facto* school segregation. However, the Supreme Court has allowed the lower courts to use certain evidentiary presumptions that make intentional segregation easier to prove.[451]

American citizenship has been recognized as a "suspect class" when employed by the states, but not when employed by the federal government.[452] The reason for this distinction lies in the bestowal of plenary power on the federal government over the admission and exclusion of aliens. According to this reasoning, if the states could penalize ("discriminate against") someone based on her lack of US citizenship, then they could do through the back door what they could not do through the front, that is, regulate immigration.[453]

The recognition of alienage as a suspect class has meant that non-US citizens are automatically eligible for benefits conferred by state and local agencies unless the agencies can prove that the discrimination furthers a compelling state interest. This is virtually impossible to do. Consequently, foreigners, whether legally in the United States or not, enjoy rights equal to American citizens to receive state welfare benefits,[454] to gain admission to professions regulated by the states, including the legal profession,[455] to demand financial assistance from the states for higher education,[456] and to secure employment in most state civil service positions.[457] The only compelling interest that the Supreme Court has recognized to date is the protection of "democratic political institutions" from which aliens have traditionally been excluded. (Ironically, this exclusion is one of the reasons for granting "suspect" status to aliens; see Justice Stone's remark above.) Accordingly, non-citizens may be denied the right to vote, to stand for public office, and to serve on juries. The Supreme Court has upheld narrowly drawn exclusions of non-citizens from the professions of police officer and public school teacher.[458]

b. Quasi-Suspect Classifications

Intermediate scrutiny in the equal protection context is employed for discrimination against illegitimate children and discrimination based on gender. Because the interests of the state need only rise to the level of important (not compelling) state interests, and because the "fit" between ends and means need only be

---

451   See Keyes v. School Dist. No. 1, 413 U.S. 189 (1973). In so doing it has "legislated" guidelines for school administrators and judges. See Swann v. Charlotte-Mecklenburg Board of Education, 402 U.S. 1 (1971).

452   Mathews v. Diaz, 426 U.S. 67 (1976), upholding federal denials of Medicare under the rational basis test.

453   See Toll v. Moreno, 458 U.S. 1 (1982).

454   Graham v. Richardson, 403 U.S. 365 (1971).

455   In re Griffiths, 413 U.S. 717 (1973).

456   Nyquist v. Mauclet, 432 U.S. 1 (1977).

457   Sugarman v. Dougall, 413 U.S. 634 (1973).

458   Foley v. Connelie, 435 U.S. 291 U.S. 291 (1978); Ambach v. Norwick, 441 U.S. 68 (1979).

substantial (not necessary), the state enjoys more discretion under intermediate than under strict scrutiny. Unfortunately, the gradations are difficult to apply. Consequently, the outcomes of controversies judged under intermediate scrutiny are more difficult to predict than under strict scrutiny, where measures are almost always invalidated, and under minimal scrutiny, where measures are almost always upheld as valid.

Very few governmental measures discriminate on the basis of legitimacy. Consequently, there have been relatively few opportunities for courts to rule on the constitutionality of such measures. The Supreme Court has struck down state laws excluding illegitimate children from receiving workers' compensation benefits on the death of their fathers and from maintaining wrongful death actions.[459] The Supreme Court also struck down a state law that provided child support only to legitimate children.[460] On the other hand, a state may deny a right of intestate succession to an illegitimate child if paternity is not formally determined before the father's death.[461] The important state interest was found in the need to promote the expeditious disposition of property at death. (The advent of relatively inexpensive DNA analysis may have rendered this interest moot.) Immigration provisions that exclude illegitimate children (and illegitimate fathers) from receiving preferences have also been upheld.[462] Note, however, that this last example of discrimination was subject to a lower level of review because of Congress's plenary power over immigration.

Statutes routinely declare that a child born to a married woman is irrebutably presumed to be the child of the mother's husband.[463] Yet studies betray that many children in intact families were not sired by their mothers' husbands.[464] Does the statutory declaration of legitimacy unconstitutionally discriminate in favor of illegitimate children? Adopted children sometimes desire to know the identity of their genetic parents for medical reasons. Can the legislature or Supreme Court constitutionally recognize a right of adopted children to such information without simultaneously bestowing that right on legitimate children?

Quite a number of cases charging gender discrimination have reached the courts. These too are judged under intermediate scrutiny. To date, all measures that deny benefits to, or impose extra burdens upon, women have been held

---

459 Weber v. Aetna Casualty & Surety Co., 406 U.S. 164 (1972); Levy v. Louisiana, 391 U.S. 68 (1968).

460 Gomez v. Perez, 409 U.S. 535 (1973).

461 Lallix v. Lallix, 439 U.S. 259 (1978).

462 Fiallo v. Bell, 430 U.S. 787 (1977).

463 E.g., Cal. Evid. Code § 7540, upheld in Michael H. v. Gerald D., 491 U.S. 110 (1989), criticized in Hadek.

464 In some urban areas more than one fourth of the children were sired by someone other than the father of record. Wright, Moral Animal at 70.

unconstitutional.[465] A potential exception to the last statement are laws that exclude pregnancy from state disability benefits.[466] Title VII of the federal Civil Rights Act of 1964 makes it unlawful for an employer "to discriminate against any individual with respect to his compensation, terms, conditions, or privileges of employment, because of such individual's race, color, religion, sex, or national origin."[467] Under Title VII, premiums for employer-sponsored health insurance must be identical for men and women even though claims by women are higher.[468] The state of Montana bans the use of gender in determining premiums for every type of insurance.[469] Are these statutes constitutional?

Laws that confer benefits upon women at the expense of men, such as those just mentioned, have almost always been upheld. Property tax exemptions for widows, but not widowers, have been ruled constitutional,[470] as have more generous mandatory discharge procedures in the military,[471] and more generous Social Security payments to women.[472] Other examples include exempting women from statutory rape laws,[473] from mandatory road construction,[474] and from military conscription.[475] One case even upheld the practice of paying women professors more than men in order to attract more women to the university.[476]

On occasion laws that confer benefits upon women have been ruled unconstitutional. Laws that prescribe lower drinking ages for women,[477] that exclude former wives from the legal obligation to pay alimony (spousal support), that grant only women a right to refuse consent to adoption,[478] and that limit admission to nursing classes at a state university to women[479] have all been declared unconstitutional.

---

465   E.g., Reed v. Reed, 404 U.S. 1 (1972), Frontiero v. Richardson, 411 U.S. 677 (1973), and United States v. Virginia, 516 U.S. 515 (1996).

466   Geduldig v. Aiello, 417 U.S. 484 (1974).

467   42 U.S.C. §§ 2000e-2(a)(1).

468   See Gaulding.

469   Mont. Code Ann. § 49-2-309.

470   Kahn v. Shevin, 416 U.S. 351 (1974).

471   Schlessinger v. Ballard, 419 U.S. 498 (1975).

472   Califano v. Webster, 430 U.S. 313 (1977).

473   Michael M. v. Sonoma County Superior Court, 450 U.S. 57 (1981).

474   Butler v. Perry, 240 U.S. 328 (1916), overruling a challenge under the 13th Amendment, and holding that a state may require all able-bodied men between the ages of 21 and 45 to work on road construction.

475   Rostker v. Goldberg, 453 U.S. 57 (1981), and according unwed mothers, but not fathers, the right to sue for the child's wrongful death. Parham v. Hughes, 441 U.S. 347 (1979).

476   Winkes v. Brown University, 747 F.2d 792 (1st Cir. 1984).

477   Craig v. Boren, 429 U.S. 190 (1976).

478   Caban v. Mohammed, 441 U.S. 380 (1979).

479   Mississippi University for Women v. Hogan, 458 U.S. 718 (1982).

Because discrimination in favor of females is judged by intermediate scrutiny, but that in favor of particular races is assessed according to strict scrutiny, a program that benefits women is easier to justify from a constitutional standpoint than one that benefits African Americans. Is this constitutionally defensible? African Americans constitute 12 percent of the population. They are disproportionately underrepresented among registered voters,[480] and earn disproportionately less than non-blacks. Women (12 percent of whom are black) constitute a majority of the American population, are disproportionately over-represented among registered voters,[481] and control over half of the wealth, according to recent reports.[482]

To summarize, laws that intentionally disadvantage illegitimate children are usually judged unconstitutional. There are apparently no laws that give an advantage to illegitimate children at the expense of legitimate, but there are a number of laws that intentionally benefit females at the expense of males. These discriminations are almost upheld. All of the measures reviewed by the Supreme Court that intentionally benefit men to the disadvantage of women, except those directly relating to pregnancy, have been ruled unconstitutional. Would the results of these cases have been any different had strict scrutiny been applied?

Should intermediate scrutiny be extended to other groups, or does doing so lead to tribalization of constitutional rights? What about the poor? For example, *Boddie v. Connecticut*[483] ruled (under the due process clause) that states may not charge court fees to indigents seeking to dissolve their marriages. But states may charge for abortions.[484] Would extending intermediate scrutiny to the poor jeopardize social programs?

Should heightened scrutiny be extended to the elderly? The Supreme Court has held that age is not a suspect classification.[485] Federal statutory law protects workers over the age of 40, and has virtually eliminated all mandatory retirement.[486]

---

480 See U.S. Bureau of the Census, Table 2. Regions—Reported Voting and Registration, by Race, Hispanic Origin, Sex, and Age, for the United States and Regions: November 1994 (Release date: June 4, 1996).

481 See U.S. Bureau of the Census, Table 2. Regions—Reported Voting and Registration, by Race, Hispanic Origin, Sex, and Age, for the United States and Regions: November 1994 (Release date: June 4, 1996).

482 Deutsche Presse-Agentur, Nov. 24, 1998.

483 401 U.S. 371 (1971).

484 Harris v. McRae, 448 U.S. 297 (1980).

485 Massachusetts Board of Retirement v. Murgia, 427 U.S. 307 (1976).

486 Age Discrimination in Employment Act, 29 U.S.C. §§ 621-634, criticized in Issacharoff & Harris and in Epstein.

What about the physically disabled and the mentally retarded? Some commentators maintain that the Americans with Disabilities Act of 1990[487] requires courts to employ strict scrutiny to judge classifications based on a disability.[488] In *Cleburne v. Cleburne Living Center, Inc.*[489] a city ordinance required that one obtain a special use permit to establish group homes for the mentally retarded, but not to open a dormitory for university students. The Supreme Court found no rational basis for the distinction and invalidated the ordinance.

The case that follows was chosen to conclude this book because it contains issues from both the first and second parts of the book, and because it illustrates the fluidity of the rhetoric and concepts of due process (liberty) and equal protection. In ruling California's statute unconstitutional, does the Supreme Court use due process or equal protection analysis? What level of scrutiny is being employed? Notice that Congress apparently considered California's approach to be constitutional. Why might members of Congress from other states find California's approach unobjectionable?

CASE: Saenz v. Roe
526 U.S. 489 (1999)

Justice STEVENS delivered the opinion of the Court.

In 1992, California enacted a statute limiting the maximum welfare benefits available to newly arrived residents. The scheme limits the amount payable to a family that has resided in the State for less than 12 months to the amount payable by the State of the family's prior residence. The questions presented by this case are whether the 1992 statute was constitutional when it was enacted and, if not, whether an amendment to the Social Security Act enacted by Congress in 1996 affects that determination.

I

California is not only one of the largest, most populated, and most beautiful States in the Nation; it is also one of the most generous. Like all other States, California has participated in several welfare programs authorized by the Social Security Act and partially funded by the Federal Government. Its programs, however, provide a higher level of benefits and serve more needy citizens than those of most other States. In one year the most expensive of those programs, Aid to Families with Dependent Children (AFDC), which was replaced in 1996 with Temporary Assistance to Needy Families

---

487   42 U.S.C. § 12101 et seq. See also PGA Tour, Inc. v. Martin, 121 S.Ct. 1879 (2001), in which the ADA was held to invalidate a prohibition against the use of golf cars in a professional golf tournament by a disabled golfer.

488   Perlin at p. 949, n. 16.

489   470 U.S. 1002 (1985).

(TANF), provided benefits for an average of 2,645,814 persons per month at an annual cost to the State of $2.9 billion. In California the cash benefit for a family of two—a mother and one child—is $456 a month, but in the neighboring State of Arizona, for example, it is only $275.

In 1992, in order to make a relatively modest reduction in its vast welfare budget, the California Legislature enacted § 11450.03 of the state Welfare and Institutions Code. That section sought to change the California AFDC program by limiting new residents, for the first year they live in California, to the benefits they would have received in the State of their prior residence. Because in 1992 a state program either had to conform to federal specifications or receive a waiver from the Secretary of Health and Human Services in order to qualify for federal reimbursement, § 11450.03 required approval by the Secretary to take effect. In October 1992, the Secretary issued a waiver purporting to grant such approval.

On December 21, 1992, three California residents who were eligible for AFDC benefits filed an action in the Eastern District of California challenging the constitutionality of the durational residency requirement in § 11450.03. Each plaintiff alleged that she had recently moved to California to live with relatives in order to escape abusive family circumstances. One returned to California after living in Louisiana for seven years, the second had been living in Oklahoma for six weeks and the third came from Colorado. Each alleged that her monthly AFDC grant for the ensuing 12 months would be substantially lower under § 11450.03 than if the statute were not in effect. Thus, the former residents of Louisiana and Oklahoma would receive $190 and $341 respectively for a family of three even though the full California grant was $641; the former resident of Colorado, who had just one child, was limited to $280 a month as opposed to the full California grant of $504 for a family of two.

The District Court issued a temporary restraining order and, after a hearing, preliminarily enjoined implementation of the statute. District Judge Levi found that the statute "produces substantial disparities in benefit levels and makes no accommodation for the different costs of living that exist in different states." Relying primarily on our decisions in *Shapiro v. Thompson* . . ., and *Zobel v. Williams* . . ., he concluded that the statute placed "a penalty on the decision of new residents to migrate to the State and be treated on an equal basis with existing residents." . . . In his view, if the purpose of the measure was to deter migration by poor people into the State, it would be unconstitutional for that reason. And even if the purpose was only to conserve limited funds, the State had failed to explain why the entire burden of the saving should be imposed on new residents. The Court of Appeals summarily affirmed for the reasons stated by the District Judge. . . .

. . . [Section] 11450.03 remained inoperative until after Congress enacted the Personal Responsibility and Work Opportunity Reconciliation Act of 1996 [PRWORA]. . . . PRWORA replaced the AFDC program with TANF. The new statute expressly authorizes any State that receives a block grant under TANF to "apply to a family the rules (including benefit amounts) of the [TANF] program . . . of another State if the family has moved to the State from the other State and has resided in the State for less than 12 months." 42 U.S.C. § 604(c) (1994 ed., Supp. II). . . .

. . .

II

On April 1, 1997, the two respondents filed this action in the Eastern District of California making essentially the same claims asserted by the plaintiffs in *Anderson v. Green*, but also challenging the constitutionality of PRWORA's approval of the durational residency requirement. . . . Reasoning that PRWORA permitted, but did not require, States to impose durational residency requirements, Judge Levi concluded that the existence of the federal statute did not affect the legal analysis in his prior opinion in Green.

. . .

Without finally deciding the merits, the Court of Appeals affirmed his issuance of a preliminary injunction. . . . It agreed with the District Court's view that the passage of PRWORA did not affect the constitutional analysis. . . . Although the decision of the Court of Appeals is consistent with the views of other federal courts that have addressed the issue, we granted certiorari because of the importance of the case. . . . We now affirm.

III

The word "travel" is not found in the text of the Constitution. Yet the "constitutional right to travel from one State to another" is firmly embedded in our jurisprudence. *United States v. Guest*. . . . Indeed, as Justice Stewart reminded us in *Shapiro v. Thompson* . . . the right is so important that it is "assertable against private interference as well as governmental action . . . a virtually unconditional personal right, guaranteed by the Constitution to us all." . . .

In Shapiro, we reviewed the constitutionality of three statutory provisions that denied welfare assistance to residents of Connecticut, the District of Columbia, and Pennsylvania, who had resided within those respective jurisdictions less than one year immediately preceding their applications for assistance. Without pausing to identify the specific source of the right, we began by noting that the Court had long "recognized that the nature of our Federal Union and our constitutional concepts of personal liberty unite to require that all citizens be free to travel throughout the length and breadth of our land uninhibited by statutes, rules, or regulations which unreasonably burden or restrict this movement." . . . We squarely held that it was "constitutionally impermissible" for a State to enact durational residency requirements for the purpose of inhibiting the migration by needy persons into the State. We further held that a classification that had the effect of imposing a penalty on the exercise of the right to travel violated the Equal Protection Clause "unless shown to be necessary to promote a compelling governmental interest," . . . and that no such showing had been made.

In this case California argues that § 11450.03 was not enacted for the impermissible purpose of inhibiting migration by needy persons and that, unlike the legislation reviewed in Shapiro, it does not penalize the right to travel because new arrivals are not ineligible for benefits during their first year of residence. California submits that, instead of being subjected to the strictest scrutiny, the statute should be upheld if it is supported by a rational basis and that the State's legitimate interest in saving over $10 million a year satisfies that test. . . .

IV

The "right to travel" discussed in our cases embraces at least three different components. It protects the right of a citizen of one State to enter and to leave another State, the right to be treated as a welcome visitor rather than an unfriendly alien when temporarily present in the second State, and, for those travelers who elect to become permanent residents, the right to be treated like other citizens of that State.

It was the right to go from one place to another, including the right to cross state borders while en route, that was vindicated in *Edwards v. California* . . . (1941), which invalidated a state law that impeded the free interstate passage of the indigent. We reaffirmed that right in *United States v. Guest* . . . (1966), which afforded protection to the " 'right to travel freely to and from the State of Georgia and to use highway facilities and other instrumentalities of interstate commerce within the State of Georgia.'" . . . Given that § 11450.03 imposed no obstacle to respondents' entry into California, we think the State is correct when it argues that the statute does not directly impair the exercise of the right to free interstate movement. For the purposes of this case, therefore, we need not identify the source of that particular right in the text of the Constitution. The right of "free ingress and regress to and from" neighboring States, which was expressly mentioned in the text of the Articles of Confederation, may simply have been "conceived from the beginning to be a necessary concomitant of the stronger Union the Constitution created." . . .

The second component of the right to travel is, however, expressly protected by the text of the Constitution. The first sentence of Article IV, § 2, provides:

> "The Citizens of each State shall be entitled to all Privileges and Immunities of Citizens in the several States."

Thus, by virtue of a person's state citizenship, a citizen of one State who travels in other States, intending to return home at the end of his journey, is entitled to enjoy the "Privileges and Immunities of Citizens in the several States" that he visits. This provision removes "from the citizens of each State the disabilities of alienage in the other States." *Paul v. Virginia* . . . (1868) ("[W]ithout some provision . . . removing from citizens of each State the disabilities of alienage in the other States, and giving them equality of privilege with citizens of those States, the Republic would have constituted little more than a league of States; it would not have constituted the Union which now exists"). It provides important protections for nonresidents who enter a State whether to obtain employment, *Hicklin v. Orbeck* . . ., to procure medical services . . ., *Doe v. Bolton* . . ., or even to engage in commercial shrimp fishing, *Toomer v. Witsell*. . . . Those protections are not "absolute," but the Clause "does bar discrimination against citizens of other States where there is no substantial reason for the discrimination beyond the mere fact that they are citizens of other States." . . . There may be a substantial reason for requiring the nonresident to pay more than the resident for a hunting license, see *Baldwin v. Fish and Game Comm'n of Mont.* . . ., or to enroll in the state university, see *Vlandis v. Kline* . . ., but our cases have not identified any acceptable reason for qualifying the protection afforded by the Clause for "the 'citizen of State A who ventures into State B' to settle there and establish a home." Zobel . . . (O'CONNOR, J., concurring in judgment). Permissible justifications for discrimination between residents and nonresidents are simply inapplicable to a nonresident's exercise of the right to move into another State and become a resident of that State.

What is at issue in this case, then, is this third aspect of the right to travel—the right of the newly arrived citizen to the same privileges and immunities enjoyed by other citizens of the same State. That right is protected not only by the new arrival's status as a state citizen, but also by her status as a citizen of the United States. That additional source of protection is plainly identified in the opening words of the Fourteenth Amendment:

> "All persons born or naturalized in the United States, and subject to the jurisdiction thereof, are citizens of the United

States and of the State wherein they reside. No State shall make or enforce any law which shall abridge the privileges or immunities of citizens of the United States; . . . ."

Despite fundamentally differing views concerning the coverage of the Privileges or Immunities Clause of the Fourteenth Amendment, most notably expressed in the majority and dissenting opinions in the Slaughter-House Cases . . . (1872), it has always been common ground that this Clause protects the third component of the right to travel. Writing for the majority in the Slaughter-House Cases, Justice Miller explained that one of the privileges conferred by this Clause "is that a citizen of the United States can, of his own volition, become a citizen of any State of the Union by a bona fide residence therein, with the same rights as other citizens of that State." . . . Justice Bradley, in dissent, used even stronger language to make the same point: "The states have not now, if they ever had, any power to restrict their citizenship to any classes or persons. A citizen of the United States has a perfect constitutional right to go to and reside in any State he chooses, and to claim citizenship therein, and an equality of rights with every other citizen; and the whole power of the nation is pledged to sustain him in that right. He is not bound to cringe to any superior, or to pray for any act of grace, as a means of enjoying all the rights and privileges enjoyed by other citizens." . . .

That newly arrived citizens "have two political capacities, one state and one federal," adds special force to their claim that they have the same rights as others who share their citizenship.[490] Neither mere rationality nor some intermediate standard of review should be used to judge the constitutionality of a state rule that discriminates against some of its citizens because they have been domiciled in the State for less than a year. The appropriate standard may be more categorical than that articulated in Shapiro . . ., but it is surely no less strict.

V

. . .

Disavowing any desire to fence out the indigent, California has instead advanced an entirely fiscal justification for its multitiered scheme. The enforcement of § 11450.03 will save the State approximately $10.9 million a year. The

---

490   [footnote 17 in the decision] "Federalism was our Nation's own discovery. The Framers split the atom of sovereignty. It was the genius of their idea that our citizens would have two political capacities, one state and one federal, each protected from incursion by the other. The resulting Constitution created a legal system unprecedented in form and design, establishing two orders of government, each with its own direct relationship, its own privity, its own set of mutual rights and obligations to the people who sustain it and are governed by it." U.S. Term Limits, Inc. v. Thornton . . . (KENNEDY, J., concurring)

question is not whether such saving is a legitimate purpose but whether the State may accomplish that end by the discriminatory means it has chosen. An evenhanded, across-the-board reduction of about 72 cents per month for every beneficiary would produce the same result. But our negative answer to the question does not rest on the weakness of the State's purported fiscal justification. It rests on the fact that the Citizenship Clause of the Fourteenth Amendment expressly equates citizenship with residence: "That Clause does not provide for, and does not allow for, degrees of citizenship based on length of residence." Zobel. . . . It is equally clear that the Clause does not tolerate a hierarchy of 45 subclasses of similarly situated citizens based on the location of their prior residence. Thus § 11450.03 is doubly vulnerable: Neither the duration of respondents' California residence, nor the identity of their prior States of residence, has any relevance to their need for benefits. Nor do those factors bear any relationship to the State's interest in making an equitable allocation of the funds to be distributed among its needy citizens. As in Shapiro, we reject any contributory rationale for the denial of benefits to new residents:

> "But we need not rest on the particular facts of these cases. Appellants' reasoning would logically permit the State to bar new residents from schools, parks, and libraries or deprive them of police and fire protection. Indeed it would permit the State to apportion all benefits and services according to the past tax contributions of its citizens." . . .

. . . In short, the State's legitimate interest in saving money provides no justification for its decision to discriminate among equally eligible citizens.

VI

The question that remains is whether congressional approval of durational residency requirements in the 1996 amendment to the Social Security Act somehow resuscitates the constitutionality of § 11450.03. That question is readily answered, for we have consistently held that Congress may not authorize the States to violate the Fourteenth Amendment. Moreover, the protection afforded to the citizen by the Citizenship Clause of that Amendment is a limitation on the powers of the National Government as well as the States.

. . .

Citizens of the United States, whether rich or poor, have the right to choose to be citizens "of the State wherein they reside." U.S. Const., Amdt. 14, § 1. The States, however, do not have any right to select their citizens. The Fourteenth Amendment, like the Constitution itself, was, as Justice Cardozo put it, "framed upon the theory that the peoples of the several states must sink or swim together, and that in the long run prosperity and salvation are in union and not division.". . .

The judgment of the Court of Appeals is affirmed.

It is so ordered.

[Dissents by Rehnquist and Thomas omitted.]

Attachments

Attachment A: The Articles of Confederation (ratified 1781) Nov. 15, 1777

To all to whom these Presents shall come, we the undersigned Delegates of the States affixed to our Names send greeting.

Articles of Confederation and perpetual Union between the states of New Hampshire, Massachusetts Bay, Rhode Island and Providence Plantations, Connecticut, New York, New Jersey, Pennsylvania, Delaware, Maryland, Virginia, North Carolina, South Carolina and Georgia.

I. The Stile of this Confederacy shall be "The United States of America".

II. Each state retains its sovereignty, freedom, and independence, and every power, jurisdiction, and right, which is not by this Confederation expressly delegated to the United States, in Congress assembled.

III. The said States hereby severally enter into a firm league of friendship with each other, for their common defense, the security of their liberties, and their mutual and general welfare, binding themselves to assist each other, against all force offered to, or attacks made upon them, or any of them, on account of religion, sovereignty, trade, or any other pretense whatever.

IV. The better to secure and perpetuate mutual friendship and intercourse among the people of the different States in this Union, the free inhabitants of each of these States, paupers, vagabonds, and fugitives from justice excepted, shall be entitled to all privileges and immunities of free citizens in the several States; and the people of each State shall free ingress and regress to and from any other State, and shall enjoy therein all the privileges of trade and commerce, subject to the same duties, impositions, and restrictions as the inhabitants thereof respectively, provided that such restrictions shall not extend so far as to prevent the removal of property imported into any State, to any other State, of which the owner is an inhabitant; provided also that no imposition, duties or restriction shall be laid by any State, on the property of the United States, or either of them.

If any person guilty of, or charged with, treason, felony, or other high misdemeanor in any State, shall flee from justice, and be found in any of the United States, he shall, upon demand of the Governor or executive power of the State from which he fled, be delivered up and removed to the State having jurisdiction of his offense.

Full faith and credit shall be given in each of these States to the records, acts, and judicial proceedings of the courts and magistrates of every other State.

V. For the most convenient management of the general interests of the United States, delegates shall be annually appointed in such manner as the legislatures of each State shall direct, to meet in Congress on the first Monday in November, in every year, with a power reserved to each State to recall its delegates, or any of them, at any time within the year, and to send others in their stead for the remainder of the year.

No State shall be represented in Congress by less than two, nor more than seven members; and no person shall be capable of being a delegate for more than three years in any term of six years; nor shall any person, being a delegate, be capable of holding any office under the United States, for which he, or another for his benefit, receives any salary, fees or emolument of any kind.

Each State shall maintain its own delegates in a meeting of the States, and while they act as members of the committee of the States.

In determining questions in the United States in Congress assembled, each State shall have one vote.

Freedom of speech and debate in Congress shall not be impeached or questioned in any court or place out of Congress, and the members of Congress shall be protected in their persons from arrests or imprisonments, during the time of their going to and from, and attendence on Congress, except for treason, felony, or breach of the peace.

VI. No State, without the consent of the United States in Congress assembled, shall send any embassy to, or receive any embassy from, or enter into any conference, agreement, alliance or treaty with any King, Prince or State; nor shall any person holding any office of profit or trust under the United States, or any of them, accept any present, emolument, office or title of any kind whatever from any King, Prince or foreign State; nor shall the United States in Congress assembled, or any of them, grant any title of nobility.

No two or more States shall enter into any treaty, confederation or alliance whatever between them, without the consent of the United States in Congress assembled, specifying accurately the purposes for which the same is to be entered into, and how long it shall continue.

No State shall lay any imposts or duties, which may interfere with any stipulations in treaties, entered into by the United States in Congress assembled, with any King, Prince or State, in pursuance of any treaties already proposed by Congress, to the courts of France and Spain.

No vessel of war shall be kept up in time of peace by any State, except such number only, as shall be deemed necessary by the United States in Congress assembled, for the defense of such State, or its trade; nor shall any body of forces be kept up by any State in time of peace, except such number only, as in the judgement of the United States in Congress assembled, shall be deemed requisite to garrison the forts necessary for the defense of such State; but every State shall always keep up a well-regulated and disciplined militia, sufficiently armed and accoutered, and shall provide and constantly have ready for use, in public stores, a due number of filed pieces and tents, and a proper quantity of arms, ammunition and camp equipage.

No State shall engage in any war without the consent of the United States in Congress assembled, unless such State be actually invaded by enemies, or shall have received certain advice of a resolution being formed by some nation of Indians to invade such State, and the danger is so imminent as not to admit of a delay till the United States in Congress assembled can be consulted; nor shall any State grant commissions to any ships or vessels of war, nor letters of marque or reprisal, except it be after a declaration of war by the United States in Congress assembled, and then only against the Kingdom or State and the subjects thereof, against which war has been so declared, and under such regulations as shall be established by the United States in Congress assembled, unless such State be infested by pirates, in which case vessels of war may be fitted out for that occasion, and kept so long as the danger shall continue, or until the United States in Congress assembled shall determine otherwise.

VII. When land forces are raised by any State for the common defense, all officers of or under the rank of colonel, shall be appointed by the legislature of each State respectively, by whom such forces shall be raised, or in such manner as such State shall direct, and all vacancies shall be filled up by the State which first made the appointment.

VIII. All charges of war, and all other expenses that shall be incurred for the common defense or general welfare, and allowed by the United States in Congress assembled, shall be defrayed out of a common treasury, which shall be supplied by the several States in proportion to the value of all land within each State, granted or surveyed for any person, as such land and the buildings and improvements thereon shall be estimated according to such mode as the United States in Congress assembled, shall from time to time direct and appoint.

The taxes for paying that proportion shall be laid and levied by the authority and direction of the legislatures of the several States within the time agreed upon by the United States in Congress assembled.

IX. The United States in Congress assembled, shall have the sole and exclusive right and power of determining on peace and war, except in the cases mentioned in the sixth article—of sending and receiving ambassadors—entering into treaties and alliances, provided that no treaty of commerce shall be made whereby the legislative power of the respective States shall be restrained from imposing such imposts and duties on foreigners, as their own people are subjected to, or from prohibiting the exportation or importation of any species of goods or commodities whatsoever—of establishing rules for deciding in all cases, what captures on land or water shall be legal, and in what manner prizes taken by land or naval forces in the service of the United States shall be divided or appropriated—of granting letters of marque and reprisal in times of peace—appointing courts for the trial of piracies and felonies commited on the high seas and establishing courts for receiving and determining finally appeals in all cases of captures, provided that no member of Congress shall be appointed a judge of any of the said courts.

The United States in Congress assembled shall also be the last resort on appeal in all disputes and differences now subsisting or that hereafter may arise between two or more States concerning boundary, jurisdiction or any other causes whatever; which authority shall always be exercised in the manner following. Whenever the legislative or executive authority or lawful agent of any State in controversy with another shall present a petition to Congress stating the matter in question and praying for a hearing, notice thereof shall be given by order of Congress to the legislative or executive authority of the other State in controversy, and a day assigned for the appearance of the parties by their lawful agents, who shall then be directed to appoint by joint consent, commissioners or judges to constitute a court for hearing and determining the matter in question: but if they cannot agree, Congress shall name three persons out of each of the United States, and from the list of such persons each party shall alternately strike out one, the petitioners beginning, until the number shall be reduced to thirteen; and from that number not less than seven, nor more than nine names as Congress shall direct, shall in the presence of Congress be drawn out by lot, and the persons whose names shall be so drawn or any five of them, shall be commissioners or judges, to hear and finally determine the controversy, so always as a major part of the judges who shall hear the cause shall agree in the determination: and if either party shall neglect to attend at the day appointed, without showing reasons, which Congress shall judge sufficient, or being present shall refuse to strike, the Congress shall proceed to nominate three persons out of each State, and the secretary of Congress shall strike in behalf of such party absent or refusing; and the judgement and sentence of the court to be appointed, in the manner before prescribed, shall be final and conclusive; and if any of the parties shall refuse to submit to the authority of such court, or to appear or defend their claim or cause, the court shall nevertheless proceed to pronounce sentence, or judgement, which shall in like manner be final and decisive, the judgement or sentence and other proceedings being in either case transmitted to Congress, and lodged among the acts of Congress for the security of the parties concerned: provided that every commissioner, before he sits in judgement, shall take an oath to be administered by one of the judges of the supreme or superior court of the State, where the cause shall be tried, 'well and truly to hear and determine the matter in question, according to the best of his judgement, without favor, affection or hope of reward': provided also, that no State shall be deprived of territory for the benefit of the United States.

All controversies concerning the private right of soil claimed under different grants of two or more States, whose jurisdictions as they may respect such lands, and the States which passed such grants are adjusted, the said grants or either of them being at the same time claimed to have originated antecedent to such settlement of jurisdiction, shall on the petition of either party to the Congress of the United States, be finally determined as near as may be in the same manner as is before presecribed for deciding disputes respecting territorial jurisdiction between different States.

The United States in Congress assembled shall also have the sole and exclusive right and power of regulating the alloy and value of coin struck by their own authority, or by that of the respective States—fixing the standards of weights and measures throughout the United States—regulating the trade and managing all affairs with the Indians, not members of any of the States, provided that the legislative right of any State within its own limits be not infringed or violated—establishing or regulating post offices from one State to another, throughout all the United States, and exacting such postage on the papers passing through the same as may be requisite to defray the expenses of the said office—appointing all officers of the land forces, in the service of the United States, excepting regimental officers—appointing all the officers of the naval forces, and commissioning all officers whatever in the service of the United States—making rules for the government and regulation of the said land and naval forces, and directing their operations.

The United States in Congress assembled shall have authority to appoint a committee, to sit in the recess of Congress, to be denominated 'A Committee of the States', and to consist of one delegate from each State; and to appoint such other committees and civil officers as may be necessary for managing the general affairs of the United States under their direction

- to appoint one of their members to preside, provided that no person be allowed to serve in the office of president more than one year in any term of three years; to ascertain the necessary sums of money to be raised for the service of the United States, and to appropriate and apply the same for defraying the public expenses

- to borrow money, or emit bills on the credit of the United States, transmitting every half-year to the respective States an account of the sums of money so borrowed or emitted

- to build and equip a navy—to agree upon the number of land forces, and to make requisitions from each State for its quota, in proportion to the number of white inhabitants in such State; which requisition shall be binding, and thereupon the legislature of each State shall appoint the regimental officers, raise the men and cloath, arm and equip them in a solid-like manner, at the expense of the United States; and the officers and men so cloathed, armed and equipped shall march to the place appointed, and within the time agreed on by the United States in Congress assembled. But if the United States in Congress assembled shall, on consideration of circumstances judge proper that any State should not raise men, or should raise a smaller number of men than the quota thereof, such extra number shall be raised, officered, cloathed, armed and equipped in the same manner as the quota of each State, unless the legislature of such State shall judge that such extra number cannot be safely spread out in the same, in which case they shall raise, officer, cloath, arm and equip as many of such extra number as they judge can be safely spared. And the officers and men so cloathed, armed, and equipped, shall march to the place appointed, and within the time agreed on by the United States in Congress assembled.

The United States in Congress assembled shall never engage in a war, nor grant letters of marque or reprisal in time of peace, nor enter into any treaties or alliances, nor coin money, nor regulate the value thereof, nor ascertain the sums and expenses necessary for the defense and welfare of the United States, or any of them, nor emit bills, nor borrow money on the credit of the United States, nor appropriate money, nor agree upon the number of vessels of war, to be built or purchased, or the number of land or sea forces to be raised, nor appoint a commander in chief of the army or navy, unless nine States assent to the same: nor shall a question on any other point, except for adjourning from day to day be determined, unless by the votes of the majority of the United States in Congress assembled.

The Congress of the United States shall have power to adjourn to any time within the year, and to any place within the United States, so that no period of adjournment be for a longer duration than the space of six months, and shall publish the journal of their proceedings monthly, except such parts thereof relating to treaties, alliances or military operations, as in their judgement require secrecy; and the yeas and nays of the delegates of each State on any question shall be entered on the journal, when it is desired by any delegates of a State, or any of them, at his or their request shall be furnished with a transcript of the said journal, except such parts as are above excepted, to lay before the legislatures of the several States.

X. The Committee of the States, or any nine of them, shall be authorized to execute, in the recess of Congress, such of the powers of Congress as the United States in Congress assembled, by the consent of the nine States, shall from time to time think expedient to vest them with; provided that no power be delegated to the said Committee, for the exercise of which, by the Articles of Confederation, the voice of nine States in the Congress of the United States assembled be requisite.

XI. Canada acceding to this confederation, and adjoining in the measures of the United States, shall be admitted into, and entitled to all the advantages of this Union; but no other colony shall be admitted into the same, unless such admission be agreed to by nine States.

XII. All bills of credit emitted, monies borrowed, and debts contracted by, or under the authority of Congress, before the assembling of the United States, in pursuance of the present confederation, shall be deemed and considered as a charge against the United States, for payment and satisfaction whereof the said United States, and the public faith are hereby solemnly pleged.

XIII. Every State shall abide by the determination of the United States in Congress assembled, on all questions which by this confederation are submitted to them. And the Articles of this Confederation shall be inviolably observed by every State, and the Union shall be perpetual; nor shall any alteration at any time hereafter be made in any of them; unless such alteration be agreed to in a Congress of the United States, and be afterwards confirmed by the legislatures of every State.

And Whereas it hath pleased the Great Governor of the World to incline the hearts of the legislatures we respectively represent in Congress, to approve of, and to authorize us to ratify the said Articles of Confederation and perpetual Union. Know Ye that we the undersigned delegates, by virtue of the power and authority to us given for that purpose, do by these presents, in the name and in behalf of our respective constituents, fully and entirely ratify and confirm each and every of the said Articles of Confederation and perpetual Union, and all and singular the matters and things therein contained: And we do further solemnly plight and engage the faith of our respective constituents, that they shall abide by the determinations of the United States in Congress assembled, on all questions, which by the said Confederation are submitted to them. And that the Articles thereof shall be inviolably observed by the States we respectively represent, and that the Union shall be perpetual.

In Witness whereof we have hereunto set our hands in Congress. Done at Philadelphia in the State of Pennsylvania the ninth day of July in the Year of our Lord One Thousand Seven Hundred and Seventy-Eight, and in the Third Year of the independence of America.

Agreed to by Congress 15 November 1777

In force after ratification by Maryland, 1 March 1781

Attachment B: Declaration of Independence

Action of Second Continental Congress, July 4, 1776

The unanimous Declaration of the thirteen United States of America

WHEN in the Course of human Events, it becomes necessary for one People to dissolve the Political Bands which have connected them with another, and to assume among the Powers of the Earth, the separate and equal Station to which the Laws of Nature and of Nature's God entitle them, a decent Respect to the Opinions of Mankind requires that they should declare the causes which impel them to the Separation.

WE hold these Truths to be self-evident, that all Men are created equal, that they are endowed by their Creator with certain unalienable Rights, that among these are Life, Liberty and the Pursuit of Happiness—That to secure these Rights, Governments are instituted among Men, deriving their just Powers from the Consent of the Governed, that whenever any Form of Government becomes destructive of these Ends, it is the Right of the People to alter or to abolish it, and to institute new Government, laying its Foundation on such Principles, and organizing its Powers in such Form, as to them shall seem most likely to effect their Safety and Happiness. Prudence, indeed, will dictate that Governments long established should not be changed for light and transient Causes; and accordingly all Experience hath shewn, that Mankind are more disposed to suffer, while Evils are sufferable, than to right themselves by abolishing the Forms to which they are accustomed. But when a long Train of Abuses and Usurpations, pursuing invariably the same Object, evinces a Design to reduce them under absolute Despotism, it is their Right, it is their Duty, to throw off such Government, and to provide new Guards for their future Security. Such has been the patient Sufferance of these Colonies; and such is now the Necessity which constrains them to alter their former Systems of Government. The History of the present King of Great-Britain is a History of repeated Injuries and Usurpations, all having in direct Object the Establishment of an absolute Tyranny over these States. To prove this, let Facts be submitted to a candid World.

HE has refused his Assent to Laws, the most wholesome and necessary for the public Good.

HE has forbidden his Governors to pass Laws of immediate and pressing Importance, unless suspended in their Operation till his Assent should be obtained; and when so suspended, he has utterly neglected to attend to them.

HE has refused to pass other Laws for the Accommodation of large Districts of People, unless those People would relinquish the Right of Representation in the Legislature, a Right inestimable to them, and formidable to Tyrants only.

HE has called together Legislative Bodies at Places unusual, uncomfortable, and distant from the Depository of their public Records, for the sole Purpose of fatiguing them into Compliance with his Measures.

HE has dissolved Representative Houses repeatedly, for opposing with manly Firmness his Invasions on the Rights of the People.

HE has refused for a long Time, after such Dissolutions, to cause others to be elected; whereby the Legislative Powers, incapable of the Annihilation, have returned to the People at large for their exercise; the State remaining in the mean time exposed to all the Dangers of Invasion from without, and the Convulsions within.

HE has endeavoured to prevent the Population of these States; for that Purpose obstructing the Laws for Naturalization of Foreigners; refusing to pass others to encourage their Migrations hither, and raising the Conditions of new Appropriations of Lands.

HE has obstructed the Administration of Justice, by refusing his Assent to Laws for establishing Judiciary Powers.

HE has made Judges dependent on his Will alone, for the Tenure of their Offices, and the Amount and Payment of their Salaries.

HE has erected a Multitude of new Offices, and sent hither Swarms of Officers to harrass our People, and eat out their Substance.

HE has kept among us, in Times of Peace, Standing Armies, without the consent of our Legislatures.

HE has affected to render the Military independent of and superior to the Civil Power.

HE has combined with others to subject us to a Jurisdiction foreign to our Constitution, and unacknowledged by our Laws; giving his Assent to their Acts of pretended Legislation:

FOR quartering large Bodies of Armed Troops among us;

FOR protecting them, by a mock Trial, from Punishment for any Murders which they should commit on the Inhabitants of these States:

FOR cutting off our Trade with all Parts of the World:

FOR imposing Taxes on us without our Consent:

FOR depriving us, in many Cases, of the Benefits of Trial by Jury:

FOR transporting us beyond Seas to be tried for pretended Offences:

FOR abolishing the free System of English Laws in a neighbouring Province, establishing therein an arbitrary Government, and enlarging its Boundaries, so as to render it at once an Example and fit Instrument for introducing the same absolute Rules into these Colonies:

FOR taking away our Charters, abolishing our most valuable Laws, and altering fundamentally the Forms of our Governments:

FOR suspending our own Legislatures, and declaring themselves invested with Power to legislate for us in all Cases whatsoever.

HE has abdicated Government here, by declaring us out of his Protection and waging War against us.

HE has plundered our Seas, ravaged our Coasts, burnt our Towns, and destroyed the Lives of our People.

HE is, at this Time, transporting large Armies of foreign Mercenaries to compleat the Works of Death, Desolation, and Tyranny, already begun with circumstances of Cruelty and Perfidy, scarcely parallcled in the most barbarous Ages, and totally unworthy the Head of a civilized Nation.

HE has constrained our fellow Citizens taken Captive on the high Seas to bear Arms against their Country, to become the Executioners of their Friends and Brethren, or to fall themselves by their Hands.

HE has excited domestic Insurrections amongst us, and has endeavoured to bring on the Inhabitants of our Frontiers, the merciless Indian Savages, whose known Rule of Warfare, is an undistinguished Destruction, of all Ages, Sexes and Conditions.

IN every stage of these Oppressions we have Petitioned for Redress in the most humble Terms: Our repeated Petitions have been answered only by repeated Injury. A Prince, whose Character is thus marked by every act which may define a Tyrant, is unfit to be the Ruler of a free People.

NOR have we been wanting in Attentions to our British Brethren. We have warned them from Time to Time of Attempts by their Legislature to extend an unwarrantable Jurisdiction over us. We have reminded them of the Circumstances of our Emigration and Settlement here. We have appealed to their native Justice and Magnanimity, and we have conjured them by the Ties of our common Kindred to disavow these Usurpations, which, would inevitably interrupt our Connections and Correspondence. They too have been deaf to the Voice of Justice and of Consanguinity. We must, therefore, acquiesce in the Necessity, which denounces our Separation, and hold them, as we hold the rest of Mankind, Enemies in War, in Peace, Friends.

WE, therefore, the Representatives of the UNITED STATES OF AMERICA, in GENERAL CONGRESS, Assembled, appealing to the Supreme Judge of the World for the Rectitude of our Intentions, do, in the Name, and by Authority of the good People of these Colonies, solemnly Publish and Declare, That these United Colonies are, and of Right ought to be, FREE AND INDEPENDENT STATES; that they are absolved from all Allegiance to the British Crown, and that all political Connection between them and the State of Great-Britain, is and ought to be totally dissolved; and that as FREE AND INDEPENDENT STATES, they have full Power to levy War, conclude Peace, contract Alliances, establish Commerce, and to do all other Acts and Things which INDEPENDENT STATES may of right do. And for the support of this Declaration, with a firm Reliance on the Protection of divine Providence, we mutually pledge to each other our Lives, our Fortunes, and our sacred Honor.

Attachment C: The Constitution of the United States of America (ratified 1788)

We the People of the United States, in Order to form a more perfect Union, establish Justice, insure domestic Tranquility, provide for the common defence, promote the general Welfare, and secure the Blessings of Liberty to ourselves and our Posterity, do ordain and establish this Constitution for the United States of America.

Article I

Section 1. All legislative Powers herein granted shall be vested in a Congress of the United States, which shall consist of a Senate and House of Representatives.

Section 2. The House of Representatives shall be composed of Members chosen every second Year by the People of the several States, and the Electors in each State shall have the Qualifications requisite for Electors of the most numerous Branch of the State Legislature.

No Person shall be a Representative who shall not have attained to the Age of twenty five Years, and been seven Years a Citizen of the United States, and who shall not, when elected, be an Inhabitant of that State in which he shall be chosen.

Representatives and direct Taxes shall be apportioned among the several States [which may be included within this Union, according to their respective Numbers, which shall be determined by adding to the whole Number of free Persons, including those bound to Service for a Term of Years, and excluding Indians not taxed, three fifths of all other Persons.] The actual Enumeration shall be made within three Years after the first Meeting of the Congress of the United States, and within every subsequent Term of ten Years, in such Manner as they shall by Law direct. The Number of Representatives shall not exceed one for every thirty Thousand, but each State shall have at Least one Representative; and until such enumeration shall be made, the State of New Hampshire shall be entitled to chuse three, Massachusetts eight, Rhode-Island and Providence Plantations one, Connecticut five, New-York six, New Jersey four, Pennsylvania eight, Delaware one, Maryland six, Virginia ten, North Carolina five, South Carolina five, and Georgia three.

When vacancies happen in the Representation from any State, the Executive Authority thereof shall issue Writs of Election to fill such Vacancies.

The House of Representatives shall chuse their Speaker and other Officers; and shall chuse their Speaker and other Officers; and shall have the sole Power of Impeachment.

Section 3. The Senate of the United States shall be composed of two Senators from each State, [chosen by the Legislature thereof], for six Years; and each Senator shall have one Vote.

Immediately after they shall be assembled in Consequence of the first Election, they shall be divided as equally as may be into three Classes. The Seats of the Senators of the first Class shall be vacated at the Expiration of the second Year, of the second Class at the Expiration of the fourth Year, and of the third Class at the Expiration of the sixth Year, so that one third may be chosen every second Year; and if Vacancies happen by Resignation, or otherwise, during the Recess of the Legislature of any State, the Executive thereof may make temporary Appointments until the next Meeting of the Legislature, which shall then fill such Vacancies.

No Person shall be a Senator who shall not have attained to the Age of thirty Years, and been nine Years a Citizen of the United States, and who shall not, when elected, be an Inhabitant of that State for which he shall be chosen.

The Vice President of the United States shall be President of the Senate, but shall have no Vote, unless they be equally divided.

The Senate shall chuse their other Officers, and also a President pro tempore, in the Absence of the Vice President, or when he shall exercise the Office of President of the United States.

The Senate shall have the sole Power to try all Impeachments. When sitting for that Purpose, they shall be on Oath or Affirmation. When the President of the United States is tried, the Chief Justice shall preside: And no Person shall be convicted without the Concurrence of two thirds of the Members present.

Judgment in Cases of Impeachment shall not extend further than to removal from Office, and disqualification to hold and enjoy any Office of honor, Trust or Profit under the United States: but the Party convicted shall nevertheless be liable and subject to Indictment, Trial, Judgment and Punishment, according to Law.

Section 4. The Times, Places and Manner of holding Elections for Senators and Representatives, shall be prescribed in each State by the Legislature thereof; but the Congress may at any time by Law make or alter such Regulations, [except as to the Places of chusing Senators].

The Congress shall assemble at least once in every Year, unless they shall by Law appoint a different Day.

Section 5. Each House shall be the Judge of the Elections, Returns and Qualifications of its own Members, and a Majority of each shall constitute a Quorum to do Business; but a smaller Number may adjourn from day to day, and may be authorized to compel the Attendance of absent Members, in such Manner, and under such Penalties as each House may provide.

Each House may determine the Rules of its Proceedings, punish its Members for disorderly Behaviour, and, with the Concurrence of two thirds, expel a Member.

Each House shall keep a Journal of its Proceedings, and from time to time publish the same, excepting such Parts as may in their Judgment require Secrecy; and the Yeas and Nays of the Members of either House on any question shall, at the Desire of one fifth of those Present, be entered on the Journal.

Neither House, during the Session of Congress, shall, without the Consent of the other, adjourn for more than three days, nor to any other Place than that in which the two Houses shall be sitting.

Section 6. The Senators and Representatives shall receive a Compensation for their Services, to be ascertained by Law, and paid out of the Treasury of the United States. They shall in all Cases, except Treason, Felony and Breach of the Peace, be privileged from Arrest during their Attendance at the Session of their respective Houses, and in going to and returning from the same; and for any Speech or Debate in either House, they shall not be questioned in any other Place.

No Senator or Representative shall, during the Time for which he was elected, be appointed to any civil Office under the Authority of the United States, which shall have been created, or the Emoluments whereof shall have been encreased during such time; and no Person holding any Office under the United States, shall be a Member of either House during his Continuance in Office.

Section 7. All Bills for raising Revenue shall originate in the House of Representatives; but the Senate may propose or concur with Amendments as on other Bills.

Every Bill which shall have passed the House of Representatives and the Senate, shall, before it become a Law, be presented to the President of the United States: If he approve he shall sign it, but if not he shall return it, with his Objections to that House in which it shall have originated, who shall enter the Objections at large on their Journal, and proceed to reconsider it. If after such Reconsideration two thirds of that House shall agree to pass the Bill, it shall be sent, together with the Objections, to the other House, by which it shall likewise be reconsidered, and if approved by two thirds of that House, it shall become a Law. But in all such Cases the Votes of both Houses shall be determined by yeas and Nays, and the Names of the Persons voting for and against the Bill shall be entered on the Journal of each House respectively. If any Bill shall not be returned by the President within ten Days (Sundays excepted) after it shall have been presented to him, the Same shall be a Law, in like Manner as if he had signed it, unless the Congress by their Adjournment prevent its Return, in which Case it shall not be a Law.

Every Order, Resolution, or Vote to which the Concurrence of the Senate and House of Representatives may be necessary (except on a question of Adjournment) shall be presented to the President of the United States; and before the Same shall take Effect, shall be approved by him, or being disapproved by him, shall be repassed by two thirds of the Senate and House of Representatives, according to the Rules and Limitations prescribed in the Case of a Bill.

Section 8. The Congress shall have Power To lay and collect Taxes, Duties, Imposts and Excises, to pay the Debts and provide for the common Defence and general Welfare of the United States; but all Duties, Imposts and Excises shall be uniform throughout the United States;

To borrow Money on the credit of the United States;

To regulate Commerce with foreign Nations, and among the several States, and with the Indian Tribes;

To establish an uniform Rule of Naturalization, and uniform Laws on the subject of Bankruptcies throughout the United States;

To coin Money, regulate the Value thereof, and of foreign Coin, and fix the Standard of Weights and Measures;

To provide for the Punishment of counterfeiting the Securities and current Coin of the United States;

To establish Post Offices and post Roads;

To promote the Progress of Science and useful Arts, by securing for limited Times to Authors and Inventors the exclusive Right to their respective Writings and Discoveries;

To constitute Tribunals inferior to the supreme Court;

To define and punish Piracies and Felonies committed on the high Seas, and Offences against the Law of Nations;

To declare War, grant Letters of Marque and Reprisal, and make Rules concerning Captures on Land and Water;

To raise and support Armies, but no Appropriation of Money to that Use shall be for a longer Term than two Years;

To provide and maintain a Navy;

To make Rules for the Government and Regulation of the land and naval Forces;

To provide for calling forth the Militia to execute the Laws of the Union, suppress Insurrections and repel Invasions;

To provide for organizing, arming, and disciplining, the Militia, and for governing such Part of them as may be employed in the Service of the United States, reserving to the States respectively, the Appointment of the Officers, and the Authority of training the Militia according to the discipline prescribed by Congress;

To exercise exclusive Legislation in all Cases whatsoever, over such District (not exceeding ten Miles square) as may, by Cession of particular States, and the Acceptance of Congress, become the Seat of the Government of the United States, and to exercise like Authority over all Places purchased by the Consent of the Legislature of the State in which the Same shall be, for the Erection of Forts, Magazines, Arsenals, dock-Yards, and other needful Buildings;— And

To make all Laws which shall be necessary and proper for carrying into Execution the foregoing Powers, and all other Powers vested by this Constitution in the Government of the United States, or in any Department or Officer thereof.

Section 9. The Migration or Importation of such Persons as any of the States now existing shall think proper to admit, shall not be prohibited by the Congress prior to the Year one thousand eight hundred and eight, but a Tax or duty may be imposed on such Importation, not exceeding ten dollars for each Person.

The Privilege of the Writ of Habeas Corpus shall not be suspended, unless when in Cases of Rebellion or Invasion the public Safety may require it.

No Bill of Attainder or ex post facto Law shall be passed.

No Capitation, or other direct, Tax shall be laid, unless in Proportion to the Census or Enumeration herein before directed to be taken.

No Tax or Duty shall be laid on Articles exported from any State.

No Preference shall be given by any Regulation of Commerce or Revenue to the Ports of one State over those of another; nor shall Vessels bound to, or from, one State, be obliged to enter, clear, or pay Duties in another.

No Money shall be drawn from the Treasury, but in Consequence of Appropriations made by Law; and a regular Statement and Account of the Receipts and Expenditures of all public Money shall be published from time to time.

No Title of Nobility shall be granted by the United States: And no Person holding any Office of Profit or Trust under them, shall, without the Consent of the Congress, accept of any present, Emolument, Office, or Title, of any kind whatever, from any King, Prince, or foreign State.

Section 10. No State shall enter into any Treaty, Alliance, or Confederation; grant Letters of Marque and Reprisal; coin Money; emit Bills of Credit; make any Thing but gold and silver Coin a Tender in Payment of Debts; pass any Bill of Attainder, ex post facto Law, or Law impairing the Obligation of Contracts, or grant any Title of Nobility.

No State shall, without the Consent of the Congress, lay any Imposts or Duties on Imports or Exports, except what may be absolutely necessary for executing it's inspection Laws; and the net Produce of all Duties and Imposts, laid by any State on Imports or Exports, shall be for the Use of the Treasury of the United States; and all such Laws shall be subject to the Revision and Controul of the Congress.

No State shall, without the Consent of Congress, lay any Duty of Tonnage, keep Troops, or Ships of War in time of Peace, enter into any Agreement or Compact with another State, or with a foreign Power, or engage in War, unless actually invaded, or in such imminent Danger as will not admit of delay.

Article II.

Section 1. The executive Power shall be vested in a President of the United States of America. He shall hold his Office during the Term of four Years, and, together with the Vice President, chosen for the same Term, be elected, as follows:

Each State shall appoint, in such Manner as the Legislature thereof may direct, a Number of Electors, equal to the whole Number of Senators and Representatives to which the State may be entitled in the Congress: but no Senator or Representative, or Person holding an Office of Trust or Profit under the United States, shall be appointed an Elector.

[The Electors shall meet in their respective States, and vote by Ballot for two Persons, of whom one at least shall not be an Inhabitant of the same State with themselves. And they shall make a List of all the Persons voted for, and of the Number of Votes for each; which List they shall sign and certify, and transmit sealed to the Seat of the Government of the United States, directed to the President of the Senate. The President of the Senate shall, in the Presence of the Senate and House of Representatives, open all the Certificates, and the Votes shall then be counted. The Person having the greatest Number of Votes shall be the President, if such Number be a Majority of the whole Number of Electors appointed; and if there be more than one who have such Majority, and have an equal Number of Votes, then the House of Representatives shall immediately chuse by Ballot one of them for President; and if no Person have a Majority, then from the five highest on the List the said House shall in like Manner chuse the President. But in chusing the President, the Votes shall be taken by States, the Representation from each State having one Vote; a quorum for this Purpose shall consist of a Member or Members from two thirds of the States, and a Majority of all the States shall be necessary to a Choice. In every Case, after the Choice of the President, the Person having the greatest Number of Votes of the Electors shall be the Vice President. But if there should remain two or more who have equal Votes, the Senate shall chuse from them by Ballot the Vice President].

The Congress may determine the Time of chusing the Electors, and the Day on which they shall give their Votes; which Day shall be the same throughout the United States.

No Person except a natural born Citizen, or a Citizen of the United States, at the time of the Adoption of this Constitution, shall be eligible to the Office of President; neither shall any Person be eligible to that Office who shall not have attained to the Age of thirty five Years, and been fourteen Years a Resident within the United States.

In Case of the Removal of the President from Office, or of his Death, Resignation, or Inability to discharge the Powers and Duties of the said Office, the Same shall devolve on the Vice President, and the Congress may by Law provide for the Case of Removal, Death, Resignation or Inability, both of the President and Vice President, declaring what Officer shall then act as President, and such Officer shall act accordingly, until the Disability be removed, or a President shall be elected.

The President shall, at stated Times, receive for his Services, a Compensation, which shall neither be increased nor diminished during the Period for which he shall have been elected, and he shall not receive within that Period any other Emolument from the United States, or any of them.

Before he enter on the Execution of his Office, he shall take the following Oath or Affirmation:—"I do solemnly swear (or affirm) that I will faithfully execute the Office of President of the United States, and will to the best of my Ability, preserve, protect and defend the Constitution of the United States."

Section 2. The President shall be Commander in Chief of the Army and Navy of the United States, and of the Militia of the several States, when called into the actual Service of the United States; he may require the Opinion, in writing, of the principal Officer in each of the executive Departments, upon any Subject relating to the Duties of their respective Offices, and he shall have Power to grant Reprieves and Pardons for Offences against the United States, except in Cases of Impeachment.

He shall have Power, by and with the Advice and Consent of the Senate, to make Treaties, provided two thirds of the Senators present concur; and he shall nominate, and by and with the Advice and Consent of the Senate, shall appoint Ambassadors, other public Ministers and Consuls, Judges of the supreme Court, and all other Officers of the United States, whose Appointments are not herein otherwise provided for, and which shall be established by Law: but the Congress may by Law vest the Appointment of such inferior Officers, as they think proper, in the President alone, in the Courts of Law, or in the Heads of Departments.

The President shall have Power to fill up all Vacancies that may happen during the Recess of the Senate, by granting Commissions which shall expire at the End of their next Session.

Section 3. He shall from time to time give to the Congress Information of the State of the Union, and recommend to their Consideration such Measures as he shall judge necessary and expedient; he may, on extraordinary Occasions, convene both Houses, or either of them, and in Case of Disagreement between them, with Respect to the Time of Adjournment, he may adjourn them to such Time as he shall think proper; he shall receive Ambassadors and other public Ministers; he shall take Care that the Laws be faithfully executed, and shall Commission all the Officers of the United States.

Section 4. The President, Vice President and all civil Officers of the United States, shall be removed from Office on Impeachment for, and Conviction of, Treason, Bribery, or other high Crimes and Misdemeanors.

Article III.

Section 1. The judicial Power of the United States shall be vested in one supreme Court, and in such inferior Courts as the Congress may from time to time ordain and establish. The Judges, both of the supreme and inferior Courts, shall hold their Offices during good Behaviour, and shall, at stated Times, receive for their Services a Compensation, which shall not be diminished during their Continuance in Office.

Section 2. The judicial Power shall extend to all Cases, in Law and Equity, arising under this Constitution, the Laws of the United States, and Treaties made, or which shall be made, under their Authority;—to all Cases affecting Ambassadors, other public Ministers and Consuls;—to all Cases of admiralty and maritime Jurisdiction;—to Controversies to which the United States shall be a Party;—to Controversies between two or more States;—between a State and Citizens of another State;—between Citizens of different States;—between Citizens of the same State claiming Lands under Grants of different States, and between a State, or the Citizens thereof, and foreign States, [Citizens or Subjects].

In all Cases affecting Ambassadors, other public Ministers and Consuls, and those in which a State shall be Party, the supreme Court shall have original Jurisdiction. In all the other Cases before mentioned, the supreme Court shall have appellate Jurisdiction, both as to Law and Fact, with such Exceptions, and under such Regulations as the Congress shall make.

The Trial of all Crimes, except in Cases of Impeachment, shall be by Jury; and such Trial shall be held in the State where the said Crimes shall have been committed; but when not committed within any State, the Trial shall be at such Place or Places as the Congress may by Law have directed.

Section 3. Treason against the United States shall consist only in levying War against them, or in adhering to their Enemies, giving them Aid and Comfort. No Person shall be convicted of Treason unless on the Testimony of two Witnesses to the same overt Act, or on Confession in open Court.

The Congress shall have Power to declare the Punishment of Treason, but no Attainder of Treason shall work Corruption of Blood, or Forfeiture except during the Life of the Person attainted.

Article IV.

Section 1. Full Faith and Credit shall be given in each State to the public Acts, Records, and judicial Proceedings of every other State. And the Congress may by general Laws prescribe the Manner in which such Acts, Records and Proceedings shall be proved, and the Effect thereof.

Section 2. The Citizens of each State shall be entitled to all Privileges and Immunities of Citizens in the several States.

A Person charged in any State with Treason, Felony, or other Crime, who shall flee from Justice, and be found in another State, shall on Demand of the executive Authority of the State from which he fled, be delivered up, to be removed to the State having Jurisdiction of the Crime.

[No Person held to Service or Labour in one State, under the Laws thereof, escaping into another, shall, in Consequence of any Law or Regulation therein, be discharged from such Service or Labour, but shall be delivered up on Claim of the Party to whom such Service or Labour may be due.]

Section 3. New States may be admitted by the Congress into this Union; but no new State shall be formed or erected within the Jurisdiction of any other State; nor any State be formed by the Junction of two or more States, or Parts of States, without the Consent of the Legislatures of the States concerned as well as of the Congress.

The Congress shall have Power to dispose of and make all needful Rules and Regulations respecting the Territory or other Property belonging to the United States; and nothing in this Constitution shall be so construed as to Prejudice any Claims of the United States, or of any particular State.

Section 4. The United States shall guarantee to every State in this Union a Republican Form of Government, and shall protect each of them against Invasion; and on Application of the Legislature, or of the Executive (when the Legislature cannot be convened), against domestic Violence.

Article V.

The Congress, whenever two thirds of both Houses shall deem it necessary, shall propose Amendments to this Constitution, or, on the Application of the Legislatures of two thirds of the several States, shall call a Convention for proposing Amendments, which, in either Case, shall be valid to all Intents and Purposes, as Part of this Constitution, when ratified by the Legislatures of three fourths of the several States, or by Conventions in three fourths thereof, as the one or the other Mode of Ratification may be proposed by the Congress; Provided that no Amendment which may be made prior to the Year One thousand eight hundred and eight shall in any Manner affect the first and fourth Clauses in the Ninth Section of the first Article; and that no State, without its Consent, shall be deprived of its equal Suffrage in the Senate.

Article VI.

All Debts contracted and Engagements entered into, before the Adoption of this Constitution, shall be as valid against the United States under this Constitution, as under the Confederation.

This Constitution, and the Laws of the United States which shall be made in Pursuance thereof; and all Treaties made, or which shall be made, under the Authority of the United States, shall be the supreme Law of the Land; and the Judges in every State shall be bound thereby, any Thing in the Constitution or Laws of any State to the Contrary notwithstanding.

The Senators and Representatives before mentioned, and the Members of the several State Legislatures, and all executive and judicial Officers, both of the United States and of the several States, shall be bound by Oath or Affirmation, to support this Constitution; but no religious Test shall ever be required as a Qualification to any Office or public Trust under the United States.

Article VII.

The Ratification of the Conventions of nine States, shall be sufficient for the Establishment of this Constitution between the States so ratifying the Same.

Done in Convention by the Unanimous Consent of the States present the Seventeenth Day of September in the Year of our Lord one thousand seven hundred and Eighty seven and of the Independence of the United States of America the Twelfth In Witness whereof We have hereunto subscribed our Names,

Attachment C-1: The Bill of Rights (ratified 1791)

The Conventions of a number of the States having, at the time of adopting the Constitution, expressed a desire, in order to prevent misconstruction or abuse of its powers, that further declaratory and restrictive clauses should be added, and as extending the ground of public confidence in the Government will best insure the beneficent ends of its institution;

Resolved, by the Senate and House of Representatives of the United States of America, in Congress assembled, two-thirds of both Houses concurring, that the following articles be proposed to the Legislatures of the several States, as amendments to the Constitution of the United States; all or any of which articles, when ratified by three-fourths of the said Legislatures, to be valid to all intents and purposes as part of the said Constitution, namely:

Amendment I

Congress shall make no law respecting an establishment of religion, or prohibiting the free exercise thereof; or abridging the freedom of speech, or of the press; or the right of the people peaceably to assemble, and to petition the Government for a redress of grievances.

Amendment II

A well regulated Militia, being necessary to the security of a free State, the right of the people to keep and bear Arms, shall not be infringed.

Amendment III

No Soldier shall, in time of peace be quartered in any house, without the consent of the Owner, nor in time of war, but in a manner to be prescribed by law.

Amendment IV

The right of the people to be secure in their persons, houses, papers, and effects, against unreasonable searches and seizures, shall not be violated, and no Warrants shall issue, but upon probable cause, supported by Oath or affirmation, and particularly describing the place to be searched, and the persons or things to be seized.

Amendment V

No person shall be held to answer for a capital, or otherwise infamous crime, unless on a presentment or indictment of a Grand Jury, except in cases arising in the land or naval forces, or in the Militia, when in actual service in time of War or public danger; nor shall any person be subject for the same offence to be twice put in jeopardy of life or limb; nor shall be compelled in any criminal case to be a witness against himself, nor be deprived of life, liberty, or property, without due process of law; nor shall private property be taken for public use, without just compensation.

Amendment VI

In all criminal prosecutions, the accused shall enjoy the right to a speedy and public trial, by an impartial jury of the State and district wherein the crime shall have been committed, which district shall have been previously ascertained by law, and to be informed of the nature and cause of the accusation; to be confronted with the witnesses against him; to have compulsory process for obtaining witnesses in his favor, and to have the Assistance of Counsel for his defence.

Amendment VII

In Suits at common law, where the value in controversy shall exceed twenty dollars, the right of trial by jury shall be preserved, and no fact tried by a jury, shall be otherwise re-examined in any Court of the United States, than according to the rules of the common law.

Amendment VIII

Excessive bail shall not be required, nor excessive fines imposed, nor cruel and unusual punishments inflicted.

Amendment IX

The enumeration in the Constitution, of certain rights, shall not be construed to deny or disparage others retained by the people.

Amendment X

The powers not delegated to the United States by the Constitution, nor prohibited by it to the States, are reserved to the States respectively, or to the people.

Attachment C-2: Constitutional Amendments 11-27

Amendment XI (1795)

The judicial power of the United States shall not be construed to extend to any suit in law or equity, commenced or prosecuted against one of the United States by Citizens of another State, or by Citizens or Subjects of any Foreign State.

Amendment XII (1804)

The Electors shall meet in their respective states and vote by ballot for President and Vice-President, one of whom, at least, shall not be an inhabitant of the same state with themselves; they shall name in their ballots the person voted for as President, and in distinct ballots the person voted for as Vice-President, and they shall make distinct lists of all persons voted for as President, and of all persons voted for as Vice-President, and of the number of votes for each, which lists they shall sign and certify, and transmit sealed to the seat of the government of the United States, directed to the President of the Senate;—The President of the Senate shall, in the presence of the Senate and House of Representatives, open all the certificates and the votes shall then be counted;—the person having the greatest number of votes for President, shall be the President, if such number be a majority of the whole number of electors appointed; and if no person have such majority, then from the persons having the highest numbers not exceeding three on the list of those voted for as President, the House of Representatives shall choose immediately, by ballot, the President. But in choosing the President, the votes shall be taken by states, the representation from each state having one vote; a quorum for this purpose shall consist of a member or members from two-thirds of the states, and a majority of all the states shall be necessary to a choice. And if the House of Representatives shall not choose a President whenever the right of choice shall devolve upon them, [before the fourth day of March next following], then the Vice-President shall act as President, as in the case of the death or other constitutional disability of the President—The person having the greatest number of votes as Vice-President, shall be the Vice-President, if such number be a majority of the whole number of electors appointed, and if no person have a majority, then from the two highest numbers on the list, the Senate shall choose the Vice-President; a quorum for the purpose shall consist of two-thirds of the whole number of Senators, and a majority of the whole number shall be necessary to a choice. But no person constitutionally ineligible to the office of President shall be eligible to that of Vice-President of the United States.

Amendment XIII (1865)

Section 1. Neither slavery nor involuntary servitude, except as a punishment for crime whereof the party shall have been duly convicted, shall exist within the United States, or any place subject to their jurisdiction.

Section 2. Congress shall have power to enforce this article by appropriate legislation.

Amendment XIV (1868)

Section 1. All persons born or naturalized in the United States and subject to the jurisdiction thereof, are citizens of the United States and of the State wherein they reside. No State shall make or enforce any law which shall abridge the privileges or immunities of citizens of the United States; nor shall any State deprive any person of life, liberty, or property, without due process of law; nor deny to any person within its jurisdiction the equal protection of the laws.

Section 2. Representatives shall be apportioned among the several States according to their respective numbers, counting the whole number of persons in each State, [excluding Indians not taxed]. But when the right to vote at any election for the choice of electors for President and Vice President of the United States, Representatives in Congress, the Executive and Judicial officers of a State, or the members of the Legislature thereof, is denied to any of the male inhabitants of such State, being twenty-one years of age, and citizens of the United States, or in any way abridged, except for participation in rebellion, or other crime, the basis of representation therein shall be reduced in the proportion which the number of such male citizens shall bear to the whole number of male citizens twenty-one years of age in such state.

Section 3. No person shall be a Senator or Representative in Congress, or elector of President and Vice President, or hold any office, civil or military, under the United States, or under any State, who, having previously taken an oath, as a member of Congress, or as an officer of the United States, or as a member of any State legislature, or as an executive or judicial officer of any State, to support the Constitution of the United States, shall have engaged in insurrection or rebellion against the same, or given aid or comfort to the enemies thereof. But Congress may by a vote of two-thirds of each House, remove such disability.

Section 4. The validity of the public debt of the United States, authorized by law, including debts incurred for payment of pensions and bounties for services in suppressing insurrection or rebellion, shall not be questioned. But neither the United States nor any State shall assume or pay any debt or obligation incurred in aid of insurrection or rebellion against the United States, or any claim for the loss or emancipation of any slave; but all such debts, obligations and claims shall be held illegal and void.

Section 5. The Congress shall have power to enforce, by appropriate legislation, the provisions of this article.

Amendment XV (1870)

Section 1. The right of citizens of the United States to vote shall not be denied or abridged by the United States or by any State on account of race, color, or previous condition of servitude.

Section 2. The Congress shall have power to enforce this article by appropriate legislation.

Amendment XVI (1913)

The Congress shall have power to lay and collect taxes on incomes, from whatever source derived, without apportionment among the several States, and without regard to any census of enumeration.

Amendment XVII (1913)

The Senate of the United States shall be composed of two Senators from each State, elected by the people thereof, for six years; and each Senator shall have one vote. The electors in each State shall have the qualifications requisite for electors of the most numerous branch of the State legislatures.

When vacancies happen in the representation of any State in the Senate, the executive authority of such State shall issue writs of election to fill such vacancies: Provided, That the legislature of any State may empower the executive thereof to make temporary appointments until the people fill the vacancies by election as the legislature may direct.

This amendment shall not be so construed as to affect the election or term of any Senator chosen before it becomes valid as part of the Constitution.

Amendment XVIII (1919)

[*Section 1.* After one year from the ratification of this article the manufacture, sale, or transportation of intoxicating liquors within, the importation thereof into, or the exportation thereof from the United States and all territory subject to the jurisdiction thereof for beverage purposes is hereby prohibited.]

[*Section 2.* The Congress and the several States shall have concurrent power to enforce this article by appropriate legislation.]

Section 3. This article shall be inoperative unless it shall have been ratified as an amendment to the Constitution by the legislatures of the several States, as provided in the Constitution, within seven years from the date of the submission hereof to the States by the Congress.

Amendment XIX (1920)

The right of citizens of the United States to vote shall not be denied or abridged by the United States or by any State on account of sex.

Congress shall have power to enforce this article by appropriate legislation.

Amendment XX (1933)

Section 1. The terms of the President and Vice President shall end at noon on the 20th day of January, and the terms of Senators and Representatives at noon on the 3d day of January, of the years in which such terms would have ended if this article had not been ratified; and the terms of their successors shall then begin.

Section 2. The Congress shall assemble at least once in every year, and such meeting shall begin at noon on the 3d day of January, unless they shall by law appoint a different day.

Section 3. If, at the time fixed for the beginning of the term of the President, the President elect shall have died, the Vice President elect shall become President. If a President shall not have been chosen before the time fixed for the beginning of his term, or if the President elect shall have failed to qualify, then the Vice President elect shall act as President until a President shall have qualified; and the Congress may by law provide for the case wherein neither a President elect nor a Vice President elect shall have qualified, declaring who shall then act as President, or the manner in which one who is to act shall be selected, and such person shall act accordingly until a President or Vice President shall have qualified.

Section 4. The Congress may by law provide for the case of the death of any of the persons from whom the House of Representatives may choose a President whenever the right of choice shall have devolved upon them, and for the case of the death of any of the persons from whom the Senate may choose a Vice President whenever the right of choice shall have devolved upon them.

Section 5. Sections 1 and 2 shall take effect on the 15th day of October following the ratification of this article.

Section 6. This article shall be inoperative unless it shall have been ratified as an amendment to the Constitution by the legislatures of three-fourths of the several states within seven years from the date of its submission.

Amendment XXI (1933)

Section 1. The eighteenth article of amendment to the Constitution of the United States is hereby repealed.

Section 2. The transportation or importation into any State, Territory, or possession of the United States for delivery or use therein of intoxicating liquors, in violation of the laws thereof, is hereby prohibited.

Section 3. This article shall be inoperative unless it shall have been ratified as an amendment to the Constitution by conventions in the several States, as provided in the Constitution, within seven years from the date of the submission hereof to the States by the Congress.

Amendment XXII (1951)

Section 1. No person shall be elected to the office of the President more than twice, and no person who has held the office of President, or acted as President, for more than two years of a term to which some other person was elected President shall be elected to the office of the President more than once. But this Article shall not apply to any person holding the office of President when this Article was proposed by the Congress, and shall not prevent any person who may be holding the office of President, or acting as President, during the term within which this Article becomes operative from holding the office of President or acting as President during the remainder of such term.

Section 2. This Article shall be inoperative unless it shall have been ratified as an amendment to the Constitution by the legislatures of three-fourths of the several States within seven years from the date of its submission to the States by the Congress.

Amendment XXIII (1961)

Section 1. The District constituting the seat of Government of the United States shall appoint in such manner as the Congress may direct:

A number of electors of President and Vice President equal to the whole number of Senators and Representatives in Congress to which the District would be entitled if it were a State, but in no event more than the least populous State; they shall be in addition to those appointed by the States, but they shall be considered, for the purposes of the election of President and Vice President, to be electors appointed by a State; and they shall meet in the District and perform such duties as provided by the twelfth article of amendment.

Section 2. The Congress shall have power to enforce this article by appropriate legislation.

Amendment XXIV (1964)

Section 1. The right of citizens of the United States to vote in any primary or other election for President or Vice President, for electors for President or Vice President, or for Senator or Representative in Congress, shall not be denied or abridged by the United States or any State by reason of failure to pay any poll tax or other tax.

Section 2. The Congress shall have power to enforce this article by appropriate legislation.

Amendment XXV (1967)

Section 1. In case of the removal of the President from office or of his death or resignation, the Vice President shall become President.

Section 2. Whenever there is a vacancy in the office of the Vice President, the President shall nominate a Vice President who shall take office upon confirmation by a majority vote of both Houses of Congress.

Section 3. Whenever the President transmits to the President pro tempore of the Senate and the Speaker of the House of Representatives his written declaration that he is unable to discharge the powers and duties of his office, and until he transmits to them a written declaration to the contrary, such powers and duties shall be discharged by the Vice President as Acting President.

Section 4. Whenever the Vice President and a majority of either the principal officers of the executive departments or of such other body as Congress may by law provide, transmit to the President pro tempore of the Senate and the Speaker of the House of Representatives their written declaration that the President is unable to discharge the powers and duties of his office, the Vice President shall immediately assume the powers and duties of the office as Acting President.

Thereafter, when the President transmits to the President pro tempore of the Senate and the Speaker of the House of Representatives his written declaration that no inability exists, he shall resume the powers and duties of his office unless the Vice President and a majority of either the principal officers of the executive department or of such other body as Congress may by law provide, transmit within four days to the President pro tempore of the Senate and the Speaker of the House of Representatives their written declaration that the President is unable to discharge the powers and duties of his office. Thereupon Congress shall decide the issue, assembling within forty-eight hours for that purpose if not in session. If the Congress, within twenty-one days after receipt of the latter written declaration, or, if Congress is not in session, within twenty-one days after Congress is required to assemble, determines by two-thirds vote of both Houses that the President is unable to discharge the powers and duties of his office, the Vice President shall continue to discharge the same as Acting President; otherwise, the President shall resume the powers and duties of his office.

Amendment XXVI (1971)

Section 1. The right of citizens of the United States, who are 18 years of age or older, to vote, shall not be denied or abridged by the United States or any State on account of age.

Section 2. The Congress shall have the power to enforce this article by appropriate legislation.

Amendment XXVII (1992)

No law, varying the compensation for the services of the Senators and Representatives, shall take effect, until an election of Representatives shall have intervened.

Attachment D: Individual Rights Found in the Text of the Constitution Excluding the Amendments

As collected by Professor Chemerinsky, Constitutional Law, at pp. 361-362.

Article I, § 9

The privilege of the Writ of Habeas Corpus shall not be suspended, unless when in Cases of Rebellion or Invasion, the public Safety may require it.

No Bill of Attainder or ex post facto Law shall be passed.

Article I, § 10

No State shall . . . pass any Bill of Attainder, ex post facto Law, or law impairing the Obligation of Contracts.

Article III, § 2

The trial of all Crimes, except in Cases of Impeachment, shall be by jury; and such Trial shall be held in the State where the said Crimes shall have been committed.

Article III, § 3

Treason against the United States, shall consist only in levying War against them or, in adhering to their Enemies, giving them Aid and Comfort. No person shall be convicted of Treason unless on the Testimony of two Witnesses to the same overt Act, or on Confession in open Court. The Congress shall have Power to declare the Punishment of Treason, but no Attainder of Treason shall work Corruption of Blood, or Forfeiture except during the Life of the Person attained.

Article IV, § 2

The Citizens of each State shall be entitled to all Privileges and Immunities of Citizens in the several States.

Article VI, cl. 3:

[N]o religious Test shall ever be required as a Qualification to any Office of public Trust under the United States.

Attachment E: The Gettysburg Address (Nov. 19, 1863)

Fourscore and seven years ago our fathers brought forth on this continent a new nation, conceived in liberty and dedicated to the proposition that all men are created equal. Now we are engaged in a great civil war, testing whether that nation or any nation so conceived and so dedicated can long endure. We are met on a great battlefield of that war. We have come to dedicate a portion of that field as a final resting-place for those who here gave their lives that that nation might live. It is altogether fitting and proper that we should do this. But in a larger sense, we cannot dedicate, we cannot consecrate, we cannot hallow this ground. The brave men, living and dead who struggled here have consecrated it far above our poor power to add or detract. The world will little note nor long remember what we say here, but it can never forget what they did here. It is for us the living rather to be dedicated here to the unfinished work which they who fought here have thus far so nobly advanced. It is rather for us to be here dedicated to the great task remaining before us—that from these honored dead we take increased devotion to that cause for which they gave the last full measure of devotion—that we here highly resolve that these dead shall not have died in vain, that this nation under God shall have a new birth of freedom, and that government of the people, by the people, for the people shall not perish from the earth.

Attachment F: The Emancipation Proclamation (1863)

By the President of the United States of America:

A PROCLAMATION

Whereas on the 22nd day of September, A.D. 1862, a proclamation was issued by the President of the United States, containing, among other things, the following, to wit:

> "That on the 1st day of January, A.D. 1863, all persons held as slaves within any State or designated part of a State the people whereof shall then be in rebellion against the United States shall be then, thenceforward, and forever free; and the executive government of the United States, including the military and naval authority thereof, will recognize and maintain the freedom of such persons and will do no act or acts to repress such persons, or any of them, in any efforts they may make for their actual freedom.

> "That the executive will on the 1st day of January aforesaid, by proclamation, designate the States and parts of States, if any, in which the people thereof, respectively, shall then be in rebellion against the United States; and the fact that any State or the people thereof shall on that day be in good faith represented in the Congress of the United States by members chosen thereto at elections wherein a majority of the qualified voters of such States shall have participated shall, in the absence of strong countervailing testimony, be deemed conclusive evidence that such State and the people thereof are not then in rebellion against the United States."

Now, therefore, I, Abraham Lincoln, President of the United States, by virtue of the power in me vested as Commander-In-Chief of the Army and Navy of the United States in time of actual armed rebellion against the authority and government of the United States, and as a fit and necessary war measure for supressing said rebellion, do, on this 1st day of January, A.D. 1863, and in accordance with my purpose so to do, publicly proclaimed for the full period of one hundred days from the first day above mentioned, order and designate as the States and parts of States wherein the people thereof, respectively, are this day in rebellion against the United States the following, to wit:

> Arkansas, Texas, Louisiana (except the parishes of St. Bernard, Palquemines, Jefferson, St. John, St. Charles, St. James, Ascension, Assumption, Terrebone, Lafourche, St. Mary, St. Martin, and Orleans, including the city of New Orleans), Mississippi, Alabama, Florida, Georgia, South Carolina, North Carolina, and Virginia (except the forty-eight counties designated as West Virginia, and also the counties of Berkeley,

Accomac, Morthhampton, Elizabeth City, York, Princess Anne, and Norfolk, including the cities of Norfolk and Portsmouth), and which excepted parts are for the present left precisely as if this proclamation were not issued.

And by virtue of the power and for the purpose aforesaid, I do order and declare that all persons held as slaves within said designated States and parts of States are, and henceforward shall be, free; and that the Executive Government of the United States, including the military and naval authorities thereof, will recognize and maintain the freedom of said persons.

And I hereby enjoin upon the people so declared to be free to abstain from all violence, unless in necessary self-defence; and I recommend to them that, in all case when allowed, they labor faithfully for reasonable wages.

And I further declare and make known that such persons of suitable condition will be received into the armed service of the United States to garrison forts, positions, stations, and other places, and to man vessels of all sorts in said service.

And upon this act, sincerely believed to be an act of justice, warranted by the Constitution upon military necessity, I invoke the considerate judgment of mankind and the gracious favor of Almighty God.

Attachment G: Franklin D. Roosevelt's Speech to Congress on December 8, 1941

Yesterday, December 7, 1941—a date which will live in infamy—the United States of America was suddenly and deliberately attacked by naval and air forces of the Empire of Japan.

The United States was at peace with that nation and, at the solicitation of Japan, was still in conversation with its Government and its Emperor looking toward the maintenance of peace in the Pacific. Indeed, one hour after Japanese air squadrons had commenced bombing the American island of Oahu, the Japanese Ambassador to the United States and his colleague delivered to the Secretary of State a formal reply to a recent American message. And while this reply stated that it seemed useless to continue the existing diplomatic negotiations, it contained no threat or hint of war or of armed attack.

It will be recorded that the distance of Hawaii from Japan makes it obvious that the attack was deliberately planned many days or even weeks ago. During the intervening time the Japanese Government has deliberately sought to deceive the United States by false statements and expressions of hope for continued peace.

The attack yesterday on the Hawaiian Islands has caused severe damage to American naval and military forces. I regret to tell you that very many American lives have been lost. In addition American ships have been reported torpedoed on the high seas between San Francisco and Honolulu.

Yesterday the Japanese Government also launched an attack against Malaya. Last night Japanese forces attacked Hong Kong. Last night Japanese forces attacked Guam. Last night Japanese forces attacked the Philippine Islands. Last night the Japanese attacked Wake Island. And this morning the Japanese attacked Midway Island.

Japan has, therefore, undertaken a surprise offensive extending throughout the Pacific area. The facts of yesterday and today speak for themselves. The people of the United States have already formed their opinions and well understand the implications to the very life and safety of our nation.

As Commander-in-Chief of the Army and Navy, I have directed that all measures be taken for our defense.

Always will we remember the character of the onslaught against us. No matter how long it may take us to overcome this premeditated invasion, the American people in their righteous might will win through to absolute victory.

I believe that I interpret the will of the Congress and of the people when I assert that we will not only defend ourselves to the uttermost but will make it very certain that this form of treachery shall never again endanger us.

Hostilities exist. There is no blinking at the fact that our people, our territory and our interests are in grave danger.

With confidence in our armed forces—with the unbounding determination of our people—we will gain the inevitable triumph—so help us God.

I ask that the Congress declare that since the unprovoked and dastardly attack by Japan on Sunday, December seventh 1941, a state of war has existed between the United States and the Japanese Empire.

Attachment H: San Diego City Council Resolution Number R-294727

(R-2001-1300)

RESOLUTION NUMBER R-294727

ADOPTED ON APR 02 2001

WHEREAS, certain references to African Americans, Latinos, Asian Americans, and Native Americans as "minorities" have conveyed negative connotations that imply inferiority and inequity among Americans; and

WHEREAS, the City of San Diego celebrates the rich history of all Americans, and acknowledges the positive contributions to American society that all ethnic groups have made; and

WHEREAS, the City of San Diego applauds initiatives across the country to promote equal opportunities for all Americans, regardless of ethnicity; and

WHEREAS, the City of San Diego supports building communities where fairness and equality of opportunity are upheld; NOW, THEREFORE,

BE IT RESOLVED, by the Council of the City of San Diego that this Council, for and on behalf of the people of San Diego, does hereby state that all citizens of the United States, regardless of ethnicity, are Americans, and that the use of the term "minorities" to identify ethnic groups yields perceived implications of being inferior or less than.

BE IT FURTHER RESOLVED, that the City of San Diego discontinue the use of the term "minority" in reference to any citizen or ethnic group.

APPROVED: CASEY GWINN, City Attorney

By _____

    Stuart H. Swett
    Senior Deputy City Attorney

SHS:smf
3/22/01
Or.Dept:Mayor
R-2001-1300
Form=proclaim.res

Bibliography

Bibliography of most important books consulted in the preparation of this edition, whether or not cited in the text. Articles listed are those cited in the text.

Ackerman, Bruce A., We the People: Foundations (1991)

American Jurisprudence (2d ed. 1998)

Black, Jr., Charles L., Impeachment: A Handbook (1974)

Bork, Robert H., The Tempting of America: The Political Seduction of the Law (1990)

Chemerinsky, Erwin, *Parity Reconsidered: Defining a Role for the Federal Judiciary*, 36 University of California Los Angeles Law Review 233 (1988)

Chemerinsky, Erwin, Constitutional Law: Principles and Policies (1997)

Choper, Jesse H., Judicial Review and the National Political Process (1980)

Currie, David P., The Constitution of the Federal Republic of Germany (1994)

Dahl, Robert, On Democracy (1999)

Daniels, Roger, Concentration Camps North America: Japanese in the United States and Canada during World War II (reprint ed. 1993)

Eberle, Edward J., *Public Discourse in Contemporary Germany*, 47 Case Western Reserve 797 (1977)

Ely, John Hart, Democracy and Distrust (1980)

Epstein, Richard A., Forbidden Grounds: The Case Against Employment Discrimination Laws (1992)

Farber, Daniel A. & Suzanna Sherry, A History of the American Constitution (1990)

Farrand, Max, The Records of the Federal Convention of 1787, vol. 1 (1913)

Fiss, Owen, *Groups and the Equal Protection Clause*, 5 Philosophy & Public Affairs 107 (1976)

Fletcher, George P., Basic Concepts of Legal Thought (1996)

Friedman, Lawrence M., A History of American Law (2d ed. 1985)

Gardner, James A., *The Positivist Revolution that Wasn't: Constitutional Universalism in the States*, 4 Roger Williams Law Review 109 (1998)

Gaulding, Jill, *Note: Race, Sex, and Genetic Discrimination in Insurance: What's Fair?*, 80 Cornell Law Review 1646 (1995)

Gottovi, Sara L., *United States v. Lopez, Theoretical Bang and Whimper? An Illustrative Analysis Based on Lower Court Treatment of the Child Support Recovery Act*, 38 William & Mary Law Review 677 (1997)

Gunther, Gerald, *Foreword: In Search of Evolving Doctrine on a Changing Court: A Model for a Newer Equal Protection*, 86 Harvard Law Review 1 (1972)

Gunther, Gerald, and Kathleen M. Sullivan, Constitutional Law (13th ed. 1997)

Hadek, David V., *Why the Policy Behind the Irrebuttable Presumption of Paternity Will Never Die*, 26 Southwestern University Law Review 359 (1997)

Hall, Kermit, William Wiecek, & Paul Finkelman, American Legal History: Cases and Materials (1991)

Hamilton, Alexander, John Jay, and James Madison, The Federalist: A Commentary on The Constitution of the United States, being A Collection of Essays written in Support of the Constitution agreed upon September 17, 1787, by The Federal Convention (H.C. Lodge, ed. 1888)

Hasday, Jill Elaine, *Federalism and the Family Reconstructed*, 45 University of California Los Angeles Law Review 1297 (1998)

Hayek, Friedrich A., The Constitution of Liberty (1960)

Hughes, Charles Evans, Speech before the Elmira [N.Y.] Chamber of Commerce, May 3, 1907, in Addresses and Papers of Charles Evans Hughes 133 (1908)

Issacharoff, Samuel & Erica Worth Harris, *Is Age Discrimination Really Age Discrimination?: The ADEA's Unnatural Solution*, 72 New York University Law Review 780 (1997)

Jackson, Vicki C., *Federalism and the Uses and Limits of Law: Printz and Principle?*, 111 Harvard Law Review 2180 (1998)

Jaffa, Harry V., Original Intent and the Framers of the Constitution: A Disputed Question (1994)

Kahn, Paul W., *Commentary: Interpretation and Authority in State Constitutionalism,* 106 Harvard Law Review 1147 (1993)

Koh, Harold, The National Security Constitution (1990)

Kramer, Larry, *The Lawmaking Power of the Federal Courts*, 12 Pace L. Rev. 263 (1992)

Lawrence, Michael A., Toward a More Coherent Dormant Commerce Clause: A Proposal Unitary Framework, 21 Harvard Journal of Law and Public Policy 395 (1998)

Larson, Lex K., Employment Discrimination, vol. 3 (2d ed. 1994)

Locke, John, Of Civil Government (London 1936)

Lundmark, Thomas, *East Germans' Conversion to Democracy*, 20 Fordham International Law Journal 384 (1996)

Lundmark, Thomas, *Forms and Legitimacy of States*, 6 Juridisk Tidskrift vid Stockholms Universitet 647 (1994-95)

Lundmark, Thomas, Free Speech Meets Free Enterprise in The United States and Germany,

Lundmark, Thomas, Juristische Technik und Methodik des Common Law (Münster 1998)

Lundmark, Thomas & John B. McNeece, *State and Local Government Participation in Solving Environmental Problems at the U.S.-Mexican Border*, 3 Journal of Environmental Law & Practice 37 (1995)

Lundmark, Thomas, Landscape, Recreation, and Takings in German and American Law (Stuttgart 1997)

Lundmark, Thomas, *Regulation of Private Logging in California*, 5 Ecology Law Quarterly 139 (1975)

Lundmark, Thomas, *Systemizing Environmental Law of a German Model*, 7 Dickenson Journal of Environmental Law and Policy 1 (1998).

Lundmark, Thomas, *Die Freiheit der Werbung und der Grundsatz der Verhältnismäßigkeit in der amerikanischen Rechtsprechung*, 1994 Verwaltungs-Archiv 522

Lupu, Ira C., *Untangling the Strands of the Fourteenth Amendment*, 77 Michigan Law Review 981 (1979)

Maloney, Kerrie E., *Gender-Motivated Violence and the Commerce Clause: The Civil Rights Provision of the Violence Against Women Act After Lopez*, 96 Columbia Law Review 1876 (1996)

Massey, Calvin, *Getting There: A Brief History of the Politics of Supreme Court Appointments*, 19 Hastings Constitutional Law Quarterly 1 (1991)

McKinley, Stacey L., *The Violence Against Women Act After United States v. Lopez: Will Domestic Violence Jurisdiction be Returned to the States?*, 44 Cleveland State Law Review 345 (1996)

McTaggart, Kelli C., *The Violence Against Women Act: Recognizing a Federal Civil Right to be Free from Violence*, 86 Georgetown Law Journal 1123 (1998)

Merryman, John Henry, *The French Deviation*, 44 American Journal of Comparative Law 109 (1996)

Mikva, Abner J., *Doubting Our Claims to Democracy*, 39 Arizona Law Review 793 (1997)

Montesquieu, Charles Louis de Secondat, De l'esprit des loix, ou du rapport que les loix doivent avoir avec la constitution de chaque gouvernement, les moeurs, le climat, la religion, le commerce, 1-3 (1749)

Mosk, Richard M., *The Jurisprudence of Ratings Symposium Part I: Motion Picture Ratings in the United States*, 15 Cardozo Arts & Entertainment Law Journal 135 (1997)

Nowak, John E. & Ronald D. Rotunda, Constitutional Law (5th ed. 1995).

Perlin, Michael L., *Individual Rights and Reasonable Accommodations under the Americans with Disabilities Act: "Make Promises by the Hour": Sex, Drugs, the ADA, and Psychiatric Hospitalization*, 46 DePaul Law Review 947 (1997)

Ross, William G., *The Supreme Court Appointment Process: A Search for a Synthesis*, 57 Albany Law Review 993 (1994)

Rotunda, Ronald D., *Independent Counsel and the Charges of Leaking: A Brief Case Study*, 68 Fordham Law Review 869 (1999)

Rubin, Edward L. & Malcolm Feeley, *Federalism: Some Notes on a National Neurosis*, 41 University of California Los Angeles Law Review 903 (1994)

Rubin, Edward L., *The Fundamentality and Irrelevance of Federalism*, 13 Georgia State University Law Review 1009 (1997)

Shaman, Jeffrey, *Cracks in the Structure: The Coming Breakdown of the Levels of Scrutiny*, 45 Ohio State Law Journal 161 (1984)

Simon, Larry G., *The Authority of the Framers of the Constitution: Can Original Interpretation Be Justified?*, 73 California Law Review 1482 (1985).

Singer, Joseph William, *No Right to Exclude: Public Accommodations and Private Property*, 90 Northwestern University Law Review 1283 (1996)

Smith, Rogers M., Liberalism and American Constitutional Law (1990)

Solimine, Michael E. & James L. Walker, *Federalism, Liberty and State Constitutional Law*, 23 Ohio Northern University Law Review 1457 (1997)

Stone, Geoffrey R., Louis M. Seidman, Cass R. Sunstein, and Mark V. Tushnet, Constitutional Law (3d ed. 1996)

Treanor, William Michael, *Fame, The Founding, and the Power to Declare War*, 82 Cornell L. Rev. 694 (1997)

Tribe, Laurence H., American Constitutional Law (3d ed. 1991)

United States Department of Commerce, Census Bureau, 1992 Census of the Government, Volume I: Government Organization, Number II: Popularly Elected Officials (issued June 1995)

Williams, Robert F., *State Constitutional Law Processes*, 24 William & Mary Law Review 169 (1983)

Wright, Robert, The Moral Animal: Evolutionary Psychology and Everyday Life (1995)

Table of Cases

Excerpted cases are in **boldface type**.